# Accounting, Finance, Sustainability, Governance & Fraud: Theory and Application

**Series Editor**

Kıymet Tunca Çalıyurt, Iktisadi ve Idari Bilimler Fakultes, Trakya University Balkan Yerleskesi, Edirne, Turkey

This Scopus indexed series acts as a forum for book publications on current research arising from debates about key topics that have emerged from global economic crises during the past several years. The importance of governance and the will to deal with corruption, fraud, and bad practice, are themes featured in volumes published in the series. These topics are not only of concern to businesses and their investors, but also to governments and supranational organizations, such as the United Nations and the European Union. Accounting, Finance, Sustainability, Governance & Fraud: Theory and Application takes on a distinctive perspective to explore crucial issues that currently have little or no coverage. Thus the series integrates both theoretical developments and practical experiences to feature themes that are topical, or are deemed to become topical within a short time. The series welcomes interdisciplinary research covering the topics of accounting, auditing, governance, and fraud.

More information about this series at http://www.springer.com/series/13615

Aswini Kumar Mishra · Vairam Arunachalam ·
Sanket Mohapatra · Dennis Olson
Editors

# The Financial Landscape of Emerging Economies

## Current State, Challenges and Solutions

Springer

*Editors*
Aswini Kumar Mishra
Department of Economics
Birla Institute of Technology and Science
Goa, India

Vairam Arunachalam
Trulaske College of Business
University of Missouri
Columbia, MO, USA

Sanket Mohapatra
Indian Institute of Management Ahmedabad
Ahmedabad, Gujarat, India

Dennis Olson
Zayed University
Abu Dhabi, United Arab Emirates

ISSN 2509-7873 ISSN 2509-7881 (electronic)
Accounting, Finance, Sustainability, Governance & Fraud: Theory and Application
ISBN 978-3-030-60007-5 ISBN 978-3-030-60008-2 (eBook)
https://doi.org/10.1007/978-3-030-60008-2



This Springer imprint is published by the registered company Springer Nature Switzerland AG
The registered company address is: Gewerbestrasse 11, 6330 Cham, Switzerland

# Preface

As per the International Monetary Fund (IMF)'s recent *World Economic Outlook Update* (*June 2020: A Crisis Like No Other, An Uncertain Recovery, June 24, 2020*), projects the global growth at –4.9% in 2020, 1.9 percentage points below April 2020, World Economic Outlook (WEO) forecast. The COVID-19 pandemic has had a more adverse impact on activity in the first half of 2020 than expected, and the recovery is projected to be more gradual than previously forecasted. In 2021, global growth is projected at 5.4%. Overall, this would leave 2021 GDP some 6½ percentage points lower than in the pre-COVID-19 projections of January 2020. Whilst the ultimate growth outcome is still uncertain, and an even worse scenario is possible if it takes longer to bring the health crisis under control, the pandemic will result in output contractions across the vast majority of emerging market and developing economies (EMDEs). The adverse impact on low-income households is particularly acute, imperilling the significant progress made in reducing extreme poverty in the world since the 1990s. Thus, the immediate policy urgencies are to alleviate human costs and attenuate the near-term economic losses. Further, to make future economies more resilient, many countries will need systems that can build and retain more human and physical capital during the recovery.

Against this backdrop, this volume comprises papers by leading academicians, scholars, and practitioners from India and abroad to provide different perspectives to drive financial growth and economic development in emerging economies. The volume presents empirical analysis, theoretical concepts, and policy implications by offering a detailed analysis of the current financial landscape of emerging economies including those from India.

Chapter 1 is about "The Evolving Financial Landscape in Emerging Market and Developing Economies". The authors Sanket Mohapatra and Aswini Kumar Mishra analyse the changing contours of the financial sector and the challenges faced by these countries in recent years. This chapter finds that in these countries, banks and domestic equity markets still continue to be vital as a source of financing for the corporate sector, bond markets. The paper suggests that with prudent macroeconomic policies and additional development of analytical frameworks and policy prescriptions for financial market regulation, financial stability can be further achieved whilst balancing the goals of financial development and broader financial inclusion. Finally, the chapter discusses financial inclusion (that includes digital and traditional) and suggests further promoting access to and usage of formal financial services to maximize society's overall welfare.

Chapter 2 contributed by Kundan Kumar, Zeeshan Nezami Ansari, and Rajendra Narayan attempts to explore the possible interdependence between the business cycle and the financial cycle in India during 1996-Q1 to 2018-Q3 using quarterly data of macroeconomic variables, namely real GDP, credit to GDP ratio, real house prices, real equity prices, and real effective exchange rate. The frequency filter technique of Christiano–Fitzgerald and the Turning point analysis of Bry–Boschan have been used to generate the cyclical components of the variables and identify peaks and troughs in the data, respectively. The degree of co-movement between two cycles is found by Harding and Pagan technique. To explore the long-run relation between the business cycle and the financial cycle, the spectral Granger causality test (Breitung and Candelon) has been conducted. The empirical finding reveals that the cyclical component of the financial variable Granger causes the cyclical component of the gross domestic product in the medium as well as long run and vice versa.

Chapter 3 by Sobhesh Kumar Agarwalla, Joshy Jacob*, Jayanth R. Varma, and Ellapulli Vasudevan examines the return dynamics of the high-beta and low-beta assets in the Indian market. The flatness in CAPM in the Indian market implies that a portfolio long in low-beta assets and short in high-beta assets would earn positive returns. The "Betting against beta" factor (BAB factor) similar to the conceptualization by Frazzini and Pedersen (2014) is used to examine the emerging market which has severe financing constraints relative to the markets examined by Frazzini and Pedersen. The findings reveal that the BAB factor earns significant positive returns in the Indian market, and the returns of the BAB factor dominate the return of the size, value, and momentum factors. They also find that the stocks with higher volatility earn relatively lower returns. These findings indicate the overweighting of riskier assets by leverage constrained investors in the Indian market.

In Chap. 4, Abhisek Mishra and Byomakesh Debata highlight the dynamic relationship between economic policy uncertainty (EPU) and stock market volatility in a pure order-driven emerging stock market. Considering the non-linear EPU–volatility relationship, this study uses the GARCH family of models to capture the impact of policy uncertainty on stock market volatility for two major indices of the Indian stock market, i.e., SENSEX and NIFTY from April-2002 to March-2019. Empirical estimates reveal that economic policy uncertainty is an essential determinant of stock market volatility, and higher EPU leads to a significant increase in volatility. The results provide a thorough understanding of the EPU–volatility relationship which would help policymakers to design countervailing strategies to reduce the unnecessary uncertainty essential for maintaining financial market stability.

In Chap. 5, Manogna R. Leshma and Aswini Kumar Mishra investigate the long-run and short-run interaction between the select agricultural commodities and Fast-Moving Consumer Goods (FMCG) stock index by applying daily data using the autoregressive distributive lag (ARDL) bound test. They investigate the co-integration relationship in an emerging economy like India, where agriculture is a top priority, suggesting that the prices of these commodities affect the stock market and domestic inflation. The findings indicate the absence of co-integration between the National Commodity and Derivative Exchange (NCDEX) agricultural commodities and the Bombay Stock Exchange (BSE) FMCG index. Additionally, this study uses the Toda and Yamamoto approach of the Granger causality test to analyse the causal relationship between variables under study. The evidence reveals the absence of a causal relationship between the FMCG index and agricultural commodities except for cottonseed, rapeseed, mustard, and jeera, furthermore, confirming only the unidirectional causal relationship from these commodities to the FMCG index. This analysis provides an opportunity for investors to hedge their risk due to the absence of causality and co-integration between the FMCG index and agricultural commodities by diversifying their portfolio in both the markets.

Chapter 6 by Abhijit Ranjan Das and Soma Panja explores the influence of emotion in investment decision-making from a theoretical perspective. They aim to strengthen the theoretical underpinning of the relationship between emotion and investment decision-making. The paper argues that emotion acts as a crucial antecedent for making a better investment decision since the investment decision-making is done under the condition of risk and uncertainty. The paper further argues that emotion has a significant role in investment decision-making and for being a successful investor, one should not only depend on the market fundamentals but should also be aware of one's own emotion. The authors conclude that successful investors control and regulate their emotion carefully for making advantageous decisions and does not only depends on their self-emotions.

In Chap. 7, Vedant Bhardwaj and Aswini Kumar Mishra provide insight on the decomposition of the sources of inequality in credit availability from both informal and formal sources in India. Using data from 2002 to 2012, they decompose the inequality of credit availability in India at the household level, the regional level, and the state level using multilevel modelling. Their findings are crucial in understanding the variance in informal credit compared to variance in formal credit. It is interesting to find that most of the variance in both informal and formal credit stems from mainly the variance between households. Furthermore, they provide substantial evidence regarding the influence of household-, regional-, and state-level characteristics on the availability of formal and informal credit in India.

In Chap. 8, Sumit Saurav reviews the critical aspects of corporate governance in emerging economies from the perspective of Principal–Principal (PP) conflict. The author focuses on the Principal-Principal conflicts as the dominant form of governance conflicts which is different from the traditional Principal-Agent (PA) conflicts. The weak institutional structure prevalent in the emerging economies acts as a root cause of this type of conflict which results in concentrated ownership in the form of family control and business group structure. The chapter uses the extant literature on PP conflicts to describe and decipher their characteristics, institutional antecedents, and organizational consequences. The author concludes that emerging countries have to come up with improvised solutions suitable to their institutional environment since traditional approaches would not solve the PP conflicts prevalent in emerging countries.

In Chap. 9, Riyanka Baral and Debasis Patnaik explore the influence of board composition on agency cost and its governance outcomes in large and small commercial banks in India They measure board composition under the category of board structure, board independence, and board committee. A sample consisting of 35 Indian commercial banks during the years 2008–2018 was used in the study using Multiple Linear Regression analysis. The study in Chap. 9 shows that in large banks board structure, board independence, and board committee influence agency costs, whilst in the case of small banks, board structure and board committee impact agency cost. Thus, this study reveals the vital role of board composition and its impact on the agency cost of large and small banks.

In Chap. 10, Sushma Verma and Samik Shome assess the airline bankruptcy in India in the time when an important corporate like Jet Airways was grounded due to severe financial crises. An early warning signal of financial distress is critical as the airline companies operate in a dynamic and competitive environment. The study by authors uses various bankruptcy predicting models, viz., Altman Model, Pilarski Model, Fuzzy Logic Model, and Kroeze Model and attempts to analyse the financial situation of select airline companies in India. They observe that different models have given more or less similar predictions and grades for different air carriers in India. This final chapter is of vital relevance considering the contribution of the aviation sector to the national growth and series of bankruptcy instances in this sector.

We are grateful to the authors for making their studies available for this edited volume. We sincerely hope that the studies included in this volume will stimulate academic debates and lead to further analytical advances in the domains of the changing contours of the financial landscape of emerging economies.

Goa, India — Aswini Kumar Mishra
Columbia, USA — Vairam Arunachalam
Ahmedabad, India — Sanket Mohapatra
Abu Dhabi, United Arab Emirates — Dennis Olson

# Acknowledgements

This Volume in Springer Series contains ten (10) selected papers covering a wide range of topics in financial economics including risk management, financial markets, corporate governance, and bankruptcy out of which seven papers were presented at the 2nd International Conference on Economics & Finance (ICEF-2020) held at Birla Institute of Technology and Science, Pilani-K K Birla Goa Campus, Goa, India, during Jan 23–25 2020, especially the financial landscape of emerging economies. The event aimed at stimulating critical thinking and sharing knowledge across emerging themes towards sustainable development, finance and trade, business and innovation, and related fields.

Eminent speakers like Jeffrey C. Thomson, President and CEO of IMA® (Institute of Management Accountants); Prof. Avanidhar (Subra) Subrahmanyam, Distinguished Professor of Finance, Goldyne and Irwin Hearsh Chair in Money and Banking, The John E. Anderson Graduate School of Management, University of California at Los Angeles(UCLA); Dr. Hamza Ali Malik, Director, Macroeconomic Policy and Financing for Development Division, United Nations Economic and Social Commission for Asia and the Pacific (United Nations ESCAP); Dr. Sweta Chaman Saxena, Chief, Macroeconomic Policy and Analysis, Macroeconomic Policy and Financing for Development, UN Economic and Social Commission for Asia and the Pacific (UN-ESCAP); Prof. Sanket Mohapatra, Economics Area Chairperson, IIM Ahmedabad; Prof. Sujeet K. Sharma, Associate Professor, Informations System & Analytics, IIM Trichy; Dr. Joyojeet Pal, Principal Researcher, Microsoft Research India; Prof. Prakash Singh, Professor in Finance & Accounting IIM, Lucknow; and Mr. Jaywardhan Semwal, Vice President, Corporate Financial Accounting, Hewlett Packard Enterprise delivered distinguished lectures on this occasion. The event was supported by National Bank for Agriculture and Rural Development (NABARD), and Institute of Management Accountants (IMA®) provided an avenue for disseminating information on contemporary research and future practices in economics.

This volume presents empirical analysis, theoretical concepts, and policy implications by offering a detailed analysis of the current financial landscape of emerging economies including those from India. An edited book such as this also required the cooperation and dedication of its many contributing authors. Apart from penning excellent chapters, the authors were always prompt in their responses. We are also indebted to the anonymous referees and members of the scientific committee for providing insightful reviews with many useful comments and suggestions.

This book deserves the mentioning of a few colleagues and research scholars whose indefatigable efforts helped us in compiling this book. We would particularly like to thank (in no particular order) for the help and cooperation received from Dr. Ch. V. V. S. N. V. Prasad, Dr. Ritika Jaiswal, Dr. Richa Shukla, Prof. Mridula Goel, Prof. Debasis Patnaik, Mr. Rammohan Menon, Mr. Abhishek Kumar Sinha, and Ms. Manogna R. Leshma. We would also like to acknowledge the support we received from Prof. Raghurama G, Director, BITS Pilani-K K Birla Goa Campus in organizing the above-mentioned event and this book is an outcome of it.

Most importantly, we would like to thank Springer editor, Nitza Jones-Sepulveda and Assistant Editor, Faith Su for their enthusiasm, advice, and encouragement.

Goa, India — Aswini Kumar Mishra
Columbia, USA — Vairam Arunachalam
Ahmedabad, India — Sanket Mohapatra
Abu Dhabi, United Arab Emirates — Dennis Olson

# Contents

1 **The Evolving Financial Landscape in Emerging Markets and Developing Economies** . . . . . 1
Sanket Mohapatra and Aswini Kumar Mishra

2 **Nexus Between Financial Cycle and Business Cycle in India** . . . . . 15
Kundan Kumar, Zeeshan Nezami Ansari, and Rajendra Narayan Paramanik

3 **Betting Against Beta in the Indian Market** . . . . . 29
Sobhesh Kumar Agarwalla, Joshy Jacob, Jayanth R. Varma, and Ellapulli Vasudevan

4 **Does Economic Policy Uncertainty Matter for Stock Market Volatility?** . . . . . 45
Abhisek Mishra and Byomakesh Debata

5 **Can the FMCG Stock Market Investors Hedge the Risk in Agricultural Commodity Markets? Empirical Evidence from India** . . . . . 55
Manogna R. Leshma and Aswini Kumar Mishra

6 **Exploring the Influence of Emotion in Investment Decision-Making: A Theoretical Perspective** . . . . . 71
Abhijit Ranjan Das and Soma Panja

7 **How Do Household and Spatial Factors Matter While Examining Inequality in Credit Availability? Evidence from an Emerging Economy** . . . . . 79
Vedant Bhardwaj and Aswini Kumar Mishra

**8 Review of Corporate Governance in Emerging Economies from the Perspective of Principal–Principal Conflict** . . . . . . . . . . . . 111
Sumit Saurav

**9 Influence of Board Composition on Agency Cost and Its Governance Outcomes** . . . . . . . . . . . . . . . . . . . . . . . . . . . . . 123
Riyanka Baral and Debasis Patnaik

**10 Assessing Airline Bankruptcy in India** . . . . . . . . . . . . . . . . . . . . . . . 149
Sushma Verma and Samik Shome

**Index** . . . . . . . . . . . . . . . . . . . . . . . . . . . . . . . . . . . . . . . . . . . . . . . . 175

# Editors and Contributors

## About the Editors

**Prof. Aswini Kumar Mishra** presently serves as the Head in the Department of Economics and an Associate Professor at BITS, Pilani-K K Birla Goa Campus, India. His research and teaching interests relate to applied econometrics, behavioural and applied development economics, and financial risk management. Dr. Mishra has published related articles in most leading scholarly journals including *International Journal of Finance & Economics*, *Journal of Quantitative Economics*, *International Economic Journal*, *Journal of Economic Studies*, *Economic Change and Restructuring*, etc.

**Prof. Vairam Arunachalam** serves as Director of the School of Accountancy & Price water house Coopers Distinguished Professor at the University of Missouri. His research and teaching interests pertain to forensic accounting, data analytics, and information systems. He is a member of the Accountancy Advisory Board at the University of Illinois at Urbana-Champaign. He is also a member of the Research Foundation of the Institute of Management Accountants (IMA). He has chaired several AACSB accounting accreditation review teams. His research has been published in several leading journals.

**Prof. Sanket Mohapatra** is a faculty at the Indian Institute of Management, Ahmedabad. He was earlier a Senior Economist with the World Bank in Washington, DC. He holds an M.A from the Delhi School of Economics and a Ph.D. from Columbia University (New York). His interests include international finance, global capital flows, sovereign and sub-sovereign credit ratings, corporate productivity, foreign debt, corporate finance in emerging economies, and international migration and remittances. He is currently an Associate Editor of *Vikalpa: The Journal for Decision Makers*. His research has been published in prominent peer-reviewed journals and he has contributed to the World Bank's flagship reports.

**Prof. Dennis Olson** is a Professor of Finance and Union National Bank Chair of Banking at Zayed University in Abu Dhabi, UAE. He holds a Ph.D. in economics from the University of Wyoming (USA) and is a Chartered Professional Accountant (CPA) in Canada. He has taught economics, finance, and accounting classes in the US, Canada, New Zealand, Denmark, Colombia, Oman, Kuwait, and the UAE. He has published in the *Journal of Banking and Finance, International Journal of Accounting, Journal of Corporate Finance, European Economic Review, International Journal of Forecasting, Economic Inquiry, Energy Economics, Emerging Markets Review*, and *Financial Review*.

## Contributors

**Sobhesh Kumar Agarwalla** Indian Institute of Management Ahmedabad, Vastrapur, Ahmedabad, Gujarat, India

**Zeeshan Nezami Ansari** Department of Humanities and Social Sciences, IIT Patna, Bihta, India

**Riyanka Baral** Department of Economics, BITS Pilani, KK Birla Goa Campus, Zuarinagar, Goa, India

**Vedant Bhardwaj** Graduate, M.Sc. in Economics and B.E. in Electronics and Instrumentation, BITS Pilani-K.K. Birla Goa Campus, Pilani, India

**Abhijit Ranjan Das** Department of Management Studies, National Institute of Technology Silchar, Silchar, India

**Byomakesh Debata** Birla Institute of Technology and Science, Pilani Campus, Vidya Vihar, Rajasthan, India

**Joshy Jacob** Indian Institute of Management Ahmedabad, Vastrapur, Ahmedabad, Gujarat, India

**Kundan Kumar** Department of Humanities and Social Sciences, IIT Patna, Bihta, India

**Manogna R. Leshma** Department of Economics, BITS Pilani KSancoale K Birla Goa Campus, Sancoale, Goa, India

**Abhisek Mishra** Nabakrushna Choudhury Centre for Development Studies, Bhubaneswar, India

**Aswini Kumar Mishra** Head of Department, Economics Department, BITS Pilani-K.K. Birla Goa Campus, Pilani, India

**Sanket Mohapatra** Indian Institute of Management Ahmedabad, Vastrapur, Ahmedabad, Gujarat, India

**Soma Panja** Department of Management Studies, National Institute of Technology Silchar, Silchar, India

**Rajendra Narayan Paramanik** Department of Humanities and Social Sciences, IIT Patna, Bihta, India

**Debasis Patnaik** Department of Economics, BITS Pilani, KK Birla Goa Campus, Zuarinagar, Goa, India

**Sumit Saurav** IIM-Ahmedabad, Vastrapur, Ahmedabad, Gujarat, India

**Samik Shome** Institute of Management, Nirma University, Ahmedabad, India

**Jayanth R. Varma** Indian Institute of Management Ahmedabad, Vastrapur, Ahmedabad, Gujarat, India

**Ellapulli Vasudevan** Department of Finance, ESCP Business School, Paris, France

**Sushma Verma** VES Institute of Management Studies and Research, Mumbai, India

# List of Figures


Fig. 1.1 Domestic credit to private sector in developing countries. *Source* World Bank. *Notes* For Europe and Central Asia, the earliest available data for 2008 data has been used instead of that for 2005. For Middle East and North Africa and Sub-Saharan Africa, the latest available data for 2016 and 2018 have been used instead of that for 2019 . . . . . . . . . . 3
Fig. 1.2 Bank branches per 100,000 adults in developing countries. *Source* World Bank . . . . . . . . . . 4
Fig. 1.3 Equity markets in developing countries. *Source* World Bank. *Notes* For Europe and Central Asia, the earliest available data for 2009 and latest available data for 2018 have been used instead of that for 2005 and 2019, respectively. For Middle East and North Africa and Sub-Saharan Africa, the latest available data for 2016 and 2018 have been used instead of that for 2019 . . . . . . . . . . 5
Fig. 1.4 Local currency bond markets in selected Asian economies. *Source* Based on data compiled by Park (2017). *Notes* South Korea is considered an emerging market by MSCI, but a high-income country by the World Bank . . . . . . . . . . 6
Fig. 1.5 Percentage of adults above the age of 15 having an account in the considered emerging lower middle-income countries. *Source* Global Findex database (2017) . . . . . . . . . . 9
Fig. 1.6 Per cent of adults (15+ age) with an account in a financial institution and those who made no deposit and withdrawal in the past one year. *Source* Global Findex database (2017). . . . . . . . . . 10
Fig. 1.7 Savings pattern amongst the adults (15+ age) having an account at a formal institution. *Note* B* represents Bangladesh. *Source* Global Findex database (2017) . . . . . . . . . . 10
Fig. 1.8 Borrowing pattern amongst the adults (15+ age) having an account at a formal institution. *Note* J* represents Jordan. *Source* Global Findex database (2017) . . . . . . . . . . 11

Fig. 1.9 Changes in Financial inclusion Indices, 2014–2017 (Level change). *Source* IMF staff calculations cited in IMF (2020) . . . . . 12
Fig. 2.1 Cyclical component of business and financial cycle: CF filter *Source* Authors' calculation . . . . . 21
Fig. 2.2 Turning point in business cycle *Source* Authors' calculation . . . . 23
Fig. 2.3 Turning point in financial cycle *Source* Authors' calculation . . . . 24
Fig. 2.4 Breitung–Candelon Spectral Granger causality *Source* Authors' calculation . . . . . 25
Fig. 3.1 Beta percentile points over time . . . . . 35
Fig. 3.2 *BAB* and 4 factor over time . . . . . 39
Fig. 7.1 Share of average formal and informal credit borrowed (2nd half of 2002 and 2012). *Source* Calculation done by authors . . . . . 84
Fig. 8.1 Principal–Principal conflicts versus Principal–Agent conflicts (Young et al. 2008) . . . . . 115
Fig. 8.2 Principal–Principal conflicts antecedents and consequences in emerging economies (Young et al. 2008) . . . . . 116
Fig. 9.1 Pictorial representation of dependent and independent variables . . . . . 129

# List of Tables


Table 2.1 Dates of turning point in BC and their summary statistics . . . 22
Table 2.2 Dates of turning point in financial cycle and their summary statistics . . . 23
Table 2.3 Lag selection-order criteria. . . . 25
Table 3.1 Summary statistics of the data . . . 32
Table 3.2 Monthly alphas for various beta-deciles and the *BAB* factor . . . 37
Table 3.3 *BAB*, Market, *HML*, *SMB* and *WML* factor returns over the years . . . 38
Table 3.4 Robustness of *BAB* Factor returns with Size, B/M, and momentum factors. . . . 40
Table 3.5 Monthly alphas for various volatility deciles . . . 40
Table 3.6 Monthly alphas of various volatility-size quintiles . . . 41
Table 4.1 Descriptive statistics and correlation matrix . . . 49
Table 4.2 GARCH, EGARCH and TGARCH estimates (with and without EPU). . . . 51
Table 5.1 Summary statistics of future and spot prices of the commodities. . . . 61
Table 5.2 Unit root test results. . . . 62
Table 5.3 Optimal lag length for pairs of agricultural commodities and BSE FMCG index. . . . 63
Table 5.4 ARDL bound results for agricultural commodities and BSE FMCG index. . . . 63
Table 5.5 Johansen cointegration test results . . . 64
Table 5.6 Granger causality test results with Toda and Yamamoto approach . . . 65
Table 7.1 Descriptive statistics for household characteristics . . . 85
Table 7.2 Fixed effect coefficient for informal credit availability in 2002 . . . 89

Table 7.3 Fixed effect coefficient for formal credit availability in 2002 .... 93
Table 7.4 Fixed effect coefficient for informal credit availability in 2012 .... 97
Table 7.5 Fixed effect coefficient for formal credit availability in 2012 .... 101
Table 7.6 Random effects for 59th (2002) and 70th round (2012) .... 105
Table 7.7 Contribution of observed variables on the variance at each level for both the rounds .... 106
Table 9.1 Definition of variables .... 131
Table 9.2 Descriptive statistics of large banks .... 133
Table 9.3 Correlation analysis of large banks .... 134
Table 9.4 Coefficients for large banks (ATR) .... 136
Table 9.5 Multiple linear regression goodness of fit for large bank (ATR) .... 137
Table 9.6 Analysis of variance (ATR) .... 137
Table 9.7 Coefficients for large banks (LR) .... 138
Table 9.8 Multiple linear regression goodness of fit for large bank (LR) .... 139
Table 9.9 Analysis of Variance (LR) .... 139
Table 9.10 Descriptive statistic for small banks .... 140
Table 9.11 Correlation analysis of small banks .... 141
Table 9.12 Coefficients for small banks (ATR) .... 142
Table 9.13 Multiple linear regression goodness of fit for the small bank (LR) .... 142
Table 9.14 Analysis of variance (ATR) .... 142
Table 9.15 Coefficients for small banks (LR) .... 143
Table 9.16 Multiple linear regression goodness of fit for the small bank (LR) .... 143
Table 9.17 Analysis of variance (LR) .... 144
Table 9.18 Comparison of both model of large and small banks .... 144
Table 10.1 Domestic and international passenger traffic in India .... 153
Table 10.2 Altman Z″ score of selected air carriers .... 159
Table 10.3 Assessment of selected air carriers based on Z″ score .... 160
Table 10.4 P-score of selected air carriers .... 161
Table 10.5 Probability of bankruptcy for selected air carriers .... 163
Table 10.6 Fuzzy logic Z scores for air carriers for 2014–2019 .... 164
Table 10.7 Assessment of risk of different air carriers based on fuzzy logic Z scores .... 165
Table 10.8 $Y_a$ scores as per Kroeze model .... 167
Table 10.9 Assessment of air carriers based on Kroeze model .... 168
Table 10.10 Consolidated scores of selected models for various air carriers .... 169

# Chapter 1
# The Evolving Financial Landscape in Emerging Markets and Developing Economies

**Sanket Mohapatra and Aswini Kumar Mishra**

**Abstract** Emerging Markets and Developing Economies (EMDEs) have been a significant driver of global growth in the twenty-first century. This paper analyses the changing contours of the financial sector and the challenges faced by EMDEs in recent years. In these countries, banks and domestic equity markets still continue to be vital as a source of financing for the corporate sector, bond markets. Amongst developing regions, South Asia had the largest equity market capitalization as a share of GDP in 2019, and the growth of corporate bond markets has been facilitated by improved macroeconomic stability, better regulation of bond markets, and protection of retail investors. Finally, the findings relating to financial inclusion (that includes digital and traditional) suggest further promoting access to and usage of formal financial services to maximize society's overall welfare.

**Keywords** Emerging markets and developing economies · Equity and bond market · Financial development · Financial inclusion

## 1.1 Introduction

The financial landscape of Emerging Markets and Developing Economies (EMDEs) has changed significantly since the early 2000s. This period has witnessed an increase in the depth, liquidity, and sophistication of financial markets in developing countries. While banks and domestic equity markets continue to remain important as a source of financing for the corporate sector, bond markets and foreign financing have become increasingly important. The increased integration of domestic and foreign

S. Mohapatra (✉) · A. K. Mishra
Indian Institute of Management Ahmedabad, Vastrapur, Ahmedabad 380015, Gujarat, India
e-mail: sanketm@iima.ac.in

A. K. Mishra
Department of Economics, BITS Pilani, K K Birla Goa Campus, Sancoale 403726, Goa, India
e-mail: aswini@goa.bits-pilani.ac.in



A. K. Mishra et al. (eds.), *The Financial Landscape of Emerging Economies*,
Accounting, Finance, Sustainability, Governance & Fraud: Theory and Application,
https://doi.org/10.1007/978-3-030-60008-2_1

financial markets has benefits in the form of lower cost of financing and diversification of risk, but the increase in foreign financing (in particular, debt financing) has also brought about additional risks arising from sudden changes in foreign investors' sentiments. In addition to improved financing for the private sector, financial inclusion has risen in the policy agenda, with ubiquitous access to mobile telephony and new financial technologies (Fintech) complementing each other in lowering the cost of transactions and increasing access to basic financial services to billions of underserved populations.

In this chapter, we document various facets of the changes in the financial sector in emerging markets and developing countries, the progress made so far, and the challenges that have arisen in recent years. The next section discusses financial development and bank lending in developing countries. This is followed by a discussion of equity and bond markets in developing countries and the benefits and risks of foreign financing. Section five analyses the changing contours of financial inclusion in emerging and lower middle-income countries and the last section concludes.

## 1.2 Financial Development and Bank Lending in Emerging Countries

The financial sector in developing countries has improved significantly in terms of depth, liquidity, and access. Banks in emerging market countries play an important role in intermediating credit to the private sector (Beim & Calomiris, 2001). Banks' credit to the private sector as a share of GDP is a well-known measure of financial depth of a country (Čihák, Demirgüč-Kunt, Feyen, & Levine, 2013).[1] The extent of legal creditor protection and information-sharing institutions (such as public and private credit registries) has been shown to be associated with higher private credit to gross domestic product (Djankov, McLiesh, & Shleifer, 2007). Protection of creditor rights is usually in the form of the ability to enforce repayment and seize collateral in the event of default.[2]

Bank credit to the private sector in developing countries doubled from 51.2% of GDP in 2000 to 108.5% of GDP in 2019. However, there is substantial heterogeneity across the six developing regions (Fig. 1.1). For instance, the Latin America and the Caribbean started with private credit at 22% of GDP in 2000, which improved to 52% in 2019. South Asia's share of private credit similarly improved from 27% of GDP in 2000 to 47% in 2019. Sub-Saharan Africa, however, experienced a decline in bank credit from 55 to 45% between 2000 and 2018. By contrast, developing countries in East Asia and the Pacific region had already high level of financial depth of more

[1]The variable is defined as domestic private credit to the real sector by deposit money banks as percentage of local currency GDP (Čihák et al., 2013).

[2]Gopalakrishnan and Mohapatra (2020) argue that stronger insolvency frameworks that increase creditor rights are associated with improved credit discipline amongst firms. The authors find that the default risk of firms is lower in countries with stronger insolvency regimes.

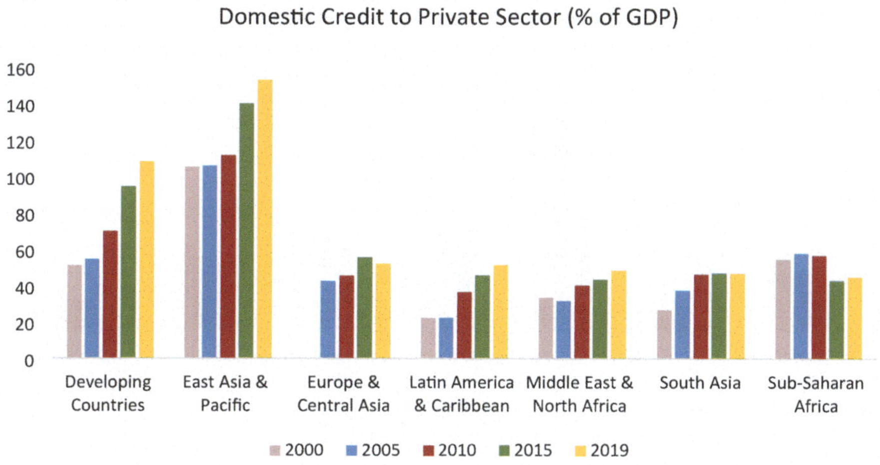


**Fig. 1.1** Domestic credit to private sector in developing countries. *Source* World Bank. *Notes* For Europe and Central Asia, the earliest available data for 2008 data has been used instead of that for 2005. For Middle East and North Africa and Sub-Saharan Africa, the latest available data for 2016 and 2018 have been used instead of that for 2019

than 105% of GDP in 2000, which further increased to 153% in 2019. The relatively large weight of East Asia and the Pacific region, particularly China, in the developing countries aggregate explains the high share of credit to GDP of developing countries as a whole.

The availability of bank branches is the highest in the developing countries in Eastern Europe (24.2 per 100,000 adults in 2018), partly owing to an expansion of Western European banks to the neighbouring countries region. Sub-Saharan Africa has the lowest number of bank branches (5 per 100,000 adults in 2018), albeit an improvement from 1.5 in 2000.

Along with an increase in credit to the private sector, the reach of bank branches in developing countries has also improved (from about 5 per 100,000 adults in 2005 to about 9 in 2018), although with variation across the developing regions (Fig. 1.2).

The experience of the global financial crisis in 2008–2009 and the episodes of country-specific banking crises (Laeven & Valencia, 2018) have highlighted the need for better regulation of the banking sector. Most developing countries have adopted the Basel II regulations on bank capital adequacy, with about 40% adopting the enhanced Basel III regulations (World Bank, 2019). The higher levels of bank capital can enhance the stability of the financial system, protect depositors, and help the banking system to absorb shocks, such as that emanating from the Covid-19 pandemic, and prevent bank failures. Nevertheless, the high levels of non-performing assets (NPAs) of banks in some developing countries are a cause for concern. NPA ratios are particularly high in India (about 9% of gross advances), Russia (10.1%), Tajikistan (about 25%), Ukraine (48.4%), and several African countries (between 10 and 25% in Angola, Congo, Central African Republic, Ghana, Kenya, and Zambia)

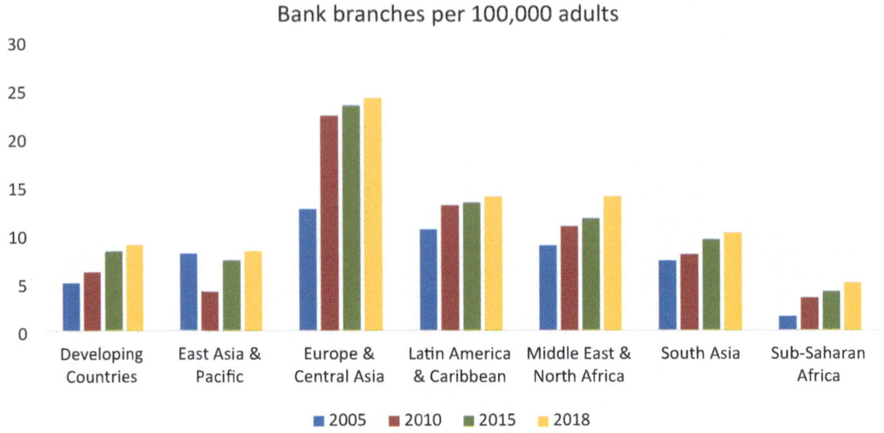


**Fig. 1.2** Bank branches per 100,000 adults in developing countries. *Source* World Bank

according to the World Bank and IMF data. High levels of banking sector NPAs impair the ability of the banks to extend credit to the corporate sector, which can translate into lower levels of investment and output.

## 1.3 Equity and Bond Markets in Developing Countries

Equity market financing is a traditional source of firm financing, usually through initial public offerings (IPOs). Modigliani and Perotti (2000) argue that the protection of minority shareholder rights is an important factor in equity capital raising by firms, and find some supportive evidence that in countries with weaker investor protection, equity markets tend to be smaller and the role of bank financing (relationship-based lending) is larger.

Overall market capitalization as a share of GDP of developing countries rose significantly from 40% in 2005 (prior to the global financial crisis) to 65% in 2010, but has declined in the subsequent years (Fig. 1.3). The large increase in equity market capitalization in the run-up to the global financial crisis can be attributed to high GDP growth rates in developing countries, buoyancy in international trade and capital flows, and expectations of continued earnings growth amongst emerging market firms. The subsequent decline is in line with a fall in the average GDP growth rates and a realignment of investors' expectations. Amongst developing regions, South Asia had the largest equity market capitalization as a share of GDP in 2019, likely owing to favourable tax treatment of equities (compared to debt), growth of domestic investor base, and greater capital account openness for foreign equity investors.

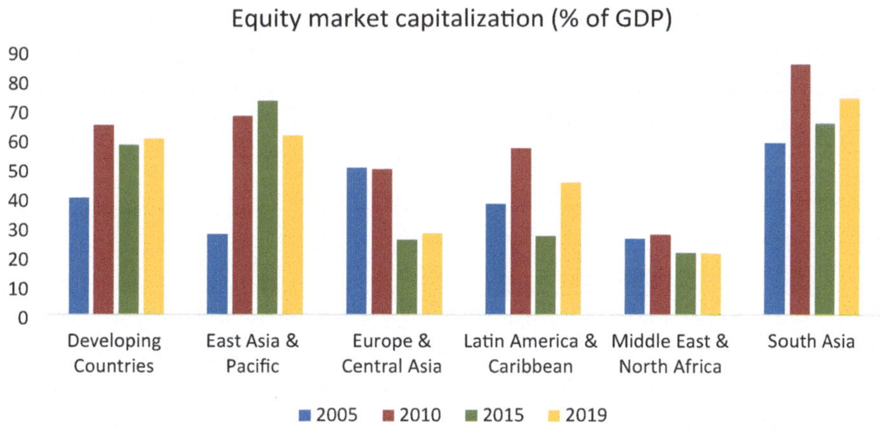


**Fig. 1.3** Equity markets in developing countries. *Source* World Bank. *Notes* For Europe and Central Asia, the earliest available data for 2009 and latest available data for 2018 have been used instead of that for 2005 and 2019, respectively. For Middle East and North Africa and Sub-Saharan Africa, the latest available data for 2016 and 2018 have been used instead of that for 2019

Bond markets can provide longer term financing, such as for infrastructure development, in developing countries (Park, 2017). Burger, Warnock, and Warnock (2012) find that emerging market economies with higher macroeconomic stability (lower inflation volatility), and stronger creditor rights have more developed local bond markets. The authors argue that improvement in creditor (bondholders') rights would support the further development of bond markets.

Government and corporate bond markets in developing countries have grown in recent decades, albeit from a relatively small base in many countries, particularly for corporate bond markets. For instance, the size of local currency bond markets in Asian economies has increased substantially in recent decades. Local currency bonds outstanding in China rose from 6% of GDP in 2005 to 62.9% in 2015, from 24.5 to 56.8% in India, and from 2.4 to 17.1% in Indonesia (Park, 2017; see Fig. 1.4). Governments have remained the largest issuers of local currency bonds in most Asian countries with the proceeds used to finance their fiscal expenditures. For instance, local currency government bonds accounted for 42.2% of GDP in India while corporate bonds accounted for only 14.6% in 2015. The growth of corporate bond markets has been facilitated by improved macroeconomic stability, better regulation of bond markets, and protection of retail investors. While Asia leads in terms of issuance of non-financial corporate bonds, there is wide variation in the countries in Latin America. Corporate bond issuance is high in some countries such as Bermuda (22%) and Jamaica (13%), but less than 1% in other countries such as Argentina, Dominican Republic, Guatemala, and Uruguay (Beck, 2016).

Park (2017) finds evidence that bond market development is related to macroeconomic performance and institutions, which can increase corporate debt issuance at longer maturities. Local currency bond markets can also help to stabilize economies

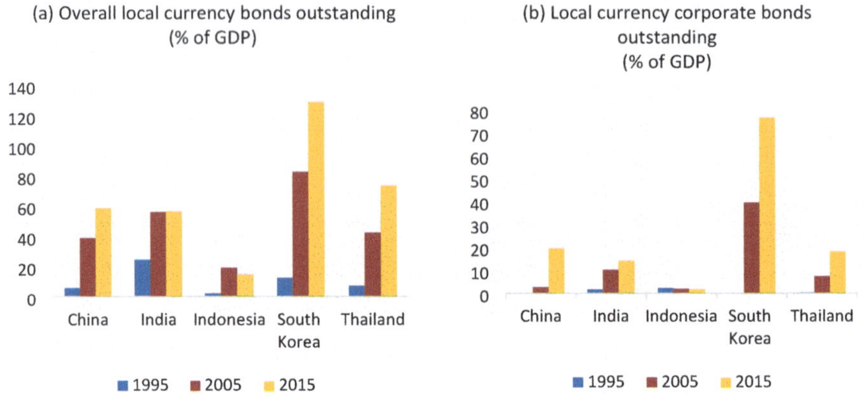


**Fig. 1.4** Local currency bond markets in selected Asian economies. *Source* Based on data compiled by Park (2017). *Notes* South Korea is considered an emerging market by MSCI, but a high-income country by the World Bank

during shocks. Park, Shin, and Tian (2019) find a negative association between the growth of local currency bond markets and the degree of currency depreciation in emerging economies during external shocks such as the global financial crisis and the taper tantrum in 2013.

## 1.4 Foreign Financing in Developing Countries: Recent Developments and Risks

In recent decades, firms in emerging market countries have relied increasingly on foreign financing in addition to domestic sources. Hale (2007) finds that domestic macroeconomic fundamentals in emerging market countries significantly affect firms' choice of international debt instrument such as loans and bonds. Caballero, Fernández, and Park (2019) find that firms in emerging market countries experienced an increase in foreign financing since the early 2000s, with a larger role for bond issuances. According to the authors, the outstanding stock of private international debt grew from about 600 billion USD in the early 2000s to 2.4 trillion USD by 2014 in 18 smaller emerging market economies. [3] Foreign currency syndicated loans have also played a role in financing corporations in emerging market economies. A study by Gong, Jiang, and Wu (2018) finds that loan spreads tend to be lower for syndicated loans denominated in a foreign currency compared to those in the local currency in many emerging economies, suggesting that international bank financing can reduce the cost of capital for emerging market firms.

[3]The 18 emerging economies in the study of Caballero et al. (2019) include Brazil, Chile, Colombia, Ecuador, Mexico, Peru, Indonesia, Korea, Malaysia, Philippines, Thailand, Czech Republic, Hungary, Poland, Russia, and Turkey, South Africa, and Israel.

In the period following the global financial crisis in 2008, loose monetary policies and quantitative easing (QE) in advanced economies resulted in increased foreign financing for firms in emerging markets and developing countries. Such effects were more pronounced for portfolio debt and equity flows to emerging economies compared to foreign direct investment (Lim & Mohapatra, 2016). Fratzscher, Lo Duca, and Straub (2018) find that the second and third quantitative easing (QE2 and QE3) measures by the US Federal Reserve led to an acceleration in portfolio flows in emerging market economies. Turner (2014) documents how a low or negative term premium in the yield curve since 2010 owing to extraordinary monetary easing in advanced economies increased international investment in local bond markets in emerging economies. According to the author, the low interest rates also encouraged foreign currency borrowing through issuance of international bond market by emerging market firms, particularly through overseas affiliates.

Increased reliance on debt financing and higher leverage ratios also bring with them additional risks. Studies using firm-level data in both advanced and developing economies have examined the effects of such changes in debt financing on firm performance. For example, in a study on 11 advanced economies, Duval, Hong, and Timmer (2020) find that more leveraged firms (firms with higher debt-to-assets ratio) prior to the global financial crisis (GFC) experienced larger fall in total factor productivity (TFP). Similar effects of leverage are likely to hold during crisis events in developing countries. Reliance on international debt financing exposes emerging market firms to global volatility. For instance, the testimony of the US Federal Reserve Chairman Ben Bernanke in the US Congress on 22 May 2013 about a "tapering" of US quantitative easing resulted in a sudden increase in capital flows out of emerging market economies and large exchange rate depreciations (Eichengreen & Gupta, 2015). Such depreciations can increase balance sheet risks for firms in emerging market countries and raise the cost of foreign debt financing in local currency terms.

## 1.5 Financial Inclusion

Financial inclusion (FI), in the broadest terms, refers to access to financial services. It is seen as one of the foremost steps towards inclusive growth and development of a nation. As defined by the United Nations Capital Development Fund (UNCDF), financial inclusion refers to the access and use of a range of appropriate and responsibly provided financial services offered in a regulated environment to individuals and enterprises. According to the World Bank (2018), financial inclusion refers to "having access to affordable and useful financial products and services to meet the needs of transactions, payments, savings, credits, and insurance delivered in a sustainable and responsible manner". Thus, the first step towards achieving total financial inclusion is to connect the adult population to the financial institutions through the bank account.

In recent years, a large strand of the literature has started exploring the subject area to attain higher financial inclusion citing the greater benefits achieved. These benefits, as mentioned by different researchers in their study, vary from providing an economic rationale to providing political rationale behind framing policies targeting financial inclusion (Karlan & Morduch, 2010). Other researches show that formal account ownership impacts saving pattern (Aportela, 1999; Zins & Weill, 2016), investments, and consumption pattern (Dupas & Robinson, 2009) and helps in attaining financial stability (Han & Melecky, 2013). A very recent study by Omar and Inaba (2020) investigates the impact of financial inclusion on reducing poverty and income inequality, and the determinants and conditional effects thereof in 116 developing countries. Results show that per capita income, ratio of Internet users, age dependency ratio, inflation, and income inequality significantly influence the level of financial inclusion in developing countries. Furthermore, the results provide robust evidence that financial inclusion significantly reduces poverty rates and income inequality in developing countries. Needless to mention, most of the developing countries in the recent decades are witnessing a sharp rise in income or wealth inequality (Mishra & Parmar, 2017; Mishra, 2018; Mishra & Kumar, 2018; Mishra, Kumar, & Sinha, 2019; Mishra & Bhardwaj, 2020).

A recent World Bank report on financial inclusion (based on Global Findex data) states that despite the various efforts taken to reach out to a different section of the society around the world, there are approximately 2 billion people who are unbanked (Demirgüç-Kunt, Klapper, Singer, Ansar, & Hess, 2018). The report further states that around half of the population above 15 years of age lacks access or does not use formal financial services. Of these, the majority dwells under the poverty line in developing nations. According to the number of researches done in the field of financial inclusion, bringing this set of the population under the umbrella of formal financial services can help reduce the poverty level and increase living standards. The World Bank's "The Little Data Book on Financial Inclusion" (2018) figures out that in the world around 68.5% of adults (age 15+) had an account in a financial institution while this number is only while for lower middle-income countries this number decreases drastically to 56.1%. This data reveals that lower middle-income countries are struggling even to make the basic infrastructure available to all of its adult population. Figure 1.5 gives us the percentage of adults (age 15+) who have an account in a financial institution in the considered lower middle-income emerging economies.

Figure 1.5 shows stark differences in the considered lower middle-income countries. On the one hand, we have countries like India and Sri Lanka, where based on the global Findex database, around 80t and 74% of the adult population, respectively, have an account at a financial institution. On the other hand, there are countries like Pakistan and Cambodia, where only 18% of the adult population have an account in a financial institution. This shows that amongst the emerging lower middle-income countries, there is a widespread disparity in terms of progress towards financial inclusion.

Having an account at a financial institution does not necessarily mean that an individual is financially included as the account itself does not ensure that the individual's demands of transaction, savings, and credit are met through the financial institutions. While looking at the data of inactive accounts (no deposit or withdrawal done in the

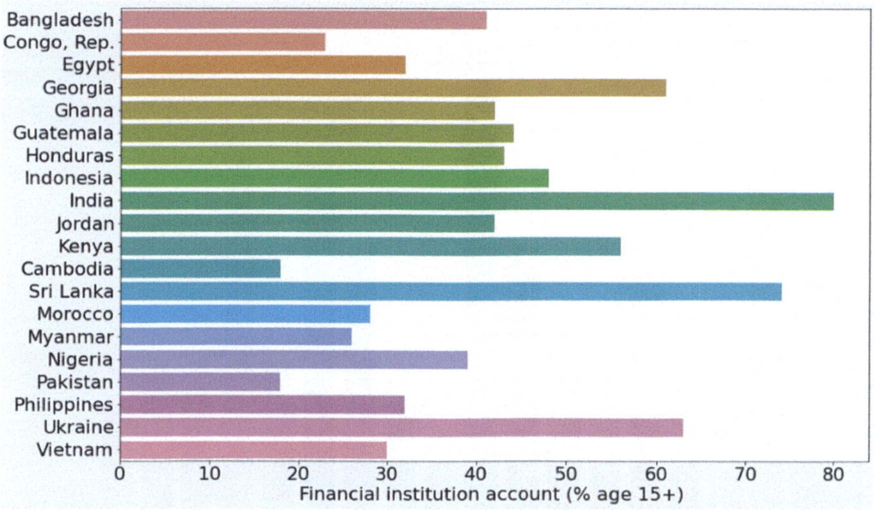


**Fig. 1.5** Percentage of adults above the age of 15 having an account in the considered emerging lower middle-income countries. *Source* Global Findex database (2017)

past one year), we observe that at the global level, 20% of adults holding an account in the financial institution have made no deposit or withdrawal in the past one year whereas this figure is 39.2% for lower middle-income countries. Figure 1.6 gives details about the inactive accounts amongst account holders in financial institutions for the considered emerging lower middle-income countries.

We observe from Fig. 1.6 that India has the highest percentage (48%) of inactive accounts amongst the adult account holders in financial institutes, whereas Ukraine has the lowest percentage of inactive accounts. We saw from Fig. 1.6 that India also has the highest percentage of adult account holders in financial institutes, which shows that just by connecting adults to the financial infrastructure does not ensure that all the barriers in the way of accessing financial services have been removed. In the case of countries like Myanmar and the Republic of Congo, we observe (from Figs. 1.5 and 1.6) that a small proportion of the adult population has been connected to financial institutions, and amongst them, around 40% of them are inactive, which paint a much dire situation.

Similarly, while exploring the pattern of savings and credit borrowing to observe the accessibility of saving and credit products, the share of the adult population that saved or borrowed from financial institutions to the percentage of the adult population as indicators has been used. At the global level, we find that 56.25% of the adults saved in a financial institution. On the other hand, merely 23.4% of adults took credit from these institutions. For the lower middle-income countries, these figures are 32.3% and 50.9% respectively.

Figure 1.7 gives the savings pattern and we observe that there is a strong positive correlation between the share of adults saving using a financial institute to save and the share of adults having accounts in financial institutes.

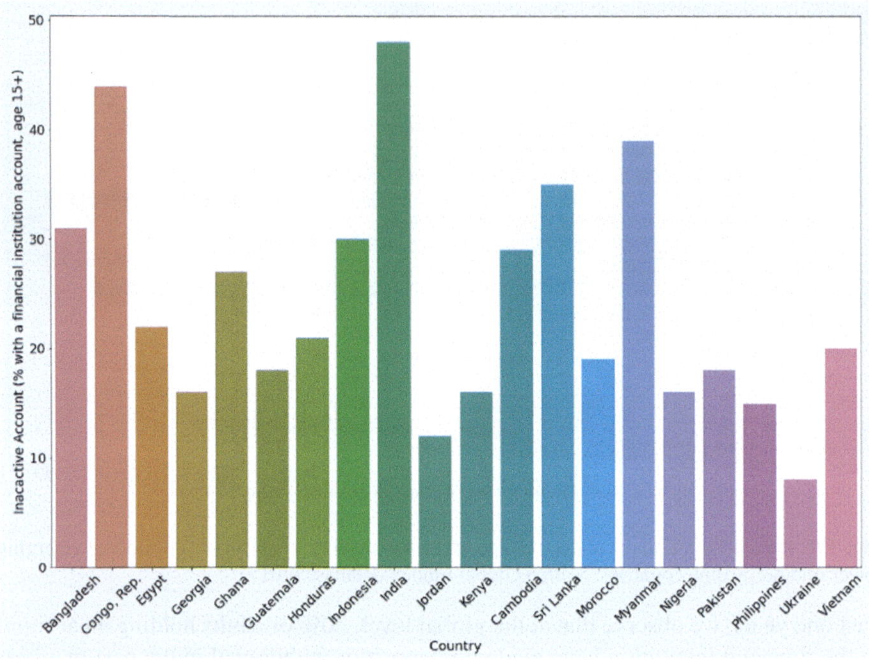


**Fig. 1.6** Per cent of adults (15+ age) with an account in a financial institution and those who made no deposit and withdrawal in the past one year. *Source* Global Findex database (2017)

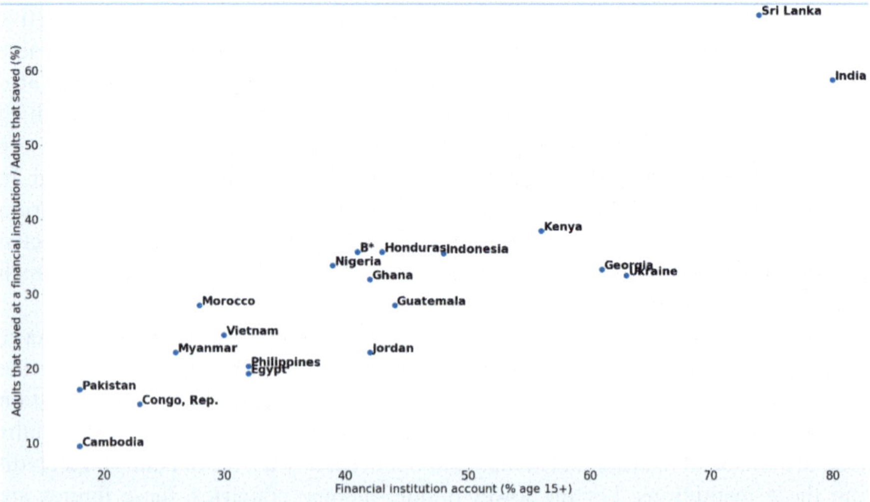


**Fig. 1.7** Savings pattern amongst the adults (15+ age) having an account at a formal institution. *Note* B* represents Bangladesh. *Source* Global Findex database (2017)

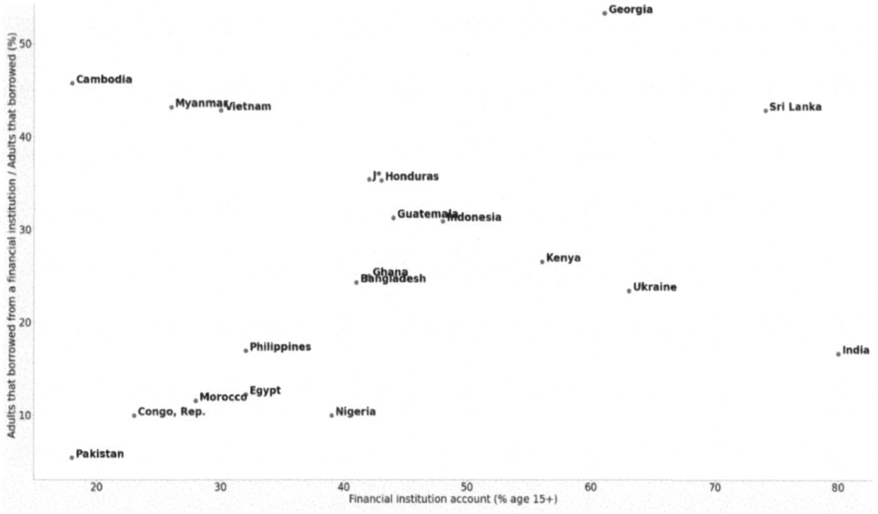


**Fig. 1.8** Borrowing pattern amongst the adults (15+ age) having an account at a formal institution. *Note* J* represents Jordan. *Source* Global Findex database (2017)

Figure 1.8 shows us the borrowing pattern in these select lower middle-income/emerging countries. We notice the correlation between the share of adults borrowing from financial institutions to the total borrowers and the share of adults having accounts in financial institutes is relatively low.

It is rather surprising as in the case of credit products, banks are very selective to ensure repayment, so borrowers are required to provide mortgages or security. The need for security acts as a barrier, especially for lower income classes. We can see that countries like Ukraine and India have connected a higher percentage of adults to financial institutions. However, the credit availability from financial institutes is still not accessible by its adult population. In contrast, Sri Lank has done both simultaneously, has connected its adult population to the financial sector, and also made credit opportunities available to them. A very recent study by the IMF (2020) also reveals the case for digital financial inclusion which varies across countries and regions. The study combines a traditional (bank-based) and a digital financial inclusion component (such as ATM and bank branches, mobile and Internet access, account holding, and usage of financial institutions/mobile account for wage and utility payments) and covers 52 emerging market and developing economies (EMDEs) with the span period of 2014–2017 for digital financial inclusion and 2011–2017 for traditional financial inclusion.

Figure 1.9 indicates that comprehensive financial inclusion (that includes digital and traditional) increase in most countries between 2014 and 2017. Countries like Benin, Ghana, and Senegal saw greater progress in digital inclusion, while others like Mongolia, Namibia, and Peru in traditional inclusion. This implies there is an

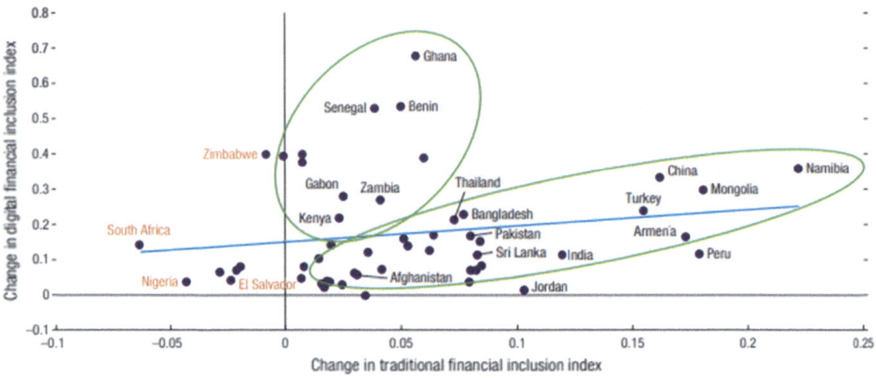


**Fig. 1.9** Changes in Financial inclusion Indices, 2014–2017 (Level change). *Source* IMF staff calculations cited in IMF (2020)

enormous potential for progress towards digital financial inclusion for most of these EMDEs. And, Fintech service providers need to play a proactive role in this regard.

## 1.6 Conclusion

The changing financial landscape of emerging markets and developing economies in the context of new global scenario entails a persistent, stronger presence of governments and/or central banks in asset pricing. This paper analyses various facets of the changes in the financial sector in emerging markets and developing countries and the challenges that have arisen in recent years. In these countries, banks and domestic equity markets still continue to be vital as a source of financing for the corporate sector. Nevertheless, foreign financing has become increasingly important with the increased integration of domestic and foreign financial markets. Amongst developing regions, South Asia had the largest equity market capitalization as a share of GDP in 2019, likely owing to favourable tax treatment of equities (compared to debt), growth of domestic investor base, and greater capital account openness for foreign equity investors. Further, the growth of corporate bond markets has been facilitated by improved macroeconomic stability, better regulation of bond markets, and protection of retail investors. While Asia leads in terms of issuance of non-financial corporate bonds, there is wide variation in the countries in Latin America. The paper suggests that with prudent macroeconomic policies and additional development of analytical frameworks and policy prescriptions for financial market regulation, financial stability can be further achieved whilst balancing the goals of financial development and broader financial inclusion. The findings relating to financial inclusion (that includes digital and traditional) imply further promoting access to and usage of formal financial services in order to maximize society's overall welfare.

## References


Aportela, F. (1999). *The effects of financial access on savings by low-income people*. MIT: Mimeo.

Beck, T. (2016). *Long-term finance in Latin America. A scoreboard model* (Discussion Paper IDBDP-476).

Beim, D. O., & Calomiris, C. W. (2001). *Emerging financial markets*. New York: McGraw-Hill/Irwin.

Burger, J. D., Warnock, F. E., & Warnock, V. C. (2012). Emerging local currency bond markets. *Financial Analysts Journal, 68*(4), 73–93.

Caballero, J., Fernández, A., & Park, J. (2019). On corporate borrowing, credit spreads and economic activity in emerging economies: An empirical investigation. *Journal of International Economics, 118*, 160–178.

Čihák, M., Demirgüč-Kunt, A., Feyen, E., & Levine, R. (2013). *Financial development in 205 economies, 1960 to 2010* (No. w18946). National Bureau of Economic Research.

Demirgüç-Kunt, A., Klapper, L., Singer, D., Ansar, S., & Hess, J. (2018). *The Global Findex Database 2017: Measuring financial inclusion and the fintech revolution*. Washington, DC: World Bank. https://doi.org/10.1596/978-1-4648-1259-0. License: Creative Commons Attribution CC BY 3.0 IGO.

Djankov, S., McLiesh, C., & Shleifer, A. (2007). Private credit in 129 countries. *Journal of Financial Economics, 84*(2), 299–329.

Dupas, P., & Robinson, J. (2009). *Savings constraints and microenterprise development: Evidence from a field experiment in Kenya* (NBER Working Papers 14693), National Bureau of Economic Research, Inc.

Duval, R., Hong, G. H., & Timmer, Y. (2020). Financial frictions and the great productivity slowdown. *The Review of Financial Studies, 33*(2), 475–503.

Eichengreen, B., & Gupta, P. (2015). Tapering talk: The impact of expectations of reduced Federal Reserve security purchases on emerging markets. *Emerging Markets Review, 25*, 1–15.

Fratzscher, M., Lo Duca, M., & Straub, R. (2018). On the international spillovers of US quantitative easing. *The Economic Journal, 128*(608), 330–377.

Gong, D., Jiang, T., & Wu, W. (2018). A foreign currency effect in the syndicated loan market of emerging economies. *Journal of International Financial Markets, Institutions and Money, 52*, 211–226.

Gopalakrishnan, B., & Mohapatra, S. (2020). Insolvency regimes and firms' default risk under economic uncertainty and shocks. *Economic Modelling* (forthcoming).

Hale, G. (2007). Bonds or loans? The effect of macroeconomic fundamentals. *The Economic Journal, 117*(516), 196–215.

Han, R., & Melecky, M. (2013). Financial inclusion for financial stability: Access to bank deposits and the growth of deposits in the global financial crisis. *Policy Research Working Papers*.

IMF-International Monetary Fund. (2020). *The promise of fintech: financial inclusion in the post COVID-19 era*/Ratna Sahay, Ulric Eriksson von Allmen, Amina Lahreche, Purva Khera, Sumiko Ogawa, Majid Bazarbash, and Kim Beaton. Monetary and Capital Markets Department. Washington, DC: International Monetary Fund.

Karlan, D., & Morduch, J. (2010). Access to finance. *Handbook of Development Economics*, 4703–4784.

Laeven, M. L., & Valencia, M. F. (2018). Systemic banking crises revisited (IMF Working Paper WP/18/2016). International Monetary Fund.

Lim, J. J., & Mohapatra, S. (2016). Quantitative easing and the post-crisis surge in financial flows to developing countries. *Journal of International Money and Finance, 68*, 331–357.

Mishra, A. K., & Parmar, V. M. (2017). Changing contours of income stratification and decomposition of income inequality: Evidence from recent longitudinal survey in India. *Journal of Quantitative Economics, 15*(2), 395–422. https://doi.org/10.1007/s40953-016-0057-0.

Mishra, A. K. (2018). Household income inequality and income mobility: implications towards equalising longer-term incomes in India. *International Economic Journal, 32*(2), 271–290. https://doi.org/10.1080/10168737.2018.1480640.

Mishra, A. K., & Kumar, A. (2018). What lies behind income inequality and income mobility in India? Implications and the way forward. *The International Journal of Social Economics, 45*(9), 1369–1384. https://doi.org/10.1108/ijse-03-2017-0119.

Mishra, A. K., Kumar, A., & Sinha, A. (2019). The shape of income distribution and decomposition of the changes in income inequality in India 2005–2012. *Journal of Economic Studies, 46*(3), 760–776.

Mishra, A. K., & Bhardwaj, V. (2020). Wealth distribution and accounting for changes in wealth inequality: empirical evidence from India, 1991–2012. *Economic Change and Restructuring*. https://doi.org/10.1007/s10644-020-09290-9.

Modigliani, F., & Perotti, E. (2000). Security markets versus bank finance: Legal enforcement and investors' protection. *International Review of Finance, 1*(2), 81–96.

Omar, M. A., & Inaba, K. (2020). Does financial inclusion reduce poverty and income inequality in developing countries? A panel data analysis. *Journal of Economic Structures, 9*(1), 37. https://doi.org/10.1186/s40008-020-00214-4.

Park, C. Y. (2017). Developing local currency bond markets in Asia. *Emerging Markets Finance and Trade, 53*(12), 2826–2844.

Park, D., Shin, K., & Tian, S. (2019). Do local currency bond markets enhance financial stability? Some empirical evidence. *Emerging Markets Finance and Trade*, 1–29.

Turner, P. (2014). The global long-term interest rate, financial risks and policy choices in EMEs (BIS Working Paper No. 441), Bank for International Settlements.

World Bank. (2018). *The little data book on financial inclusion 2018*. World Bank, Washington, DC. © World Bank. Retrieved from https://openknowledge.worldbank.org/handle/10986/29654. License: CC BY 3.0 IGO.

World Bank. (2019). *Global financial development report 2019/2020: Bank regulation and supervision a decade after the global financial crisis*. Washington DC: World Bank.

Zins, A., & Weill, L. (2016). The determinants of financial inclusion in Africa. *Review of Development Finance, 6*(1), 46–57.

# Chapter 2
# Nexus Between Financial Cycle and Business Cycle in India

**Kundan Kumar, Zeeshan Nezami Ansari, and Rajendra Narayan Paramanik**

**Abstract** The present paper attempts to explore the possible interdependence between business cycle and financial cycle in India during 1996Q1–2018Q3. Quarterly data of macroeconomic variables, namely real GDP, credit to GDP ratio, real house prices, real equity prices and real effective exchange rate have been used for the analysis. The cyclical components of the variables are generated by the frequency filter technique of Christiano–Fitzgerald. The identification of peaks and troughs has been done using turning point analysis of Bry and Boschan (National Bureau of Economic Research 1971). Degree of co-movement between two cycles is found by Harding and Pagan (Journal of Monetary Economics, 49(2):365–381 2002) technique. To explore the long-run relation between the business cycle and financial cycle, spectral Granger causalitytest (Breitung and Candelon) has been conducted. The empirical finding reveals that the cyclical component of financial variable Granger causes the cyclical component of the gross domestic product in the medium as well as long runs and vice versa.

**Keywords** Business cycle · Financial cycle · Turning point · Spectral granger causality

## 2.1 Introduction

Economic literature described business cycle (BC henceforth) as upward and downward movement of aggregate economic output over a time period and it is measured using real GDP data whereas, financial cycle (FC henceforth) maps out the expansions and contractions in the financial activities (Behera and Sharma, RBI 2019). Seminal work of Burn and Mitchell (1946) laid the foundation for empirical business cycle analysis in modern macroeconomics. Economic literature mainly documents the features of output and its different phases like recovery and recession in early studies. Later on, financial cycle gathered academic attention for further scrutiny

K. Kumar (✉) · Z. N. Ansari · R. N. Paramanik
Department of Humanities and Social Sciences, IIT Patna, Bihta, India
e-mail: kundan_1921hs03@iitp.ac.in



A. K. Mishra et al. (eds.), *The Financial Landscape of Emerging Economies*, Accounting, Finance, Sustainability, Governance & Fraud: Theory and Application,
https://doi.org/10.1007/978-3-030-60008-2_2

along with notions like political business cycle (Rogoff et al. 1988; Nordhaus et al. 1989) and their impact on the real economy. FC is generally gauged through variation in variables like credit, credit to GDP, exchange rate, etc. Notional existence of business cycle in theoretical literature necessitates empirical construct to identify the cycle from the aforementioned macro-financial variables. The battery of statistical techniques such as time series filter of Hodrick and Prescott (1997) and frequency filter of Baxter and King (1999) and Christian and Fitzgerald (2003) are proposed to extract the unobservable cyclical component from time series variables. Though modern macroeconomics has different doctrines like Keynesian and Neo-Classical thought to explain the reason for the existence of business cycle, there is growing consensus regarding nexus between FC and BC.

This paper explores possible interdependence between these two cycles in the Indian context during 1996Q1–2018Q3. Degree of co-movement between two variables has been measured with concordance correlation, and different phases of these two cycles have been chronicled. Turning point analysis of Harding and Pagan (2002) is used for the identification of peaks and troughs for the cyclical components of both variables. Further, the paper empirically validates the long-run relationship between the BC and FC using Breitung and Candelon (2006) spectral Granger causalitytest.

## 2.2 Literature Review

Though in economic literature the notion and definition of BC are well-known, the conceptualization of FC is still an emerging exercise. The literature on BC can be traced back to Burns and Mitchel (946) where they discuss the measurement of business cycle endogenously as well as exogenously. Aikman et al. (2015) used frequency-based filters to find the nexus between the credit and business cycle and concluded that length and amplitude of credit cycle are higher than business cycle, and banking crises is related to credit booms. Claessens et al. (2011) employed turning-point analysis to recognize peaks and troughs in the cyclical component of credit, property and equity prices and found long and severe cycles in these series and the cyclical behaviour of financial indicator is extremely synchronized and there is strong link between FC and BC.

Dates of classical BC and growth cycle for the Indian economy are determined by Dua and Banerji (2000). They constructed a coincidental index and found 5 recovery and 6 recession phases for the BC with a periodicity of around 6 years. Banerjee (2012) documented the relation between growth and credit cycles and found that in the pre-1980s era output is powered by credit, during the 1980s there was no nexus between output and credit and post-1991 credit is powered by output. Anusha (2015) found a strong concordance between bank credit and IIP growth cycle in the US as well as in India. It shows that output is driven by credit in the US whereas credit is driven by output in India. Suarez and Sussman (1999) discuss micro-theoretical part of BC and FC which states that the liquidation rate of firms is higher in the bust than boom. There is an asymmetric inverse relationship between the demand for equipment and price during two contrasting phases of business cycle. Lempert (1985) analysed cyclical components of several variables, and 18 variables are found to be leading indicators whereas 11 variables are lagging in terms of their relationships with peaks and troughs of business cycle. Borio (2014) examined the monetary policy and its nexus with financial cycle which is calculated on the basis of housing price and concluded that the duration and amplitude of FC increases after the financial liberalization. There are empirical works conducted for many countries regarding the concordance of BC and FC and volatility in the financial variables. Drehmann et al. (2012) found that credit, credit to output ratio and house price have more volatility than GDP. Some studies found that FC has longer duration and amplitude than BC (Behera and Sharma 2019). Avouyi-Dovi and Matheron (2005) found real GDP and stock price did not coincide in short term but in long term, there is strong co-movement between them. Winter et al. (2017) showed that in the medium term, business cycle and house price have co-movement whereas in short term there is no co-movement between them.

The measurement of Indian BC carried out by Pandey et al. (2017, 2019a) highlighted that the duration of expansion is greater than that of recession and the expansion phase has less coefficient of variation in duration than the recession phase. The research on BC and FC in case of India carried out by Behera and Sharma (2019) found that bidirectional causality between FC and BC does not exist in short term but in long term it prevails. Ghate et al. (2013) in their study observed that investment, import and nominal exchange rate are pro-cyclical to GDP whereas net export, government expenditure are anti-cyclical to GDP. The existing body of literature on financial cycle and its relation with business in India needs more empirical attention and this paper attempts to explore this unexplored work.

## 2.3 Data and Methodology

Several financial variables have been used in the literature to analyse the financial cycle. We used the following financial variables namely, credit to GDP ratio, real house prices, real effective exchange rate (reer) and real equity prices. Using the cyclical component of these variables, the present paper developed a financial index by applying principal component analysis (PCA). GDP at market price is used as a proxy to measure BC. All the variables have been deflated by consumer price index (base year 2010) to convert into their real terms and are expressed in their natural log forms. The paper considers all the variables at quarterly frequency during 1996Q1–2018Q3 and de-seasonalised using the X-12-ARIMA technique. The data is taken from a handbook on Indian economy of Reserve Bank of India (RBI) and Bank of International Settlement (BIS).

### 2.3.1 Seasonal Adjustment and Extraction of the Cyclical Component by Christiano–Fitzgerald Filter

Each series has been adjusted for seasonal fluctuations by using the X-12-ARIMA technique. Extraction of the cyclical component of both series is the next step and this has been done using the frequency filter technique of Christiano and Fitzgerald (2003). The CF filter assumes that time series $y_t$ is generated by pure random walk without drift. It is an approximation of an ideal band-pass filter which is based on the principles of the Baxter and King filter (1999). The cyclical component is estimated as follows:

$$c_t = k_0 y_t + k_1 y_{t+1} + \cdots + k_{T-1-t} y_{T-1} + \tilde{k}_{T-t} y_t + k_1 y_{t-1} + \cdots + k_{t-2} y_2 + \tilde{k}_{t-1} y_1 \tag{2.1}$$

where $t = 3, 4, \ldots, T - 2$ and

$$k_j = \frac{\sin(jc) - \sin(ja)}{\pi j}, j \geq 1$$

$$k_0 = \frac{m - n}{\pi}, n = \frac{2\pi}{p_h}, m = \frac{2\pi}{p_l}$$

$$\tilde{k}_k = -\frac{1}{2} k_0 - \sum_{j=1}^{k-1} k_j$$

where $2 \leq p_l < p_h < \infty$ and for the quarterly data $p_l$ and $p_h$ are 6 and 32, respectively. The CF filter is not symmetric because it gives different weights to each observation. In the Baxter and King filter (1999) filter, weights are considered as fixed regardless of the number of observations. The CF filter is consistent; as the sample size increases, it converges to an ideal band-pass filter.

### 2.3.2 The Dating Algorithm

Following Bry and Boschan (1971) and Harding and Pagan (2002) algorithms, turning points in business cycle as well in financial cycle are identified. This algorithm detects possible turning points as the local minima and maxima in the series. It satisfies two conditions: phases are at least $p$ quarter long and complete cycles are at least $c$ quarter long (i.e. the gap between two consecutive peaks or troughs). The use of this dating algorithm shows the potential dates of peaks and troughs along with summary statistics. The algorithm requires that peaks and troughs should be alternate, and a trough should be lower than the preceding peak and vice versa. Turning point is defined in the following way: Local peak in the time series $c_t$ occurs at time

$t$ whenever $c_t > c_{t \pm k}$ and a local trough occurs whenever $c_t < c_{t \pm k}$ where $k = 1, \ldots, k$.

Here, NBER assumes that data having a monthly frequency $K$ is set to be five and having quarterly data it is set to be two. Therefore, to apply these rules to quarterly data $K$ is set to two. After identifying the peaks and troughs by the Bry and Boschan (1971) algorithm, some basic statistics such as average duration and amplitude of the phases in individual series can be calculated.

### *2.3.3 Concordance Index*

After dating the peaks and troughs by using the algorithm of Bry and Boschan (1971), some basic statistics such as average duration and average amplitude for both FC and BC can be calculated. Concordance indicator developed by Harding and Pagan (2002) and implemented by McDermott and Scott (2000) at the IMF is used to find the concordance between BC and FC. Concordance statistics measures the proportion of time when two variables coincide at the same phase of the cycle. This statistics is nonparametric in nature. If the concordance statistics equals one then there is perfect synchronization and it implies both the series are moving together, and if it equals zero then there is perfect disconcordance which means that the series are in the opposite phase.

Suppose there is a binary variable $S_{b,t}$ for BC such that it is equal to 1 when BC is at expansion at time t and 0 otherwise. In the same way, $S_{f,t}$ for FC is equal to 1 when it is in acceleration phase and 0 otherwise. The concordance index between BC and FC is then

$$C_{b,f} = T^{-1}\left[\sum_{t=1}^{t} S_{b,t} S_{f,t} + \sum_{t=1}^{t} (1 - S_{b,t})(1 - S_{f,t})\right] \tag{2.2}$$

where $T$ is the sample size.

Thus, $C_{b,f}$ equals one denotes BC and FC are in the same phase and zero denotes both are in the opposite phase and 0.5 indicates there is a lack of symmetric relationship in the dynamics of BC and FC.

### *2.3.4 Spectral Granger Causality Test*

To examine the causal relationship whether FC Granger causes BC or not and vice versa, the spectral Granger causalitytest has been implemented. Granger (1969) causality analysis can forecast the future value of the effect variable with the help of past values of the cause variable. Based on Granger causality, Breitung and Candelon (2006) came with a test of Granger causality that is easier to implement in the frequency domain. The frequency domain (spectral analysis) decomposes the variability in a time series into periodic elements and allows researchers to determine the major frequencies that cause fluctuations in the variables. The use of this test can decide whether a specific element of the cause variable at a specific frequency let $\omega$ can be beneficial to predict the one period ahead element of effect variable at that particular frequency. Breitung and Candelon (2006) wrote the equation for $y_t$ in the VAR ($p$) system as

$$y_t = c + a_1 y_{t-1} + \cdots a_p y_{t-p} + b_1 x_{t-1} + \cdots b_p x_{t-p} + e_t \tag{2.3}$$

where $a_i = \phi_{11,i}$ and $b_i = \phi_{12,i}$. Null hypothesis of $M_{x \to y}(\omega) = 0$ is equal to

$$H_0 : K(\omega)b = 0 \tag{2.4}$$

where $b = (b1, \ldots, bp)\prime$ and $K(\omega)$ is a restriction matrix of order $2 \times p$.

$$\mathrm{K}(\omega) = \begin{bmatrix} \cos(\omega)\cos(2\omega)\ldots\cos(p\omega) \\ \sin(\omega)\sin(2\omega)\ldots\sin(p\omega) \end{bmatrix}$$

One can use the Wald test because these are the simple linear restrictions.

Suppose $\lambda = \left[c, a_1, \ldots, a_{p,} b_1, \ldots, b_p\right]\prime$ be a $m = (2p + 1) \times 1$ vector and $N$ be an $m \times m$ covariance matrix from an unrestricted regression (2.3). Then Wald statistic can be written as

$$W = (M\lambda)'\left(MNM'\right)^{-1}(M\lambda) \sim \chi_2^2 \tag{2.5}$$

where **M** is $2 \times m$ restriction matrix such that

$$M = \left[O_{2\times(p+1)} \vdots K(\omega)\right]$$

This framework can be expanded to an additional variable to avert the spurious causality and then conditionally frequency test can be calculated. Geweke (1984) suggested adding the lag values of the variables. Suppose $d_t$ is the only additional variable; so to test the null hypothesis $H_0 : M_{x \to y|d}(\omega) = 0$ one can run the regression (2.6) and may apply the testing procedure on lagged $x_t$ parameters.

$$y_t = c + \sum_{i=1}^{p} a_i y_{t-i} + \sum_{i=1}^{p} b_i x_{t-i} + \sum_{i=1}^{p} \delta_i d_{t-i} + \varepsilon_t \tag{2.6}$$

Hosoya (2001) suggested a different measure of causality. Suppose $h_t$ is the projection residual of regression of $dt$ on $y_t, y_{t-1} \ldots, y_{t-p}, x_t, x_{t-1}, \ldots, x_{t-p}$ and $d_t, d_{t-1}, \ldots, d_{t-p}$. According to him, Granger causality can be evaluated as

$$y_t = c + \sum_{i=1}^{p} a_i y_{t-i} + \sum_{i=1}^{p} b_i x_{t-i} + \sum_{i=1}^{p} \delta_i h_{t-i} + \varepsilon_t \tag{2.7}$$

According to Breitung and Candelon (2006) in this approach, $h_t$ bears contemporaneous information in *dt* and is not suitable for Granger causality because it can cause spurious causality.

## 2.4 Empirical Analysis

This section provides findings of our empirical analysis.

### 2.4.1 Extraction of Cyclic Component

Figure 2.1 superposes the cyclical component of BC and FC by using the CF filter technique.

### 2.4.2 Business Cycle and Financial Cycle Turning Points

After extracting thecyclicalcomponent, the Harding–Pagon (2002) dating algorithm is employed to find the dates of peaks and troughs. Table 2.1 shows the dates of

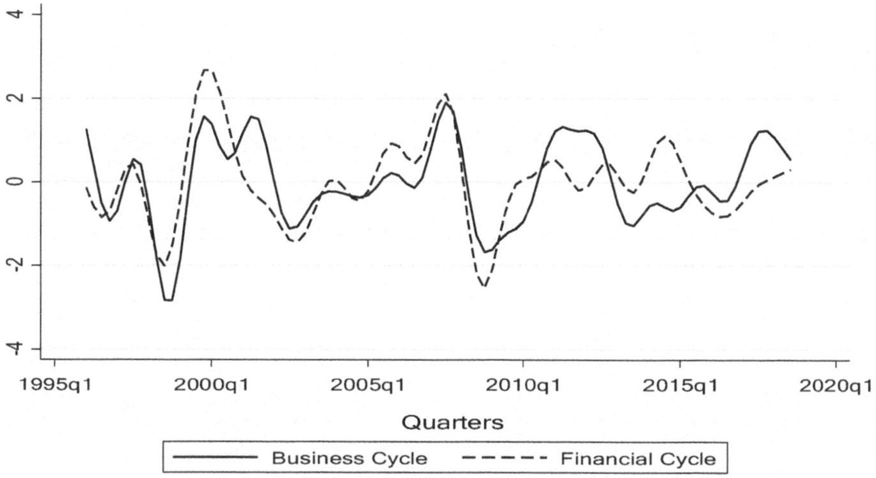


**Fig. 2.1** Cyclical component of business and financial cycle: CF filter *Source* Authors' calculation

**Table 2.1** Dates of turning point in BC and their summary statistics

| Phase | Start | End | Duration | Amplitude |
|---|---|---|---|---|
| Recession | – | 1996q4 | – | 0.93 |
| Expansion | 1996q4 | 1997q3 | 3 | 0.54 |
| Recession | 1997q3 | 1998q4 | 5 | 2.83 |
| Expansion | 1998q4 | 1999q4 | 4 | 1.57 |
| Recession | 1999q4 | 2000q3 | 3 | 0.54 |
| Expansion | 2000q3 | 2001q2 | 3 | 1.56 |
| Recession | 2001q2 | 2002q3 | 5 | 1.10 |
| Expansion | 2002q3 | 2003q4 | 5 | 0.22 |
| Recession | 2003q4 | 2004q4 | 4 | 0.36 |
| Expansion | 2004q4 | 2005q4 | 4 | 0.22 |
| Recession | 2005q4 | 2006q3 | 3 | 0.13 |
| Expansion | 2006q3 | 2007q3 | 4 | 1.90 |
| Recession | 2007q3 | 2008q4 | 5 | 1.67 |
| Expansion | 2008q4 | 2011q2 | 10 | 1.32 |
| Recession | 2011q2 | 2013q3 | 9 | 1.03 |
| Expansion | 2013q3 | 2014q2 | 3 | 0.48 |
| Recession | 2014q2 | 2014q4 | 2 | 0.67 |
| Expansion | 2014q4 | 2015q4 | 4 | 0.06 |
| Recession | 2015q4 | 2016q2 | 2 | 0.43 |
| Expansion | 2016q2 | 2017q4 | 6 | 1.24 |

| Expansion/recession | Average duration (in quarters) | Average amplitude |
|---|---|---|
| Expansion | 4.6 | 0.91 |
| Recession | 4.22 | 0.96 |

*Source* Authors' calculation

turning point in real GDP and their summary statistics. Table 2.1 and Fig. 2.2 show ten phases of recession and expansion each in the economy. The longest period of expansion is 2008Q4–2011Q2 and for recesssion it is 2011Q2–2013Q3. The average duration (in quarters) for expansion is 4.6 and for recession it is 4.22 and average amplitude of expansion is 0.91 and recession is 0.96 shows recession hurts more to the Indian economy.

Table 2.2 lists the dates of turning point in FC when the cycle is extracted by the CF filter and their summary statistics. Table 2.2 and Fig. 2.3 show nine phases of deceleration and eight phases of accelaration in FC. The longest phase of decelaration is 1999Q4–2002Q4 and the longest phase of acceleration is 2008Q4–2011Q1. The average duration (in a quarter) of accelaration is 4.87 and for decelaration it is 4.55. The average amplitude of accceleration is 1.03 and for decelaration it is 0.99. Our empirics suggest that both financial and business cycles have an equal duration in India during the period 1996Q1–2018Q3.

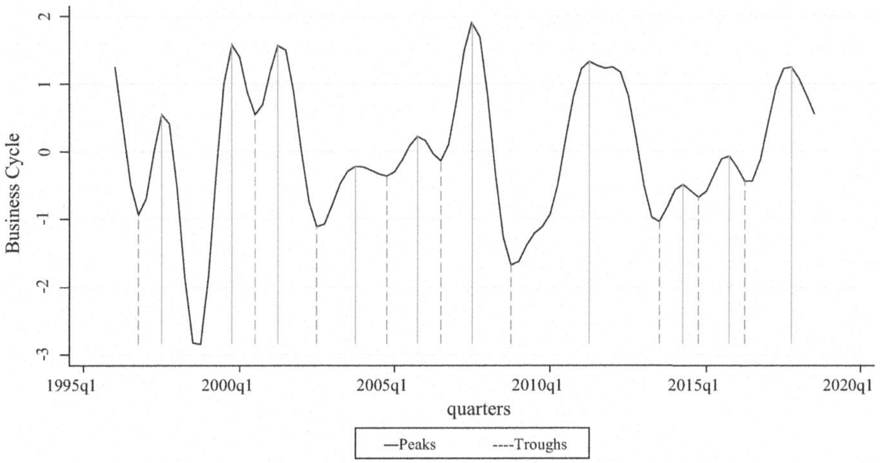


**Fig. 2.2** Turning point in business cycle *Source* Authors' calculation

**Table 2.2** Dates of turning point in financial cycle and their summary statistics

| Phase | Start | End | Duration | Amplitude |
|---|---|---|---|---|
| Decelaration | – | 1996q3 | – | 0.84 |
| Acceleration | 1996q3 | 1997q3 | 4 | 0.42 |
| Decelaration | 1997q3 | 1998q3 | 4 | 2.01 |
| Acceleration | 1998q3 | 1999q4 | 5 | 2.68 |
| Decelaration | 1999q4 | 2002q4 | 12 | 1.44 |
| Acceleration | 2002q4 | 2004q1 | 5 | 0.05 |
| Decelaration | 2004q1 | 2004q4 | 3 | 0.44 |
| Acceleration | 2004q4 | 2005q4 | 4 | 0.93 |
| Decelaration | 2005q4 | 2006q3 | 3 | 0.45 |
| Acceleration | 2006q3 | 2007q3 | 4 | 2.11 |
| Decelaration | 2007q3 | 2008q4 | 5 | 2.53 |
| Acceleration | 2008q4 | 2011q1 | 9 | 0.53 |
| Decelaration | 2011q1 | 2011q4 | 3 | 0.18 |
| Acceleration | 2011q4 | 2012q4 | 4 | 0.43 |
| Decelaration | 2012q4 | 2013q3 | 3 | 0.23 |
| Acceleration | 2013q3 | 2014q3 | 4 | 1.11 |
| Decelaration | 2014q3 | 2016q2 | 7 | 0.81 |

| Acceleration/decelaration | Average duration (in quarters) | Average amplitude |
|---|---|---|
| Acceleration | 4.87 | 1.03 |
| Decelaration | 4.55 | 0.99 |

*Source* Authors' calculation

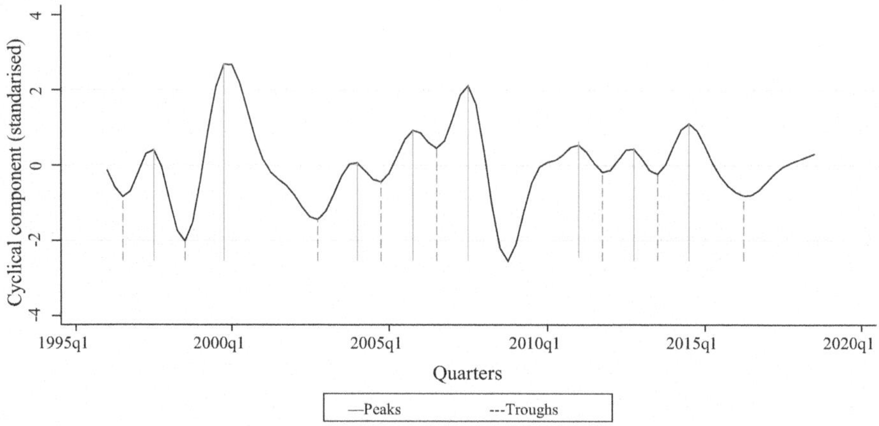


**Fig. 2.3** Turning point in financial cycle *Source* Authors' calculation

### 2.4.3 Concordance Between Business Cycle and Financial Cycle

When both series, BC and FC, accelerate anddecelerate at the same time then the concordance index is 1 whereas if they are in different phases, then the concordance is 0 and when their movements are independent then concordance is 0.5. The concordance statistics of BC and FC is found to be 0.78022 and it implies that the co-movement between these two cycles is moderately strong. After calculating the concordance between BC and FC, causal relationship between the BC and FC has been explored by using the spectral Granger causalitytest. Section 2.4.4 represents the results of spectral Granger causality.

### 2.4.4 Spectral Granger Causality Result

The selection of a suitable lag length is quite vital in time series analysis. Lag order of 4 has been suggested by the entire information criterion (Table 2.3) and for the analysis, lag order is taken on the basis of AIC.

To check the causal relationship, the spectral Granger causalitytest has been used. Figure 2.4 represents the output of the test statistics for all the frequencies in the interval (0, π). The frequency domain can be transformed into the time domain by using the formula:

$$\text{quarters} = \frac{2\pi}{\omega} \times 4$$

**Table 2.3** Lag selection-order criteria

| Lag | LL | LR | df | p | FPE | AIC | HQIC | SBIC |
|---|---|---|---|---|---|---|---|---|
| 0 | 426.083 | | | | 2.0e-07 | −9.74903 | −9.7262 | 9.69234 |
| 1 | 587.765 | 323.36 | 4 | 0.000 | 5.3e-09 | −13.3739 | −13.3054 | 13.2038 |
| 2 | 712.354 | 249.18 | 4 | 0.000 | 3.3e-10 | −16.1461 | −16.0319 | 15.8626 |
| 3 | 823.661 | 222.61 | 4 | 0.000 | 2.8e-11 | −18.6129 | −18.4531 | 18.2161 |
| 4 | 1021.88 | 396.44[a] | 4 | 0.000 | 3.3e13[a] | −23.0778[a] | −22.8723[a] | 22.5676[a] |

*Endogenous* Business cycle, financial cycle
*Exogenous* Cons
*Source* Authors' calculation
a signifies the optimal lag length for respective statistical criteria

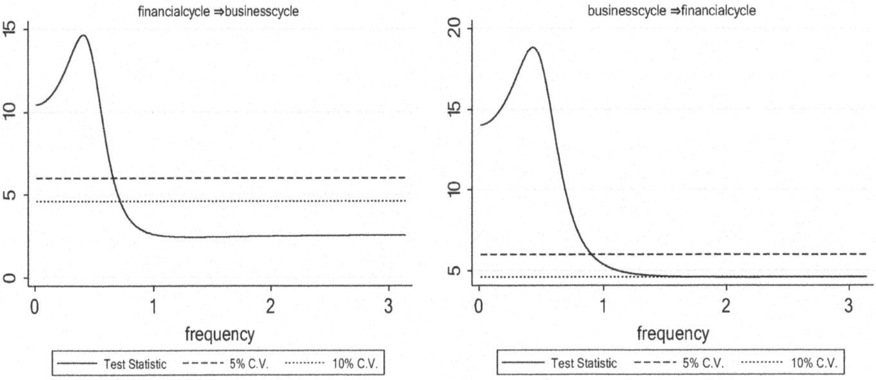


**Fig. 2.4** Breitung–Candelon Spectral Granger causality *Source* Authors' calculation

where $\omega$ is angular frequency and the multiplier 4 is used for quarterly data. The horizontal dotted line represents the critical value at 5 and 10% level of significance, respectively, for the null hypothesis of no Granger causality at frequency $\omega$. Figure 2.4 represents the direction of causality running from financial cycle to business cycle and vice versa.

There is causality at a given frequency if the values lie above the critical value. The result shows that at a given frequency in medium- and long-term financial cycles Granger cause business cycle and vice versa. This might be the fact that FC may follow a random walk; in the short run and in the long run, this causality can result from the evolution of the financial system. This result is similar to the findings of Drehmann et al. (2012) where they found FC is mainly related to BC in the medium run. The emergence of BC in India 1991 onwards was mainly due to private sector participation, reduced import duties and foreign investment (Pandey et al. 2019b). Our study also indicates that credit to GDP ratio, house price and equity price have relevant information in estimating BC. During the sample period, foreign direct investment (FDI) rose to a remarkable level, capital flows to India doubled, bank credit to the commercial sector rose up to 50% of GDP and private corporate sector's share in total bank credit also went up.

## 2.5 Conclusion

This paper attempts to find the nexus between Indian business cycle and financial cycle for the time period of 1996Q1–2018Q3. The main objective of this empirical work is to verify whether there is any co-movement between FC and BC. Business cycle is calculated using real GDP at market price and financial cycle is gauged by making an index using PCA of bank credit, real house prices, real equity prices and real effective exchange rate. Data series are seasonally adjusted using the X-12-ARIMA technique and the Christiano–Fitzgerald filter is used to extract the cyclical component from the de-seasonalized time series. Empirical findings support the existence of financial cycle in India. Further, Bry–Boschan and Harding–Pagan algorithms identified the turning points in the cyclical component of the series. We found the concordance between FC and BC is moderately strong. The result of the spectral Granger causalitytest suggests FC Granger causes BC in the medium and long runs and vice versa. This might be the fact that FC may follow a random walk, in the short run and in the long run, this causality can result from the evolution of the financial system. In order to design macro-prudential policies, monetary authorities can benefit by focusing on long-term and medium-term financial cycles.

## References


Anusha. (2015). Credit and growth cycles in India and US: Investigation in the frequency domain. In *Paper Presented at 11th ISI Annual Conference on Economic Growth and Development.*

Aikman, D., Haldane, A. G., & Nelson, B. D. (2015). Curbing the credit cycle. *The Economic Journal, 125*(585), 1072–1109.

Avouyi-Dovi, S., & Matheron, J. (2005). Interactions between business cycles, financial cycles and monetary policy: Stylised facts. *BIS papers, 22,* 273–298.

Banerjee, K. (2012). *Credit and growth cycles in India: An empirical assessment of the lead and lag behaviour* (RBI Working Paper Series No. 22).

Baxter, M., & King, R. G. (1999). Measuring business cycles: approximate band-pass filters for economic time series. *Review of Economics and Statistics, 81*(4), 575–593.

Behera, H., & Sharma, S. (2019). *Does financial cycle exist in India?* (RBI Working Paper Series No. 03).

Borio, C. (2014). The financial cycle and macroeconomics: What have we learnt? *Journal of Banking & Finance, 45,* 182–198.

Breitung, J., & Candelon, B. (2006). Testing for short-and long-run causality: A frequency-domain approach. *Journal of econometrics, 132*(2), 363–378.

Bry, G., & Boschan, C. (1971). Cyclical analysis of time series: Selected procedure and computer programs. *National Bureau of Economic Research.*

Burns, A. F., & Mitchell, W. C. (1946). *Measuring business cycles.* New York: National Bureau of Economic Research.

Christiano, L. J., & Fitzgerald, T. J. (2003). The band pass filter. *International Economic Review, 44*(2), 435–465.
Claessens, S., Kose, M. A., & Terrones, M. E. (2011). Financial cycles: What? -n? *NBER International Seminar on Macroeconomics, 7*(1), 303–344.
De Winter, J., Koopman, S. J., Hindrayanto, I., & Chouhan, A. (2017). *Modeling the business and financial cycle in a multivariate structural time series model.*
Drehmann, M., Borio, C. E., & Tsatsaronis, K. (2012). *Characterising the financial cycle: Don't lose sight of the medium term!*
Dua, P., & Banerji, A. (2000). *An index of coincident economic indicators for the Indian economy* (No. 73).
Geweke, J. F. (1984). Measures of conditional linear dependence and feedback between time series. *Journal of the American Statistical Association, 79*(388), 907–915.
Ghate, C., Pandey, R., & Patnaik, I. (2013). Has India emerged? Business cycle stylized facts from a transitioning economy. *Structural Change and Economic Dynamics, 24,* 157–172.
Granger, C. W. (1969). Investigating causal relations by econometric models and cross-spectral methods. *Econometrica: Journal of the Econometric Society*, 424–438.
Harding, D., & Pagan, A. (2002). Dissecting the cycle: A methodological investigation. *Journal of Monetary Economics, 49*(2), 365–381.
Hodrick, R. J., & Prescott, E. C. (1997). Postwar US business cycles: An empirical investigation. *Journal of Money, Credit, and Banking*, 1–16.
Hosoya, Y. (2001). Elimination of third-series effect and defining partial measures of causality. *Journal of Time Series Analysis, 22*(5), 537–554.
Lempert, L. H. (1985). Financial markets and the business cycle. *Business Economics*, 31–36.
McDermott, M. C. J., & Scott, A. (2000). Concordance in business cycles (No. 0–37). *International Monetary Fund.*
Nordhaus, W. D., Alesina, A., & Schultze, C. L. (1989). Alternative approaches to the political business cycle. *Brookings Papers on Economic Activity, 1989*(2), 1–68.
Pandey, R., Patnaik, I., & Shah, A. (2017). Dating business cycles in India. *Indian Growth and Development Review, 10*(1), 32–61.
Pandey, R., Patnaik, I., & Shah, A. (2019). *Measuring business cycle conditions in India* (No. 19/269).
Pandey, R., Patnaik, I., & Shah, A. (2019). Business cycle measurement in India. In *Business Cycles in BRICS* (pp. 121–152). Springer, Cham.
Rogoff, K., & Sibert, A. (1988). Elections and Macroeconomic policy cycles. *The Review of Economic Studies, 55*(1), 1–16.
Suarez, J., & Sussman, O. (1999). Financial distress and the business cycle. *Oxford Review of Economic Policy, 15*(3), 39–51.

# Chapter 3
# Betting Against Beta in the Indian Market

**Sobhesh Kumar Agarwalla, Joshy Jacob, Jayanth R. Varma, and Ellapulli Vasudevan**

**Abstract** Recent empirical evidence from different markets suggests that the security market line is flatter than posited by CAPM. This flatness implies that a portfolio long in low-beta assets and short in high-beta assets would earn positive returns. Frazzini and Pedersen (2014) conceptualize a *BAB* factor that tracks such a portfolio. We find that a similar *BAB* factor earns significant positive returns in India. The returns on the *BAB* factor dominate the returns on the size, value, and momentum factors. We also find that stocks with higher volatility earn relatively lower returns. These findings indicate overweighting of riskier assets by leverage constrained investors in the Indian market.

**Keywords** CAPM · Betting against beta · BAB factor · Leverage constraint · Emerging markets

**JEL classifications** G11 · G12 · G14 · G15

## 3.1 Introduction

The Sharpe–Lintner version of the capital asset pricing model (CAPM) predicts that the expected return on assets would increase with their systematic risk, measured by beta. However, empirical evidence from different markets suggests

S. K. Agarwalla · J. Jacob (✉) · J. R. Varma
Indian Institute of Management Ahmedabad, Vastrapur, Ahmedabad, Gujarat 380015, India
e-mail: joshyjacob@iimahd.ernet.in

S. K. Agarwalla
e-mail: sobhesh@iimahd.ernet.in

J. R. Varma
e-mail: jrvarma@iimahd.ernet.in

E. Vasudevan
Department of Finance, ESCP Business School, Paris, France
e-mail: vellapulli@escp.eu

 
A. K. Mishra et al. (eds.), *The Financial Landscape of Emerging Economies*, Accounting, Finance, Sustainability, Governance & Fraud: Theory and Application,
https://doi.org/10.1007/978-3-030-60008-2_3

a much flatter relation between beta and returns. Black (1972) showed that various borrowing constraints, including margin requirements, could lead to the flatness. Black suggested that one of the factors that contributes to the flatness of the security market line is overweighting of the high-beta assets by leverage constrained investors.[1] Black (1993) argued that a factor which involves shorting of the high-beta assets and being long on the low-beta assets would be priced in the market. He examined the returns to such a beta factor and found that it generated significant positive returns in excess of its risk. He also found that the beta factor earned greater returns than both the size and book-to-market factors. He further argued that "Beta is a valuable tool if the line is as steep as the CAPM predicts. It is even more valuable if the line is flat." These evidences suggest that the Sharpe–Lintner-Black model of CAPM with borrowing constraints would be a better fit of the empirical return data.

Recently, Frazzini and Pedersen (2014) re-examine this issue in a richer theoretical and empirical context and document pervasive evidence of low returns generated by the high-beta assets. They model investors with leverage and margin constraints and examine the implications for the pricing of beta. More specifically, they model a market with different types of agents: (a) agents who cannot leverage and overweight the high-beta assets, (b) agents who can leverage but face margin constraints and underweight the high-beta assets, and (c) agents who are unconstrained and lever up the low-beta assets. The model produces a flatter security market line as in Black (1972). The specific propositions of the model are as follows: (i) the slope of the security market line would depend on the tightness of the funding constraints across agents, (ii) during times of tightening funding constraints, agents de-leverage and therefore the high-beta stocks earn lower returns, (iii) when funding liquidity risk is high, betas in the cross-section are compressed toward one, and (iv) more constrained investors overweight the high-beta assets and less constrained investors underweight the high-beta assets. They develop a beta factor in the lines of Black (1993), called the "Betting against beta" factor (*BAB* factor). They find that the *BAB* factor earns significant returns using data from 20 international equity markets, treasury bond markets, credit markets, and futures markets. Their empirical evidence suggests that the relative flatness of the security market line is widespread in the world. Their *BAB* factor returns are also robust to variations in firm size and idiosyncratic risk. They find that more leverage constrained investors hold high-beta portfolios and the less constrained ones hold low-beta portfolios.

We examine the return dynamics of the high-beta and low-beta assets in the Indian market. The flatness of the security market line in India has also been documented (for instance, Ansari, 2000). The Indian market could provide interesting insights into the impact of financing constraints on the risk-return dynamics for a variety of reasons. First, the emerging markets have severe financing constraints relative to the markets examined in Frazzini and Pedersen (2014). Second, unlike most other markets, India has a very active single stock futures market. This could offer significant leverage opportunity to investors in stocks with active derivative markets. These features

[1]The other reason for the flatness suggested by Black (1972) is the use of inappropriate market proxy.

would afford a closer examination of the impact of leverage constraints on the pricing of beta and the overall risk-return relation.

Our key findings are as follows. First, the *BAB* factor earns significant positive returns in the Indian market. Second, the returns of the *BAB* factor dominate the return of the size, value, and momentum factors in India. Third, we also find that the stocks with higher volatility earn relatively lower returns. These findings indicate overweighting of riskier assets by leverage constrained investors in the Indian market.

The reminder of the paper is organized as follows. Section 3.2 describes the data used in the analysis and Sect. 3.3 details the approach used in the analysis. Section 3.4 discusses our key findings on the pricing of the beta factor and Sect. 3.5 concludes.

## 3.2 Data

We include all the stocks traded in the Bombay Stock Exchange (BSE) ever since January 1993 in the analysis. The required data is taken from the Prowess database maintained by the Centre for Monitoring Indian Economy (CMIE). While the return data of the stocks are available from January 1990, the risk-free returns are available only from January 1993. Hence, we limit the analysis to the 20.5-year period between January 1993 and June 2013. The returns on the Fama–French factors (Fama and French, 1992) and momentum (Jegadeesh and Titman, 1993) are taken from the data library of the recent paper on systematic risk factors in India by Agarwalla et al. (2013). The risk-free returns, measured as the yield on the 91-day treasury bills, are taken from the Reserve Bank of India website.[2] Sensex, the popular market value weighted index of the 30 largest stocks in India, is used as the market proxy.[3]

The summary statistics of the data is given in Table 3.1. There is a significant increase in the number of traded firms and the market capitalization over the period of analysis. On an average, about 3,500 firms trade in the market. The aggregate market capitalization ranges from ₹2.4 trillion in 1993 to ₹66.1 trillion in 2013. The average market risk premium based on Sensex is about 8% per annum. The distribution of the market capitalization of the firms suggests that 90% of the firms can be regarded as small firms as their average market capitalization over time is below ₹8 million.

[2]http://dbie.rbi.org.in/DBIE/dbie.rbi?site=statistics.

[3]It is an index maintained by the Bombay Stock Exchange.

**Table 3.1** Summary statistics of the data

| Year | Number of firms | Market cap. Percentile (₹ million) | | | Aggregate market cap. (₹ million) | Average market cap. (₹ million) | Sensex return (%) | Risk-free return (%) |
|---|---|---|---|---|---|---|---|---|
| | | 10% | 50% | 90% | | | | |
| 1993 | 2278 | 26 | 136 | 1,609 | 2,395,366 | 1,052 | 27.94 | 9.16 |
| 1994 | 3358 | 39 | 181 | 2,135 | 4,826,523 | 1,437 | 17.36 | 8.36 |
| 1995 | 4721 | 31 | 106 | 1,238 | 4,934,752 | 1,045 | −20.79 | 12.08 |
| 1996 | 5319 | 15 | 55 | 778 | 4,497,657 | 846 | −0.81 | 10.99 |
| 1997 | 4921 | 7 | 36 | 635 | 4,881,884 | 992 | 18.6 | 7.1 |
| 1998 | 4000 | 7 | 35 | 748 | 4,349,433 | 1,087 | −16.5 | 7.98 |
| 1999 | 3938 | 9 | 43 | 1,152 | 5,915,665 | 1,502 | 63.83 | 9.09 |
| 2000 | 3972 | 10 | 52 | 1,319 | 7,851,392 | 1,977 | −20.65 | 9.03 |
| 2001 | 3415 | 8 | 46 | 1,157 | 5,539,627 | 1,622 | −17.87 | 7.47 |
| 2002 | 3012 | 9 | 56 | 1,634 | 5,989,443 | 1,989 | 3.52 | 6.04 |
| 2003 | 2915 | 10 | 69 | 2,351 | 8,149,890 | 2,796 | 72.89 | 4.94 |
| 2004 | 2869 | 12 | 104 | 4,203 | 13,640,240 | 4,754 | 13.08 | 4.68 |
| 2005 | 2954 | 26 | 275 | 8,253 | 20,163,835 | 6,826 | 42.33 | 5.38 |
| 2006 | 2983 | 24 | 353 | 13,053 | 31,556,966 | 10,579 | 46.7 | 6.35 |
| 2007 | 3118 | 33 | 504 | 18,088 | 50,214,789 | 16,105 | 47.15 | 7.15 |
| 2008 | 3194 | 36 | 419 | 15,371 | 46,167,115 | 14,454 | −52.45 | 7.88 |
| 2009 | 3256 | 32 | 337 | 13,012 | 47,234,715 | 14,507 | 81.03 | 3.65 |
| 2010 | 3446 | 43 | 540 | 21,630 | 68,085,994 | 19,758 | 17.43 | 5.37 |
| 2011 | 3581 | 38 | 429 | 18,050 | 63,580,329 | 17,755 | −24.64 | 7.88 |
| 2012 | 3714 | 33 | 343 | 15,934 | 63,611,244 | 17,127 | 25.7 | 8.44 |
| 2013 | 3672 | 29 | 322 | 15,518 | 66,135,135 | 18,011 | −0.32 | 7.82 |

The table presents the year-wise market cap. percentiles (market capitalisation), aggregate market cap., and the cross-sectional average of the market cap. of all the BSE listed firms. The yearly market cap. of a firm is the average of its month-end market cap. figures. The risk-free return is the yield on the 91-day Treasury bill. The 2013 period covers only the 6-month period from 1 January to 30 June. All the return figures are annualized

## 3.3 Methodology

The pre-ranking stock betas are estimated with five-year daily stock returns and Sensex returns. We adopt the following approach for beta estimation.

$$\beta_{it} = \rho_{it} \frac{\sigma_{it}}{\sigma_{mt}} \tag{3.1}$$

where we estimate the $\rho_{it}$, the correlation between the market and stock, based on three-day cumulative excess returns over a period of 5 years to handle the possible influence of nonsynchronous trading. The stock volatility ($\sigma_{it}$) and the market volatility ($\sigma_{mt}$) are estimated as the standard deviation of the daily excess returns over a one-year period. The use of returns over a longer period for the estimation of correlation is in line with the evidence of slowly evolving correlations. To estimate the volatility, the stocks should have traded for at least 120 days in the last one year. Similarly, to estimate the correlation, the stocks should have traded for at least 750 days during the last five years.

It is well-known that regression betas are subject to estimation error (S.E. of beta). Hence, it is common in event studies and IPO literature to assume a $\beta$ of one (equal to market beta) for stocks, as regression estimates are either unreliable or impossible. However, the market beta estimate also has an error equal to the cross-sectional variation of the betas around the mean of 1. Vasicek (1973) developed a shrinkage beta estimator to combine the market beta and the stock beta in an attempt to improve the reliability of stock betas. This beta estimator is a weighted average of the two betas as given by Eq. 3.2 and is regarded as the statistically optimal estimator.

$$\beta_i^s = \beta_i w_i + \beta_m (1 - w_i) \tag{3.2}$$

where $\beta_i^s$ is the shrunk stock beta, $\beta_m$ the market beta, and $\beta_i$ the stock beta, estimated with Eq. 3.1. The weight $w_i$ of each stock is estimated as below.

$$w_i = \frac{1}{T} \sum_{t=1}^{T} \frac{\sigma_{\beta_t}^2}{\text{S.E}\,\beta_{it} + \sigma_{\beta_t}^2} \tag{3.3}$$

where $\sigma_{\beta_t}^2$ is the cross-sectional variation in the betas at time $t$, and S.E $\beta_{it}$ is the standard error of the beta estimate of stock $i$ at time $t$, estimated through regression of the daily stock returns on the market returns using five-year rolling returns.

Equation 3.2 requires $w_i$ to be estimated separately for each stock. The $w_i$ in our dataset varies from 0.6 to 0.85 and has a pooled average of 0.7. However, for simplicity and robustness, it is common in the literature to use a single value of $w_i$ for all the stocks. We take $w_i$ equal to 0.6 following Frazzini and Pedersen (2014) and Vasicek (1973). Alternative choices like $w_i$= 0.7 (the pooled average of estimated $w_i$) do not make any material difference to our results.

There are many instances in the Indian market where very large market capitalization firms, which account for a large share of the total market value, are listed through IPOs (primarily disinvestment of public sector firms). We would not be able to include such large market cap firms in the analysis for a very long period as reliable beta estimation with Eq. 3.1 requires a minimum of five-year return data. Therefore, we attempt to include them in the analysis starting from the second year of their trading by downwardly adjusting the weight given to their betas in Eq. 3.2. This adjustment is done using the relationship between the standard error (SE Beta in this case) and sample size. This adjustment leads to the following stock beta estimate, when the return data for a newly listed stock is not available for 5 years (proof given in Appendix 3.1).

$$\beta_{iN}^{s} = \frac{40}{40+N} \times \beta_m + \frac{N}{40+N} \times \beta_{iN} \tag{3.4}$$

where $\beta_{iN}^{s}$ is the shrinkage beta estimated at the end of month $N$, $\beta_m$ is the market beta (equal to 1), and $\beta_{iN}$ is the stock beta estimated with Eq. 3.1. $N$ takes value between 13 (corresponding to the first month in the second year of trading) and 60.

We follow the methodology of Frazzini and Pedersen (2014) to construct the long-short beta portfolios and to estimate the *BAB* factor returns as their approach makes the portfolio both market neutral and self-financing. For each month $t$, the stocks are divided into two groups (portfolios) based on their beta values at $t-1$. The portfolio above (below) the median is called the high-beta (low-beta) portfolio. The *BAB* factor returns ($BAB_t$) are estimated as below.

$$BAB_t = \frac{1}{\bar{\beta}_L}\left(\bar{R}_{L,t} - R_{F,t}\right) - \frac{1}{\bar{\beta}_H}\left(\bar{R}_{H,t} - R_{F,t}\right) \tag{3.5}$$

where $\overline{\beta_L}$ ($\overline{\beta_H}$) is the weighted average beta of the low-$\beta$ (high-$\beta$) portfolios. $\overline{R_{L,t}}$ ($\overline{R_{H,t}}$) is the weighted returns on the low-$\beta$ (high-$\beta$) portfolio. $R_{F,t}$ is the risk-free returns measured as the yield on the 91-day treasury bills. The weights are determined based on the beta ranks of the stocks in the portfolio. For every month $t$ in our estimation period, the weight assigned to the return of each stock, $W_i$, is estimated as follows:

$$W_i = \frac{2 \times \left|Rank_i - \overline{Rank}\right|}{\sum_{i=1}^{n} \left|Rank_i - \overline{Rank}\right|} \tag{3.6}$$

$Rank_i$ is the β-rank of stock $i$ among all the $n$ (including both high-beta and low-beta) stocks included at time period $t-1$. $\overline{Rank}$ is the mean rank. This weighting tilts the high-β (low-β) portfolio toward stocks with the highest (lowest) betas. The portfolios are reconstituted every month based on the beta values in the immediately prior month.

The performance of the *BAB* factor and of various beta-ranked portfolios are examined through calender-time regressions of the portfolio excess returns using the CAPM, 3-factor and 4-factor models as follows:

$$R_{it}^{e} = \alpha_i + \sum_{k=1}^{n} \beta_i R_{kt} + e_{it} \tag{3.7}$$

where $R_{it}^{e}$ is the excess return on portfolio $i$ during period $t$, $R_{kt}$ is the factor return during the same period, and $n$ is the number of factors (for instance, three in the Fama–French model).

Even though we attempt to estimate beta of individual stocks with less than 5 years of return data using Eq. 3.4, we avoid this approach in the initial 5 years of our sample (January 1993–December 1997), as all the stocks would then require this adjustment.

Hence, the *BAB* factor returns are estimated only for a period of 15.5 years from January 1998 to June 2013.

## 3.4 Findings and Discussion

### 3.4.1 Beta Characteristics

We observe that the high-beta stocks are relatively larger, more volatile, and have high book-to-market ratios in the Indian market. The time series average of the market value weighted betas (0.97), estimated with Eq. 3.2, is close to the market beta of one.[4] The effect of the shrinking of the stock betas toward the market beta (1.0) is more on the higher values of beta. The distribution of the shrunk betas over time is given in Fig. 3.1. The distribution indicates that there is a large cross-sectional

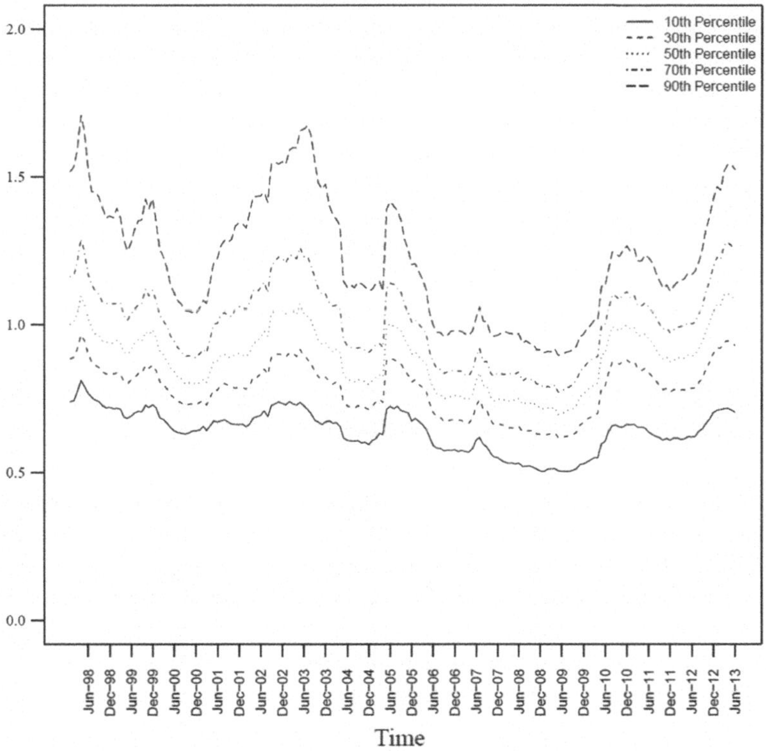


**Fig. 3.1** Beta percentile points over time

[4]The weighted betas are not strictly equal to the market beta of one as the market proxy, Sensex, does not include all the traded stocks.

variation in the betas of Indian firms. The distribution also exhibits significant time variation with a noticeable compression in the cross-sectional betas during certain periods. For instance, upper percentile of the betas significantly fell during the year 2008, which is known to be a financially constrained period. On the other hand, the lower percentile betas exhibit lower variation over time. Similar behavior of betas is documented by Frazzini and Pedersen (2014). They attribute the cross-sectional compression of the betas to funding constraints in the market.

### *3.4.2 Beta-Sorted Portfolio Returns*

The return and other characteristics of the portfolios formed on their pre-ranking betas are given in Table 3.2. The realized betas almost fully follow the rank order of their pre-ranking betas. The excess returns, Sharpe ratios, and the alphas of the 10 beta-decile portfolios decrease more or less monotonically with their ex-ante betas. For instance, the monthly CAPM alpha of the high-beta (P10) portfolio is −2.89% as compared to −0.44% of the low-beta portfolio, when equally weighted portfolio returns are used. The alphas of the beta-deciles are negative in the Indian market due to the poor performance of a large number of small stocks in all the portfolios. In fact, only about 20% of the stocks earn positive excess returns in the Indian market, which are primarily large stocks. These are reflected in the positive returns and alphas of several of the portfolios when market value weighted returns, as given in Panel B of Table 3.2. In fact, all the alphas turn less negative with market value weighted returns. Alphas estimated with calender-time regressions of the portfolio returns with 3- and 4-factor models also exhibit a similar trend. All the 3- and 4-factor alphas are negative and statistically significant for the higher beta portfolios (P8–P10).

### *3.4.3 Returns to the Market-Neutral BAB Factor*

Table 3.2 also gives the returns on the market-neutral *BAB* factor. As expected in a market-neutral portfolio, the realized beta of the *BAB* factor is very close to zero (0.09). The *BAB* portfolio on an average is equivalent to a long position of ₹1.32 on the low-beta beta portfolio and a short position of ₹0.91 on the high-beta portfolio. The *BAB* factor earns statistically and economically significant returns as suggested by its alphas. For instance, it earns a monthly alpha of 1.08% relative to the 4-factor model. These findings are similar to the results of Frazzini and Pedersen (2014) for other markets.

The yearly *BAB* factor returns and their comparison with the size, value, and momentum factor returns are given in Table 3.3. Overall, the *BAB* factor earns a positive return during the 15.5-year period (from January 1998 to June 2013) in the Indian market. For most of the years during the period, the *BAB* factor earns greater returns than the market risk premium. The average return suggests that the *BAB* factor

**Table 3.2** Monthly alphas for various beta-deciles and the *BAB* factor

| Portfolio | P1 (Low beta) | P2 | P3 | P4 | P5 | P6 | P7 | P8 | P9 | P10 (High beta) | *BAB* |
|---|---|---|---|---|---|---|---|---|---|---|---|
| Panel A: Equally weighted portfolios | | | | | | | | | | | |
| XR (over $R_F$) | 0.01 | 0.26 | 0.22 | 0.23 | −0.05 | 0.17 | −0.20 | −0.79 | −1.21 | −1.97 | 1.70*** |
| CAPM alpha | −0.44 | −0.29 | −0.39 | −0.42 | −0.72* | −0.54 | −0.96** | −1.58*** | −2.04*** | −2.89*** | 1.67*** |
| Three-factor alpha | −0.99*** | −0.79*** | −0.89*** | −0.92*** | −1.20*** | −1.10*** | −1.50*** | −2.16*** | −2.68*** | −3.61*** | 1.35*** |
| Four-factor alpha | −0.97*** | −0.67** | −0.79*** | −0.73*** | −1.00*** | −0.89*** | −1.25*** | −1.78*** | −2.32*** | −3.09*** | 1.08** |
| Beta (ex-ante) | 0.56 | 0.68 | 0.75 | 0.81 | 0.86 | 0.91 | 0.97 | 1.05 | 1.15 | 1.38 | 0.00 |
| Beta (realized) | 0.70 | 0.86 | 0.96 | 1.01 | 1.05 | 1.12 | 1.18 | 1.24 | 1.31 | 1.44 | 0.09 |
| Volatility | 31.43 | 33.37 | 34.37 | 35.70 | 36.32 | 38.94 | 40.88 | 43.51 | 47.20 | 54.71 | 23.79 |
| Sharpe ratio | 0.00 | 0.09 | 0.08 | 0.08 | −0.02 | 0.05 | −0.06 | −0.22 | −0.31 | −0.43 | 0.86 |
| Panel B: Market value weighted portfolios | | | | | | | | | | | |
| XR (over $R_F$) | 0.31 | 0.56 | 0.85* | 0.79* | 0.11 | 0.42 | 0.13 | −0.42 | −0.44 | −1.19 | 1.70*** |
| CAPM alpha | −0.17 | 0.15 | 0.32 | 0.28 | −0.45 | −0.24 | −0.45 | −1.11*** | −1.11*** | −2.01*** | 1.67*** |
| Three-factor alpha | −0.32 | 0.05 | 0.28 | 0.26 | −0.47 | −0.35 | −0.49* | −1.12*** | −1.24*** | −2.22*** | 1.35*** |
| Four-factor alpha | −0.55 | 0.01 | 0.13 | 0.05 | −0.57* | −0.30 | −0.47 | −1.19*** | −0.86** | −1.68*** | 1.08** |
| Beta (ex-ante) | 0.56 | 0.68 | 0.75 | 0.81 | 0.86 | 0.91 | 0.97 | 1.05 | 1.15 | 1.38 | 0.00 |
| Beta (realized) | 0.75 | 0.64 | 0.82 | 0.80 | 0.88 | 1.04 | 0.92 | 1.08 | 1.05 | 1.29 | 0.09 |
| Volatility | 30.73 | 24.62 | 28.36 | 28.76 | 29.40 | 33.63 | 30.01 | 35.91 | 35.81 | 45.77 | 23.79 |
| Sharpe ratio | 0.12 | 0.27 | 0.36 | 0.33 | 0.05 | 0.15 | 0.05 | −0.14 | −0.15 | −0.31 | 0.86 |

P1–P10 are the equally weighted (Panel A) or value weighted (Panel B) portfolios constructed based on the beta-deciles. Excess returns (XR) are calculated over the risk-free rate. Alpha is the intercept of the regression of the monthly portfolio excess return on the factors: (a) Market risk premium ($R_M - R_F$) (b) $SMB$ (c) $HML$ and (d) $WML$. Portfolio premium is calculated as the excess return over the risk-free rate. Monthly alphas are percentage returns. Beta (ex-ante) is the average beta estimated with and Beta (realized) is estimated from the regressions of the realized returns. Volatility (%) and Sharpe ratio are annualized figures

**Table 3.3** *BAB*, Market, *HML*, *SMB* and *WML* factor returns over the years

| Calender year | *BAB*(%) | $R_m - R_f$ (%) | *SMB*(%) | *HML*(%) | *WML*(%) |
|---|---|---|---|---|---|
| 1998 | −1.71 | −22.66 | 14.57 | −7.41 | 4.96 |
| 1999 | −4.30 | 50.18 | 37.51 | −0.18 | 79.84 |
| 2000 | 20.74 | −27.22 | −15.82 | 12.78 | −23.57 |
| 2001 | −2.46 | −23.58 | −2.87 | 8.20 | 47.02 |
| 2002 | 22.68 | −2.37 | −17.80 | 73.07 | 15.08 |
| 2003 | 96.60 | 64.75 | 3.98 | 44.29 | 52.33 |
| 2004 | 45.43 | 8.02 | 16.91 | 37.56 | 21.15 |
| 2005 | 40.28 | 35.06 | 35.27 | 19.61 | 28.35 |
| 2006 | 17.73 | 37.94 | 3.56 | 3.20 | 35.67 |
| 2007 | 126.42 | 37.33 | 22.84 | 63.31 | 16.68 |
| 2008 | −34.21 | −55.92 | −26.55 | −17.22 | −10.61 |
| 2009 | 41.37 | 74.66 | 15.18 | 12.78 | −10.82 |
| 2010 | 50.62 | 11.45 | 7.00 | 0.11 | 17.45 |
| 2011 | 15.59 | −30.15 | 9.07 | −22.23 | 62.03 |
| 2012 | 1.71 | 15.91 | −0.32 | 5.52 | −1.26 |
| 2013 | −0.74 | −3.85 | −18.64 | −4.01 | 42.26 |
| Average | 29.10 | 11.56 | 6.84 | 15.56 | 22.29 |
| Volatility | 40.77 | 38.40 | 18.21 | 27.71 | 29.11 |

All the given return figures are annualized percentage returns. The *BAB* factor returns are estimated based on Eq. 3.5. The 4-factor returns are taken from Agarwalla et al. (2013). The values for 2013 are only for the initial 6 months. The Average and Volatility figures exclude the 2013 data

dominates the size, value, and momentum factors in the Indian market. For instance, the most dominant among the 4 factors, momentum, earns an average return of 22.3% compared to 29.1% of the *BAB* factor. The relative economic significance of the *BAB* factor returns is also reflected in Fig. 3.2 which plots the cumulative returns of the different factors.

Overall, these findings strongly suggest that there is significant overweighting of high-beta assets in the Indian market, due to leverage constraints and funding liquidity risk faced by certain investor categories. Further, the significant time variation of the *BAB* factor returns is most likely to be linked to the time variation of funding constraints in the Indian market. We also examine the robustness the *BAB* factor returns to various anomalies including, size, value, momentum, and volatility.

### 3.4.4 Robustness with Size, Value, and Momentum

The robustness of the *BAB* factor returns are examined by re-estimating the *BAB* returns on various sub-portfolios sorted on size, value, and momentum. Accordingly,

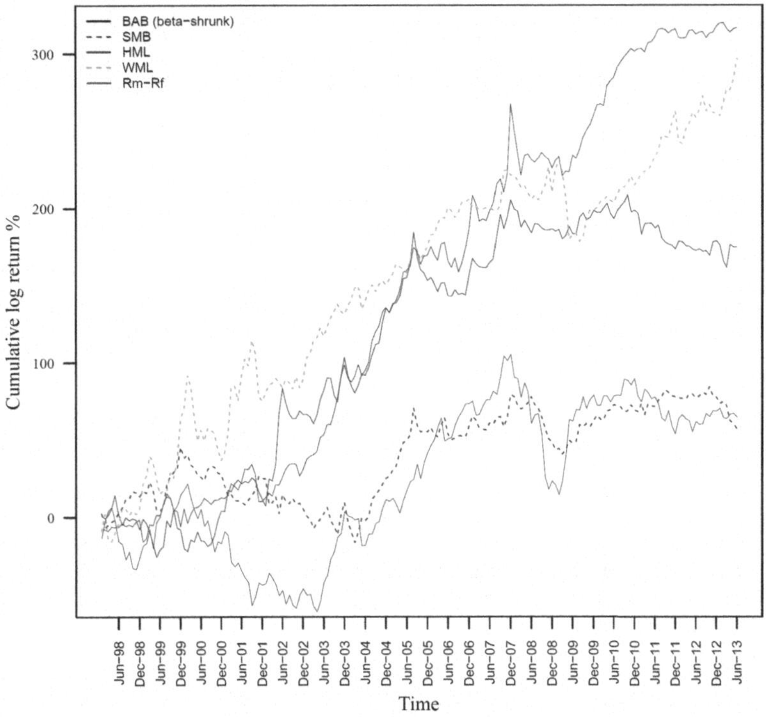


**Fig. 3.2** *BAB* and 4 factor over time

the stocks are classified into standardized groups like Value and Growth (based on B/M), Small and Big (based on size), and Winner and Loser (based on momentum). The excess returns and the 4-factor alphas of each of these sub-portfolios are given in Table 3.4. The excess returns and the alphas are positive in all the cases. As given in Panel A of the table, the *BAB* factor return are greater in the case of small stocks. On the value dimension, it appears that the *BAB* factor does not have a statistically significant alpha for the growth firms. The *BAB* factor alphas are not statistically significant for both the Winner and Loser stocks.

### *3.4.5 Beta Factor Returns and Volatility*

We find a positive correlation of 0.34 between the beta and the total volatility of stocks in the Indian market. Given this positive correlation, the *BAB* factor is likely to be related to the volatility anomaly (Ang et al., 2006, 2009; Baker et al., 2011). We carry out a preliminary analysis of the relation between total volatility and returns. We find that the low-volatility portfolios earn positive alphas and high-volatility portfolios earn negative alphas (as given in Table 3.5), particularly in the case of smaller stocks

**Table 3.4** Robustness of *BAB* Factor returns with Size, B/M, and momentum factors

| Portfolio | Excess $t$-value 4F-$\alpha$ return | $t$-value | Volatility | Sharpe ratio |
|---|---|---|---|---|
| *Panel A: Size* | | | | |
| Small firms (deciles 1–9) | 0.24*** → 2.74 → 0.21** | 2.31 | 1.20 | 0.20 |
| Big firms (decile 10) | 0.14 → 0.74 → 0.30 | 1.62 | 2.58 | 0.05 |
| *Panel B: B/M* | | | | |
| Growth firms (deciles 1–3) | 0.18 → 1.35 → 0.17 | 1.26 | 1.81 | 0.10 |
| Neutral firms (deciles 4–7) | 0.25* → 1.71 → 0.28* | 1.92 | 1.99 | 0.13 |
| Value firms (deciles 8–10) | 0.40** → 2.41 → 0.39** | 2.27 | 2.25 | 0.18 |
| *Panel C: Momentum* | | | | |
| Loser firms (deciles 1–3) | 0.13 → 1.21 → 0.17 | 1.51 | 1.50 | 0.09 |
| Medium firms (deciles 4–7) | 0.36** → 2.35 → 0.39** | 2.46 | 2.06 | 0.17 |
| Winner firms (deciles 8–10) | 0.20 → 1.19 → 0.16 | 0.89 | 2.33 | 0.09 |

For each month $t$ we sort the stocks based on size (into big and small), B/M (into value, neutral, and growth), and momentum (into winner, medium, and loser). Within each of these groups, we further sort the stocks into high- and low-beta subgroups. The Fama–French and momentum factors are taken from Agarwalla et al. (2013). The *BAB* factor returns for $t+1$ are calculated for each subgroup as described in Eq. 3.5. The 4F-$\alpha$ is the alpha from the calendar-time regressions of the monthly excess returns on the portfolios

**Table 3.5** Monthly alphas for various volatility deciles

| Porfolio | P1 (Low vol.) | P2 | P3 | P4 | P5 (High vol.) |
|---|---|---|---|---|---|
| Excess return | 0.11 | −0.28 | −0.72 | −1.25 | −2.17 |
| CAPM alpha | −0.23 | −0.68* | −1.15** | −1.71*** | −2.67*** |
| Three-factor alpha | −0.37* | −0.87*** | −1.41*** | −1.93*** | −2.86*** |
| Four-factor alpha | −0.18 | −0.56*** | −1.11*** | −1.64*** | −2.63*** |
| β (ex-ante) | 0.86 | 0.93 | 0.96 | 1.00 | 1.01 |
| Annualized volatility (ex-ante) | 42.64 | 57.09 | 68.52 | 83.20 | 115.86 |
| Sharpe ratio | 0.05 | −0.09 | −0.22 | −0.35 | −0.52 |

Portfolios P1–P5 are equally weighted portfolios constructed based on volatility quintiles. Excess returns are calculated over risk-free rate. Alpha is the intercept of regression of the portfolio excess returns over factors: (a) Market risk premium ($R_M - R_F$), (b) *SMB*, (c) *HML*, and (d) *WML*. The data includes all the firms traded in the Bombay Stock Exchange over the period from January 1998–June 2013

(Table 3.6). Even within different size groups of firms, the volatility anomaly prevails. The possible link between the *BAB* factor and the volatility anomaly in the Indian context is being examined by the authors.

**Table 3.6** Monthly alphas of various volatility-size quintiles

| Portfolio | Deciles 10 (large firms) | | | | | Deciles 1–9 (small firms) | | | | |
|---|---|---|---|---|---|---|---|---|---|---|
| | P1 | P2 | P3 | P4 | P5 | P1 | P2 | P3 | P4 | P5 |
| | (Low Vol.) | | | | (High Vol.) | (Low Vol.) | | | | (High Vol.) |
| XR (over $R_F$) | 0.34 | 0.17 | 0.06 | −0.02 | −1.42 | −0.04 | −0.34 | −0.76 | −1.30 | −2.26 |
| CAPM alpha | 0.09 | −0.17 | −0.34 | −0.48* | −1.99*** | −0.39 | −0.75* | −1.19** | −1.76*** | −2.75*** |
| Three-factor alpha | 0.06 | −0.23 | −0.45* | −0.55** | −1.92*** | −0.56*** | −0.97*** | −1.45*** | −1.98*** | −2.96*** |
| Four-factor alpha | 0.17 | −0.01 | −0.19 | −0.34 | −1.83*** | −0.34 | −0.66*** | −1.14*** | −1.71*** | −2.70*** |
| Beta (ex-ante) | 0.78 | 0.90 | 0.96 | 0.99 | 1.05 | 0.86 | 0.94 | 0.96 | 1.00 | 1.01 |
| Vol. annualized (ex-ante) | 32.28 | 41.04 | 47.83 | 56.17 | 76.24 | 45.69 | 59.74 | 70.94 | 85.58 | 118.06 |
| Sharpe ratio | 0.19 | 0.08 | 0.02 | −0.01 | −0.37 | −0.01 | −0.11 | −0.23 | −0.36 | −0.54 |

The portfolio of each month $t$ is formed by sorting the stocks first on their market capitalization (size) and then on volatility within each size group based on their estimates in the month $t - 1$. The top decile of stocks are classified as large and the remaining nine deciles are classified as small stocks. Excess returns are calculated over risk-free rate ($R_f$). Alpha is the intercept of regression of the portfolio excess return over the factors: (a) Market risk premium ($R_m - R_f$), (b) *SMB*, (c) *HML*, and (d) *WML*. The portfolio returns represent equally weighted returns. The returns on the four factors in the Indian market are taken from Agarwalla et al. (2013). The returns of each portfolio are equally weighted

## 3.5 Conclusion

We examine the return dynamics of the high-beta and the low-beta stocks in the Indian market. The relatively higher funding constraints and thier significant time variation in the Indian market create an ideal setting to bring out the nature of interactions between financing constraints, margin requirements, and the pricing of beta. We find that the market-neutral long-short portfolio (*BAB* factor), conceptualized by Frazzini and Pedersen (2014), earns significant positive returns in the Indian market. The returns of this factor dominate the size, value, and momentum factors' returns in India. The overall results suggest overweighting of the high-beta assets by leverage constrained investors in the Indian market. The authors are currently engaged in extending this research to understand the possible linkage between the *BAB* factor pricing and financial constraints in the Indian market.

# 1 Beta Shrinkage Estimator

## 1.1 Basic Bayesian Model

$$\beta^{\text{Shrunk}} = \frac{H^{Prior}}{H^{Prior} + H^{Regression}} \times \beta^{Prior} + \frac{H^{Regression}}{H^{Prior} + H^{Regression}} \times \beta^{Regression} \tag{3.8}$$

where $H^{Prior} = \frac{1}{\sigma^2_{Prior}}$ is the precision of the prior (cross-sectional estimate), $H^{Regression} = \frac{1}{\sigma^2_{Regression}}$ is the precision of the regression (sample), and $\beta^{Prior} = 1$.

## 1.2 Ratio of the Precisions in the Vasicek Model

In the Vasicek (1973) estimate, the regression estimate is based on 60 months and

$$\frac{H^{Prior}}{H^{Prior} + H^{Regression:60}} = 0.4$$

$$\frac{H^{Regression:60}}{H^{Prior} + H^{Regression:60}} = 0.6$$

$$\beta^{\text{Shrunk}} = 0.4 \times \beta^{Prior} + 0.6 \times \beta^{Regression} \tag{3.9}$$

The ratio of $H^{Prior}$ and $H^{Regression:60}$ is computed as follows:

$$\frac{H^{Prior}}{H^{Prior} + H^{Regression:60}} = 0.4$$

$$\Rightarrow H^{Prior} = 0.4 \times H^{Prior} + 0.4 \times H^{Regression.60}$$

$$\Rightarrow 0.6H^{Prior} = 0.4 \times H^{Regression.60}$$

$$\Rightarrow 1.5H^{Prior} = H^{Regression.60}$$

## 1.3 Modification for Smaller Sample Size

From basic sampling theory

$$H^{Regression:N} = \frac{N}{60} H^{Regression:60} = 1.5 \frac{N}{60} H^{Prior} = \frac{N}{40} H^{Prior} \tag{3.10}$$

As such

$$\frac{H^{Prior}}{H^{Prior} + H^{Regression:N}} = \frac{1}{1 + \frac{N}{40}} = \frac{40}{40 + N} \tag{3.11}$$

This yields the estimate

$$\beta^{Shrunk} = \frac{40}{40 + N} \times \beta^{Prior} + \frac{N}{40 + N} \times \beta^{Regression:N} \tag{3.12}$$

$\beta_m$ (market beta) is the efficient estimator of $\beta^{Prior}$. Hence, the above equation becomes

$$\beta_{iN}^{s} = \frac{40}{40 + N} \times \beta_m + \frac{N}{40 + N} \times \beta_{iN} \tag{3.13}$$

where $\beta_{iN}^{s}$ is the shrinkage beta estimated at the end of month $N$, $\beta_m$ is the market beta (equal to 1), and $\beta_{iN}$ is the stock beta as estimated following Eq. 3.1. $N$ takes value between 13 (first month in the second year of trading) and 60.

## References

Agarwalla, S. K., Jacob, J., & Varma, J. R. (2013). Four factor model in Indian equities market. Working Paper W. P. No. 2013-09-05, Indian Institute of Management, Ahmedabad.

Ang, A., Hodrick, R. J., Xing, Y., & Zhang, X. (2006). The cross-section of volatility and expected returns. *The Journal of Finance, 61*(1), 259–299.

Ang, A., Hodrick, R. J., Xing, Y., & Zhang, X. (2009). High idiosyncratic volatility and low returns: International and further us evidence. *Journal of Financial Economics, 91*(1), 1–23.

Ansari, V. A. (2000). Capital asset pricing model: Should we stop using it? *Vikalpa, 25*(1), 55–64.

Baker, M., Bradley, B., & Wurgler, J. (2011). Benchmarks as limits to arbitrage: Understanding the low-volatility anomaly. *Financial Analysts Journal, 67*(1).

Black, F. (1972). Capital market equilibrium with restricted borrowing. *Journal of Business*, 444–455.

Black, F. (1993). Beta and return. *Streetwise: The Best of The Journal of Portfolio Management*, 74.

Fama, E. F., & French, K. R. (1992). The cross-section of expected stock returns. *The Journal of Finance, 47*(2), 427–465.

Frazzini, A., & Pedersen, L. H. (2014). Betting against beta. *Journal of Financial Economics, 111*(1), 1–25.

Jegadeesh, N., & Titman, S. (1993). Returns to buying winners and selling losers: Implications for stock market efficiency. *The Journal of Finance, 48*(1), 65–91.

Vasicek, O. A. (1973). A note on using cross-sectional information in bayesian estimation of security betas. *The Journal of Finance, 28*(5), 1233–1239.

# Chapter 4
# Does Economic Policy Uncertainty Matter for Stock Market Volatility?

**Abhisek Mishra and Byomakesh Debata**

**Abstract** This study examines the dynamic relationship between economic policy uncertainty (EPU) and stock market volatility in a pure order-driven emerging stock market. Considering the non-linear EPU-volatility relationship, this study uses GARCH family of models to capture the impact of policy uncertainty on stock market volatility. Empirical estimates reveal that economic policy uncertainty is an essential determinant of stock market volatility, and higher EPU leads to significant increase in volatility. We believe, a thorough understanding the EPU-Volatility relationship can be beneficial for investors to better predict the behaviour of stock market volatility.

**Keywords** Economic policy uncertainty · GARCH models · Stock market volatility

**JEL Code** E44 · G12 · G14

## 4.1 Introduction

Stock market volatility has been a pertinent subject of interest for investors, policymakers, academic researchers and practitioners due to its implications for asset pricing, hedging, risk management, portfolio diversification, predicting future prospects of market and maintaining financial market stability (Paye, 2012; Ropach & Zhou, 2013; Antonakakis, Balcilar, Gupta, & Kyei, 2016). In the post-global financial crisis, the Economic Policy Uncertainity (EPU) has received considerable attention in finance literature. Existing studies have found that EPU has potential negative effects on various economic activities including economic growth, inflation, investment and employment (Rodrik, 1991; Bloom, Bond, & Reenen, 2007;

A. Mishra (✉)
Nabakrushna Choudhury Centre for Development Studies, Bhubaneswar, India
e-mail: abhisek.mishra@hotmail.com

B. Debata
Birla Institute of Technology and Science, Pilani Campus, Vidya Vihar, Rajasthan, India

 
A. K. Mishra et al. (eds.), *The Financial Landscape of Emerging Economies*, Accounting, Finance, Sustainability, Governance & Fraud: Theory and Application,
https://doi.org/10.1007/978-3-030-60008-2_4

Bloom, 2009; Bhagat, Ghosh, & Ranjan, 2016, Broggard & Detzel, 2015; Gulen & Ion, 2016). Specifically, in the context of stock market, it is evident that rise in EPU leads to increase in stock market volatility and reduce stock returns (Pastor & Veronesi, 2012; Antonakkis, Chatziantoniou, & Filis, 2013; Bhagat et al., 2016; Kang & Ratti, 2013; Wu, Liu, & Hsueh, 2016; Christou et al., 2017).

From the ongoing literature, it is inferred that the majority of the studies have been carried out in developed countries and the results are inconclusive. Further, the effect of EPU on stock volatility in the context of emerging economies is scantly investigated. In this conjecture, the present study is carried out to examine the effect of EPU on stock market volatility in an emerging order-driven stock market. We consider the Indian stock market as the ideal candidate for this study due to the following reasons. First, Bekaert and Harvey (2003) advocate that the market structure, regulatory environment and the level of market development in emerging market is unique. Further, emerging markets are characterised with low liquidity and high volatility (Bekaert et al., 2007; Charitou & Panayides, 2009; Damowitz, 2002; Mensi et al., 2016) and can influence the portfolio performance significantly (Lesmond, 2005). Secondly, based on security listing the Indian stock market is the second largest in the world (Debata & Mahakud, 2018). In fact, there is a significant increase in the market capitalisation to gross domestic product ratio (17.83% in 1991 to 72.4% in 2015), which further motivates to consider Indian stock market as a suitable case. We also believe that addressing this issue in an emerging stock market may yield some powerful insights and provide out-of-the-sample evidence.

To analyse the effect of EPU on stock market volatility, we use generalised autoregressive conditional heteroskedasticity (GARCH), exponential GARCH (EGARCH) and threshold GARCH (TGARCH) models. The empirical estimates provide sufficient evidence in favour of EPU for the determination of stock market volatility. In addition, we also find evidence for the existence of volatility asymmetry (leverage effect). Most of the existing literature is curved towards the developed countries and the studies on developing or emerging economies are scant. To the best of our knowledge, this is one of the early studies to examine the impact of EPU on stock market volatility in the context of Indian stock market. Thus, this study can be an endeavour to the existing literature. The rest of the paper is structured as follows. The methodology used is discussed in Sect. 4.2. Section 4.3 deals with data and variables. Results are discussed in Sects. 4.4 and 4.5 concludes.

## 4.2 Methodology

The models employed for examining the effect of EPU on stock market volatility are explained in this section. Assuming a non-linear relationship between EPU and volatility, we use GARCH class of models. The use of GARCH models helps capturing the volatility clustering and leptokurtosis. In addition, the asymmetry or leverage effect is captured using EGARCH and TGARCH models (Alberg, Shalit, &

Yosef, 2008; Oskooe & Shamsavari, 2011). Following the usual econometric estimation procedure, we diagnose the persistence of serial correlation in the time series of stock returns and conditional variance using Box-Ljung and ARCH-LM test (Kumari & Mahakud, 2015). We have also taken care of stationarity issue by using augmented Dickey–Fuller (ADF) and Philips–Perron (PP) unit root tests.

In this study, we use the economic policy uncertainty term in the conditional variance equation. It is evident from existing studies that the current stock returns are a function of the lagged stock returns. From this, one can infer that the volatility is conditioned upon the past values. Nevertheless, the use of lagged EPU in conditional framework enables us to ascertain the role of EPU for the determination of stock volatility in the GARCH specifications.

### 4.2.1 GARCH (1, 1) Model

GARCH (1, 1) is the simplest and most widely used model for studying volatility behaviour. This can be specified as follows:

$$Y_t = \vartheta_0 + \vartheta_1 Y_{t-1} + \varepsilon_t \quad \text{(Mean Equation)} \tag{4.1}$$

$$\varepsilon_t / \Omega \sim i.i.d.(0, h_t)$$

$$h_t = \omega + \sum_{i=1}^{p} \alpha_j \varepsilon_{t-i}^2 + \sum_{j=1}^{q} \beta_j h_{t-j} + \varphi EPU_{t-1} \quad \text{(Variance Equation)} \tag{4.2}$$

where $\omega > 0$ and $\alpha_i + \beta_j < 1$.

$Y_t$ is the index returns, and $EPU_{t-1}$ stands for the lagged economic policy uncertainty. $h_t$ is the conditional variance and $\varepsilon_t$ is the residual. $\alpha_i$ is the coefficients of the lagged squared residuals, $\beta_j$ is the lagged conditional variance and $\varphi$ represents the coefficient of lagged EPU.

### 4.2.2 EGARCH Model

Despite the wide popularity and usefulness of GARCH model, one of the primary limitations is that it accounts symmetric responses to both positive and negative shocks. However, financial time series responds to negative shocks more predominantly over positive shocks. In fact, the likelihood of the impact of negative news raises market volatility more than positive news of the same magnitude. Considering the importance of leverage effect, Nelson (1991) proposed exponential GARCH model, which is specified as follows:

$$Y_t = \vartheta_0 + \vartheta_1 Y_{t-1} + \varepsilon_t \quad \text{(Mean Equation)} \tag{4.3}$$

$$\varepsilon_t/\Omega \sim i.i.d.(0, h_t)$$

$$\log(\mathrm{h_t}) = \omega + \sum_{i=1}^{p} \alpha_i \left[ \left| \frac{\varepsilon_{t-i}}{\sqrt{h_{t-i}}} - E\left( \frac{\varepsilon_{t-i}}{\sqrt{h_{t-i}}} \right) \right| \right] + \sum_{k=1}^{m} \delta_k \frac{\varepsilon_{t-k}}{\sqrt{h_{t-k}}}$$
$$+ \sum_{j=1}^{q} \beta_j h_{t-j} + \varphi EPU_{t-1} \quad \text{(Variance Equation)} \tag{4.4}$$

where $\omega > 0$ and $\alpha_i + \beta_j < 1, \delta_k < 0$ implies asymmetric nature of volatility (leverage effect). In addition, $Y_t$ shows the index returns, $\log(\mathrm{h_t})$ is log of conditional variance of index returns and $\delta_k$ represents the asymmetric coefficient. $\varphi$ is the coefficient of lagged EPU. The use of logarithm of conditional variance enforces the distribution to be exponential and the estimates to be non-negative. The asymmetric behaviour of volatility, volatility persistence and impact of positive (negative) news can clearly be ascertained using EGARCH model.

### 4.2.3 TGARCH Model

Further, following Zakoian (1994), we use the threshold GARCH model to capture the leverage effect. The basic assumption is that the impact of positive (negative) news on stock volatility is different though the magnitude of the shock is same. This model looks similar to EGARCH model, but there are some fundamental differences too. TGARCH assumes volatility as a function of innovations, whereas there is no as such assumption in EGARCH specification. Secondly, unlike EGARCH which imposes a constant structure at all lags, TGARCH allows different lags to contribute differently. The model specification of TGARCH is as follows:

$$Y_t = \vartheta_0 + \vartheta_1 Y_{t-1} + \varepsilon_t \tag{4.5}$$

$$\varepsilon_t/\Omega \sim i.i.d.(0, h_t)$$

$$h_t = \omega + \sum_{i=1}^{p} \alpha_j \varepsilon_{t-i}^2 + \gamma \epsilon_{t-1}^2 d_{t-1} + \sum_{j=1}^{q} \beta_j h_{t-j} + \varphi EPU_{t-1} \tag{4.6}$$

where the dummy variable is represented by $(d_t)$, and this will be equal to 1 for $\varepsilon_t > 0$. And $d_t = 0$, when $\varepsilon_t < 0$. The good news (bad news) is represented by $\varepsilon_t > 0 (\varepsilon_t < 0)$. A coefficients capture the impact of good news, while bad news effect is represented by $(\alpha + \gamma)$. Further, when $\gamma = 0$, the volatility is considered symmetric and otherwise asymmetric. $\varphi$ shows the coefficient of lagged EPU. This model further corroborates the results of EGARCH model.

## 4.3 Data and Variables

The data and variables employed in the study are discussed in this section. This study has used the SENSEX (Benchmark index of Bombay Stock Exchange) and the S&P CNX Nifty (Benchmark index of National Stock Exchange) as the proxies for the aggregate market returns. To obtain the excess market return, the yield of 91-days T-bill was subtracted from aggregate market returns of both the indices. We use EPU index proposed by Baker, Bloom, & Davis, (2013, 2016) for Indian market in this study. EPU essentially reflects the uncertainty pertaining to policy-related economic decisions (Wu, Liu, & Hsueh, 2016; Debata & Mahakud, 2018).

The data period varies from April 2002 to March 2019 (204 monthly observations). The choice of the data period is based on the availability of continuous data. Also, it helps in avoiding the impact of the movement from Badla system to the rolling settlement cycle (T + 2) in the Indian stock market. Stock market variables are collected from Bloomberg database. The EPU index is obtained from "Measuring Economic Policy Uncertainty" by Scott Baker, Nicholas Bloom and Steven J. Davis at www.PolicyUncertainty.com.

Table 4.1 depicts the summary statistics and correlation structure among aggregate market returns (SENSEX, NIFTY) and economic policy uncertainty (LNEPU). We derive the following inferences from the above table. The aggregate market returns

**Table 4.1** Descriptive statistics and correlation matrix

| *Panel A: descriptive statistics* | | | |
|---|---|---|---|
| | SENSEX | NIFTY | EPU |
| Mean | 0.013376 | 0.012931 | 4.483 |
| Median | 0.013742 | 0.016091 | 4.503 |
| Standard deviation | 0.069977 | 0.071914 | 0.548 |
| Kurtosis | 2.104489 | 2.722245 | 2.351 |
| Skewness | −0.568 | −0.70383 | −0.112 |
| Maximum | 0.248851 | 0.247376 | 5.647 |
| Minimum | −0.27299 | −0.30666 | 3.216 |
| *Panel B: correlation matrix* | | | |
| SENSEX | 1 | 0.88 | −0.21 |
| CNXNIFTY | 0.88 | 1 | −0.29 |
| LNEPU | −0.21 | −0.29 | 1 |

*Source* Authors' own calculation

vary from −30% to 24% (as depicted from NIFTY) during the data period. In addition, we observe a strong positive correlation between the SENSEX and NIFTY, i.e. 0.88. Besides the negative correlation between market returns and economic policy uncertainty (−0.21 with SENSEX and −0.29 with NIFTY) implies that the return from the market shows a negative trend during the time of heightened policy uncertainty.

## 4.4 Result and Discussion

This section deals with the discussion of empirical results. Before we proceed for estimation of the proposed models, the stationarity of time series is checked using ADF (1981) and PP (1988) unit roots tests. Further, consistent with Diebold and Mariano (1995), optimal lag length was selected using AIC and SIC criteria. Subsequently, we estimate GARCH (1, 1), EGARCH (1, 1) and TGARCH (1, 1) models with and without economic policy uncertainty in the variance equation.

Table 4.2 reports the estimated results of GARCH (1, 1), EGARCH (1, 1) and TGARCH (1, 1) models with and without economic policy uncertainty in the variance equation. These estimations are made for both the market proxies (NIFTY, SENSEX) independently. We find that the volatility coefficients are statistically significant for all the models across with and without EPU. The results are found to be consistent for both indices. From the positive coefficients of $\alpha$ and $\beta$, we can infer that the past information such as past residuals and conditional variances influence significantly to predict volatility persistence. In addition, we find that $\alpha + \beta$ is close to 1 for most of the models which further corroborate the volatility clustering.

Furthermore, we find $\delta \neq 0$ which implies that volatility asymmetry exists. The negative value of $\delta$ ($\delta < 0$) clearly ascertains that the effect of negative shock on volatility is more pronounced over positive shock of the same magnitude. One can intuitively argue that due to the risk-averse nature of the investors, they have a tendency to sell out the stocks during market downturn aggressively in anticipation of a significant fall on stock price in future. These findings are further substantiated by the estimates of TGARCH (1, 1) model. The non-zero and positive value of $\gamma$ reveals that the effect of negative news on conditional variance is more prominent over positive news and the impact of negative shocks sustain for longer time period. The consistency of EGARCH model is further validated by the findings of TGARCH model. This holds good for both the market indices. Our empirical findings are consistent with Antonakakis, Chatziantoniou, and Filis, (2013) and Debata and Mahakud (2018) that an increase in policy uncertainty causes uncertainty on stock returns, as a result of which the volatility of stock market shoots up. Overall, we can ascertain that the EPU is a significant determinant of stock market volatility.

**Table 4.2** GARCH, EGARCH and TGARCH estimates (with and without EPU)

| | GARCH | GARCH EPU | EGARCH | EGARCH EPU | TGARCH | TGARCH EPU |
|---|---|---|---|---|---|---|
| *Panel A: estimated results for NIFTY* | | | | | | |
| C | 0.0474** | 0.0663*** | 0.0607*** | 0.0674*** | 0.1066*** | 0.0871*** |
| $\omega$ | 0.000136 | 0.00019 | −6.5754 | −9.8540*** | −0.00013*** | −0.000016 |
| $\alpha$ | 0.0989** | 0.0040 | 0.1281 | 0.1108* | 0.1329*** | 0.0582*** |
| $\beta$ | 0.8760*** | 0.9531*** | 0.8325* | −0.8305*** | 0.8403*** | 0.9312*** |
| $\alpha + \beta$ | 0.9749 | 0.96 | 0.96 | 0.94 | 0.97 | 0.99 |
| EPU | | 0.1688** | | 0.5356* | | −0.1191** |
| $\delta$ | | | −0.0444* | −0.0256* | | |
| $\gamma$ | | | | | 0.2105*** | 0.1414*** |
| LL | 197.3799 | 198.4346 | 192.8942 | 193.4193 | 203.4517 | 205.1735 |
| AIC | −2.45359 | −2.47012 | −2.38326 | −2.39251 | −2.51861 | −2.54417 |
| *Panel B: estimated results for SENSEX* | | | | | | |
| C | 0.0515** | 0.0605*** | 0.0672*** | 0.0724*** | 0.1127*** | 0.1058*** |
| $\omega$ | 0.00012 | 0.0002 | −7.217*** | −9.736*** | −0.0001*** | −0.00046 |
| $\alpha$ | 0.103586** | 0.056182* | 0.2447** | 0.2078* | 0.1383*** | 0.1287* |
| $\beta$ | 0.8723*** | 0.8970*** | 0.6451 | 0.8449*** | 0.8335*** | 0.8201*** |
| $\alpha + \beta$ | 0.98 | 0.95 | 0.89 | 0.85 | 0.97 | 0.95 |
| EPU | | 0.10475* | | 0.56852* | | 0.0915* |
| $\delta$ | | | −0.0534* | −0.02848 | | |
| $\gamma$ | | | | | 0.223*** | 0.2094** |
| LL | 203.7139 | 203.6957 | 198.584 | 198.1602 | 207.9096 | 208.0588 |
| AIC | −2.53479 | −2.53801 | −2.45588 | −2.45368 | −2.57576 | −2.5814 |

*Note* In this table, the $\omega$ denotes the constant values, $\alpha$ denotes the ARCH term, $\beta$ the GARCH term and $\alpha + \beta$ presents the stationary condition of model and volatility persistence. *EPU* demonstrates the economic policy uncertainty

***Denotes the significance level at 1%

**Denotes the significance level at 5%

*Denotes the significance level at 10%

## 4.5 Conclusion

The study investigates the effect of economic policy uncertainty on stock volatility for two major indices of Indian stock market, i.e. SENSEX and NIFTY over the period April 2002–March 2019. To do so, GARCH family of models particularly GARCH, EGARCH and TGARCH were used.

The empirical findings reveal that volatility clustering and asymmetry exist in Indian stock market. We also document that EPU is an essential determinant of stock market volatility. From the analysis, it is found that EPU is a systematic risk factor, and it plays a crucial role to understand the behaviour of stock market volatility. Our findings are consistent with Baker et al. (2013, 2016) and Liu and Zhang (2015). While analysing the leverage effect, we strongly advocate the impact of negative shock on volatility is more persistent over positive shock. Thus, the EPU-volatility relationship during the market downturn may provide some powerful insights to predict volatility conditions in times of jump and diffusion. This is one of the early studies from an emerging market perspective, particularly in Indian stock market. The findings may have some implications for policymakers and market participants. A thorough understanding of EPU-volatility relationship would help policymakers to design countervailing strategies to reduce the unnecessary uncertainty which is essential for maintaining financial market stability. For investors, inclusion of EPU along with other market fundamentals and macroeconomic conditions may help predicting volatility considerably. Knowledge on economic policy uncertainty could be helpful for practitioners to gauge and assess the future stock market performance.

## References

Alberg, D., Shalit, H., & Yosef, R. (2008). Estimating stock market volatility using asymmetric GARCH models. *Applied Financial Economics, 18*, 1201–1208.

Antonakakis, N., Balcilar, M., Gupta, R., & Kyei, C. (2016). *Components of economic policy uncertainty and predictability of US stock returns and volatility: Evidence from a non parametric causality-in-quantile approach* (Working Paper No. 201639: University of Pretoria, Department of Economics). Retrieved August 20, 2019, from https://ffejournal.files.wordpress.com/2017/12/3-ms-antonakakis-balcilar-guptat-kyei.pdf.

Antonakakis, N., Chatziantoniou, I., & Filis, G. (2013). Dynamic co-movements between stock market return and policy uncertainty. *Economics Letters, 120,* 87–92.

Baker, S., Bloom, N., & Davis, S. (2013). Measuring economic policy uncertainty (Working Paper-13-02). Stanford University.

Baker, S. R., Bloom, N., & Davis, S. (2016). Measuring economic policy uncertainty. *The Quarterly Journal of Economics, 131*(4), 1593–1636.

Bekaert, G., & Harvey, C. R. (2003). Emerging markets finance. *Journal of Empirical Finance, 10*(1–2), 3–55.

Bhagat, S., Ghosh, P., & Ranjan, S. P. (2016). Economic policy uncertainty economic growth in India. *Economic and Political Weekly, 51*(35).

Bloom, N. (2009). The impact of uncertainty shocks. *Econometrica, 77,* 623–685.

Bloom, N., Bond, S., & Reenen, J. V. (2007). Uncertainty and investment dynamics. *Review of Economic Studies, 74,* 391–415.

Broggard, J., & Detzel, A. (2015). The asset-pricing implications of government economic policy uncertainty. *Management Science, 61*(1).

Charitou, A., & Panayides, M. A. (2009). Market making in international capital markets: challenges and benefits of its implementation in emerging markets. *International Journal of Managerial Finance: Special Issue, 5*, 50–80.

Christou, C., Cunado, J., Gupta, R., & Hassapis, C. (2017). Economic policy uncertainty and stock market returns in pacific-rim countries: Evidence based on Bayesian Panel VAR model. *Journal of Multinational Financial Management, 40,* issue C:92–102.

Damowitz, I. (2002). Liquidity, Transaction cost, and Reintermediation in electronic markets. *Journal of Financial Services Research, 22,* 141–157.

Debata, B., & Mahakud, J. (2018). Interdependence between monetary policy and stock liquidity: A panel VAR approach. *Margin The Journal of Applied Economics, 12*(4), 387–413.

Deibold, F. X., & Mariano, R. S. (1995). Comparing predictive accuracy. *Journal of Business & Economic Statistics, 13*(3), 253–263.

Gulen, H., & Ion, M. (2016). Policy uncertainty and corporate investment. *The Review of Financial Studies*, 523–564.

Kang, W., & Ratti, R. A. (2013). Oil shocks, policy uncertainty and stock market returns. *Journal of International Financial Market, Institutions and Money, 26,* 305–318.

Kumari, J., & Mahakud, J. (2015). Does investor sentiment predict asset volatility? Evidence from emerging stock market India. *Journal of Behavioral and Experimental Finance, 8*, 25–39.

Lesmond, D. (2005). Liquidity of emerging markets. *Journal of Financial economics, 77*, 411–452.

Liu, L., & Zhang, T. (2015). Economic policy uncertainty and stock market volatility. *Finance Research Letters, 15*, 99–105.

Mensi, W., Hammoudesh, S., Yoon, S. M., & Nguyen, D. K. (2016). Asymmetric linkages between BRICS stock returns and country risk ratings: Evidence from dynamic panel threshold models. *Review of International Economics, 24,* 1–9.

Nelson, D. (1991). Conditional Hateroskedasticity in asset return: A new approach. *Econometrica, 49*(2), 347–370.

Oskooe, S. A. P., & Shamsavari, A. (2011). Asymmetric effects in emerging stock markets-The case of Iran stock market. *International Journal of Economics and Finance, 3*(6), 16–24.

Paye, B. S. (2012). 'Déjà Vol': Predictive regressions for aggregate stock market volatility using macroeconomic variables. *Journal of Financial Economics, 106*(3), 527–546.

Pastor, L., & Veronesi, P. (2012). Uncertainty about government policy and stock prices. *Journal of Finance, 67,* 1219–1264.

Rodrik, D. (1991). Policy uncertainty and private investment in developing countries. *Journal of Development Economics, 36,* 229–242.

Ropach, D., & Zhou, G. (2013). *Forecasting stock return.* In G. Elliot & A. Timmermann (Eds.), *Handbook of economic forecasting* (Vol. 2A, pp. 328–383). Amsterdam: Elsevier.

Wu, T.-P., Liu, S.-B., & Hsueh, S.-J. (2016). The causal relationship between economic policy uncertainty and stock market: A panel data analysis. *International Economics Journal, 30*(1), 109–122.

Zakoian, J. M. (1994). Threshold heteroskedastic models. *Journal of Economic Dynamics and control, 18*(5), 931–955.

# Chapter 5
# Can the FMCG Stock Market Investors Hedge the Risk in Agricultural Commodity Markets? Empirical Evidence from India

**Manogna R. Leshma and Aswini Kumar Mishra**

**Abstract** The emerging economy of India counts agriculture as its top priority, suggesting that the prices of these commodities affect the stock market and domestic inflation. This paper investigates the long-run and short-run interactions between the select agricultural commodities and Fast-Moving Consumer Goods (FMCG) stock index by applying daily data using the Autoregressive Distributive Lag (ARDL) bound test to investigate the cointegration relationship. The findings indicate the absence of cointegration between National Commodity and Derivative Exchange (NCDEX) agricultural commodities and Bombay Stock Exchange (BSE) FMCG index. Additionally, this study uses the Toda and Yamamoto approach of Granger causality test to analyze the causal relationship between variables under study. The evidence reveals absence of causal relationship between FMCG index and agricultural commodities except for cottonseed, rape mustard seed and jeera. Furthermore, this test confirms only unidirectional causal relationship from these commodities to FMCG index. Finally, our analysis provides an opportunity for investors to hedge their risk due to the absence of causality and cointegration between FMCG index and agricultural commodities by diversifying their portfolio in both the markets.

**Keywords** Agricultural commodities · Johansen cointegration · ARDL bound test · Causal relationship · FMCG · Toda and Yamamoto approach of granger causality test

R. L. Manogna (✉) · A. K. Mishra
Department of Economics, BITS Pilani K K Birla Goa Campus, Sancoale, Goa, India
e-mail: leshma2020@gmail.com

A. K. Mishra
e-mail: aswini@goa.bits-pilani.ac.in

 
A. K. Mishra et al. (eds.), *The Financial Landscape of Emerging Economies*, Accounting, Finance, Sustainability, Governance & Fraud: Theory and Application,
https://doi.org/10.1007/978-3-030-60008-2_5

## 5.1 Introduction

Indian economy provides major emphasis on agriculture with consistent efforts to transform the agricultural scenario of the country. Almost two-thirds of the population depend on agriculture for their livelihood. Efficient marketing of agricultural commodities has been undertaken to protect the interest of both producer and consumer. For a developing economy like India, agricultural commodities like oilseed cakes, spices and grains contribute majorly in earning a sizeable foreign currency through its exports and managing the imports. National Commodity and Derivative Exchange (NCDEX) is one of India's leading commodity exchanges which majorly trades on agricultural commodities.

The efficient market hypothesis states that the news entering the market can directly affect the perception of investors, causing them to revise their portfolio of investments and the changes immediately impact the financial markets (Tursoy and Faisal 2017). A study by Elder et al. (2012) found a very low correlation between commodity and equity prices due to which commodity becomes an asset class like bonds and stocks and thus leading to the improvement of the overall portfolio. The low correlation arises when the same news has different effects on commodity and equity prices or could lead to a negative impact on each other (Reddy and Sebastin 2009; Hammoudeh and Aleisa 2004). Studies analyzing the various determinants of the FMCG stock prices in the Indian context which has major inputs from the agricultural commodities help both the farmers and consumers along with traders in hedging against the sharp price fluctuations and portfolio diversification.

As such, this study is an attempt to examine the relationship between spot prices of nine commodities (cottonseed, castorseed, soybeanseed, rape mustard seed, turmeric, jeera, coriander, guar seed and chana) traded on NCDEX and Bombay Stock Exchange (BSE) listed FMCG index using econometric tools such as cointegration techniques and causality tests. This has significant implications for policymaking, market efficiency, risk management and trading strategies. The remaining part of the present study is structured as follows: Sect. 5.2 highlights the existing literature followed by the description of data in Sect. 5.3. Section 5.4 explains the econometric methodology used for the study and Sect. 5.5 presents the empirical findings. Section 5.6 discusses the results and finally concludes in Sect. 5.7.

## 5.2 Review of Literature

A large body of literature exists, describing the relationship between commodity market and stock market in developed economies (Ciner et al. 2013; Tursoy and Faisal 2017; Bekiros et al. 2016), but only a small proportion of literature focuses on these relationships in developing and emerging economies (Gurgun and Unalmis 2014; Baur and McDermott 2010). The investigation between the effects of oil and gold prices is plentiful among them (Bouri et al. 2017; Chittedi 2012; Tursoy and

Faisal 2017, among others). In contrast, there has been very few examining the relationship between the FMCG stock prices and the commodity markets despite speculations about the inputs of agricultural production influencing FMCG prices.

Bouri et al. (2017) examined the cointegration among the international gold, crude oil and Indian stock market using the implied volatility indices. The findings reveal the cointegration relationships among the variables with the ARDL approach. Chittedi (2012) and Naveed Raza et al. (2016) employed the ARDL model suggesting that the volatility of stock prices in India has a significant impact on the volatility of oil prices. During the period of financial distress, Souček (2013) found that the correlation between oil and stock decreased. On the other side, Urrutia and Malliaris (2005) found that during the period of financial distress, the causal relationship between crude oil and stocks becomes stronger. Thus, leading to decrease in the diversification benefits among investors.

As discussed above, studies have mainly focused on gold and crude oil relationship with stock indices. Few studies have examined the relationship between agricultural commodities and stock indices. For example, Lehecka (2014) found a weak indication of co-movement between the food prices and stock market which is synchronized with structural changes such as a change in agricultural policies, new demand due to growth in emerging markets and financialization of commodities. Ali and Gupta (2011) examined the cointegration between the future and spot prices of 16 agricultural commodities using the Johansen's cointegration method and revealed long-term cointegration between the future and spot price indices for all commodities except rice and wheat. Study by Manogna and Mishra (2020) uses Granger causality, Vector Error Correction Model (VECM) and Exponential Generalized Autoregressive Conditional Heteroskedasticity (EGARCH) to examine the price discovery and spillover effects for agricultural commodities in spot and futures markets. Diversely, Kang et al. (2013) applied Granger causality test to find the relationship between the international food commodity prices and stock exchange indices in China, mainly Shanghai stock exchange and Shenzen stock exchange indices and found that rice has a unilateral causal relationship while wheat, corn and soybean have a bilateral causal relationship with stock indices. Kaur and Dhiman (2019) investigated the effect of agricultural commodities on FMCG index listed on National Stock Exchange (NSE) using weekly data and found absence of cointegration and causality except for barley, cottonseed, jeera, mustard seed and wheat which show a unidirectional causal relationship. However, not many studies have considered the daily data with relevant time period wherein agricultural commodity markets have seen massive growth for the last five years.

To address this literature gap, this study attempts to examine the relationship between agricultural commodities and FMCG stock index of India. The relationship is explained by the mechanism that the FMCG companies which use agricultural commodities as raw material have an impact on their profits from the increase in the input cost of production and thus shrink the expected rate of return. Thus, the rise in agricultural commodity prices has a negative impact on FMCG stocks (Memdani 2014; Broadstock et al. 2012). Another mechanism could be the hike in food commodity prices pushing up the inflation in emerging countries like

India, where the food products contribute to higher share in the purchase basket of consumers (Árendáš 2005) causing the policy change by the central bank and in turn affecting the stock prices (Broadstock et al. 2012). We also extend the literature by using the ARDL bounds test and Johansen cointegration test along with Toda and Yamamoto Granger causality test to study the long-term and short-term relationships across the examined variables.

## 5.3 Data

This study uses a sample consisting of nine most liquid agricultural commodity futures traded on National Commodities and Derivatives Exchange limited (NCDEX), extracted from the Accord Fintech Private Ltd. database. The resulting sample has taken care of the missing values for all the selected nine commodities being classified as oilseeds (cottonseed, castorseed, soybeanseed and rape mustard seed), spices (turmeric, jeera and coriander) and grains (guarseed and chana). To capture the dynamics of commodity spot prices and fast-moving index prices, we have chosen the high-frequency daily data. These prices are transformed to log returns to proceed with the analysis. Daily closing prices of BSE FMCG index were collected from the official BSE website.

## 5.4 Methodology

Prior to implementing the cointegration test among the estimated variables in the model, it is important to determine the order of integration by verifying the stationarity of the series. Unit root tests using autoregressive models have been applied to check the stationarity. The most common methods Augmented Dickey–Fuller (1981) (ADF) test and the Phillips–Perron (1988) (PP) test are being employed with the presence of unit root as the null hypothesis. To meet the demand of data over long periods, both intercept and intercept with trend have been applied. Based on the Akaike Information Criteria (AIC), the lags for the ADF test and critical values are selected (Hamilton 1994).

### *5.4.1 Autoregressive Distributive Lag Bounds Test*

This study utilizes the ARDL bounds testing method presented by Pesaran et al. (2001) to investigate the cointegration among the estimated variables. Although other cointegration approaches can be applied to the series that have a unique order of cointegration, the ARDL bounds test is more flexible compared to other traditional models and can be applied to any series that has a mixed order of integration. However, it must be verified that none of the variables is integrated of order 2 or higher. The ARDL model for the standard specification between the BSE FMCG index and agricultural commodities is as follows:

$$\Delta BSE\ FMCG = \omega_1 + \sum_{i=1}^{n} \alpha_{1i} \Delta BSE\ FMCG_{t-1} + \sum_{i=1}^{n} \beta_{1i} \Delta Agri\ C_{t-1} + a_1 BSE\ FMCG_{t-1} + b_1 Agri\ C_{t-1} + \varepsilon_{1t} \tag{5.1}$$

$$\Delta Agri\ C = \omega_2 + \sum_{i=1}^{n} \alpha_{2i} \Delta BSE\ FMCG_{t-1} + \sum_{i=1}^{n} \beta_{2i} \Delta Agri\ C_{t-1} + a_2 BSE\ FMCG_{t-1} + b_2 Agri\ C_{t-1} + \varepsilon_{2t} \tag{5.2}$$

where $\Delta$ is the first difference operator, $Agri\ C$ denotes the agricultural commodities and $\varepsilon_t$ is the error term that must be white noise. In order to analyze cointegration among the selected variables, the bounds test will be applied.

### 5.4.2 *Johansen Cointegration Test*

To test for cointegration, we propose Johansen trace test and maximum eigenvalue test (Johansen 1988). As the FMCG index and agricultural prices are seen to be cointegrated of same order, the long-run relationship between the two series is tested with hypothesis that the system of equations contains, at most, r cointegrating vectors. The trace test is formulated as $\lambda(r)_t = -T\sum_{i=r+1}^{n} ln(1 - \hat{\lambda}_i)$, where $\hat{\lambda}_i$ is the $i$th largest eigenvalue. The null hypothesis for trace statistic is $r = 0$ and the results are based on a model with a constant but no time trend. The null hypothesis of no cointegration (r = 0) is rejected against the alternative $r = 1$, and the null hypothesis of $r \leq 1$ against the alternative $r = 2$.

### 5.4.3 *Toda and Yamamoto Method of Granger Causality Test*

The Granger causality test approach proposed by Toda and Yamamoto (1995) was employed to study the causal relationship between the BSE FMCG index and the agricultural commodities. This technique, also known as Augmented Granger Causality Method, can be used to analyse the econometric time series data which is integrated of a different order. Using this methodology enables us to eliminate unit root test as variables at level are used for analysis. This approach is relatively more efficient than the other traditional methods for studying causal relationship as it does not require to find out the cointegrating relationship between the variables before proceeding for detection of a causal relationship between them.

On the basis of Vector Autoregressive (VAR) model with generated k order and extra lag d, Toda and Yamamoto method is applied to detect causal relationship between the agricultural commodities and BSE FMCG Index. Here, Wald statistics is applied along with Granger causality test to study the causality between the variables under study. The following equation details the model:

$$X_t = B_0 + B_1 X_{t-1} + B_2 X_{t-2} \cdots B_k X_{t-k} + \varepsilon_t \tag{5.3}$$

where $X_t = \begin{pmatrix} X_{1t} \\ X_{2t} \end{pmatrix} = \begin{pmatrix} FI_t \\ AC_t \end{pmatrix}$ and $\varepsilon_t \sim i.i.d N(0, \mu)$. AC corresponds to the agricultural commodity prices and FI denotes the FMCG index. In order to detect the causal relationship between the variables under study, augmented level VAR in the below equation is implemented.

$$X_t = \alpha + B_1 X_{t-1} + \cdots + B_k X_{t-k} + B_{k+1} X_{t-k+1} \cdots + B_p X_{t-p} + \varepsilon_t \tag{5.4}$$

## 5.5 Empirical Findings

### *5.5.1 Descriptive Statistics*

Table 5.1 reports descriptive statistics for spot and futures prices, such as mean, standard deviation, Skewness, Kurtosis and Coefficient of Variation (CV) along with a total number of observations and sample period. The price series for cottonseed, turmeric and chana show leptokurtic behaviour conveying that the prices of these commodities were not stable during the sample period. Finally, except for chana, all the other commodities are either moderately skewed or symmetric around their respective means.

### *5.5.2 Unit Root Test Results*

Augmented Dickey–Fuller (ADF) and Phillips–Perron (PP) unit root tests have been deployed to examine the stationarity of futures and spot prices. Both the models, a) with intercept and b) with intercept and trend have been conducted to diagnose the stationarity attributes. Akaike Information Criterion (AIC) has been used for optimal lag selection for conducting these tests. Level and first difference of the commodity prices along with BSE FMCG index are used to conduct these tests. PP test is a non-parametric approach, whereas ADF is a parametric approach. At levels of prices,

**Table 5.1** Summary statistics of future and spot prices of the commodities

| Variables | | Total Obs | Mean | SD | Minimum | Maximum | Skewness | Kurtosis | CV (%) |
|---|---|---|---|---|---|---|---|---|---|
| Oil seeds | Cottonseed (₹/q) Jan ’10–Jul ’19 | 2116 | 1620.2 | 448.3 | 918.9 | 3106.2 | 0.9 | 3.3 | 27.7 |
| | Castorseed (₹/q) Jan ’17–Jul ’19 | 592 | 4703.4 | 561.1 | 3847.5 | 6210.5 | 0.5 | 2.1 | 11.9 |
| | Soybeanseed (₹/q) Jan ’09–Jul ’19 | 2493 | 3089.9 | 738.9 | 1872 | 4958 | 0 | 1.8 | 23.9 |
| | RMseed (₹/20 kg) Mar ’11–Jul ’19 | 1820 | 3926.2 | 549 | 2549.7 | 5168 | −0.2 | 2.9 | 14 |
| Spices | Turmeric (₹/q) Mar ’09-Jul ’19 | 2058 | 7542.3 | 2870.7 | 3215.6 | 17047.1 | 1.5 | 4.8 | 38.1 |
| | Jeera (₹/q) Jan ’09-Jul ’19 | 2574 | 15024.4 | 2608.7 | 10246.9 | 21093.4 | 0.2 | 2.2 | 17.4 |
| | Coriande (₹/q) Mar ’09-Jul ’19 | 2290 | 6191.9 | 2435.7 | 2636.4 | 12120.6 | 0.8 | 2.9 | 39.3 |
| Grains | Guarseed (₹/q) Dec ’13-Jul ’19 | 1028 | 4019.4 | 623.1 | 2982.7 | 5900 | 0.5 | 2.8 | 15.5 |
| | Chana (₹/q) Aug ’17-Jul ’19 | 420 | 4287.2 | 585.5 | 3400 | 6195 | 1.4 | 5 | 13.7 |
| BSE FMCG Index (₹) Jan ’09–Jul ’19 | | 2621 | 6751.9 | 2942.4 | 1802.6 | 12771.7 | 0.1 | 1.9 | 43.6 |

*Note* SD indicates standard deviation, CV indicates coefficient of variation
*Source* Author’s own calculations using Accord Fintech data

null hypothesis of non-stationarity for both the ADF and PP tests conclude that null cannot be rejected. Hence, first difference of these prices has been conducted to reveal that both the ADF and PP tests reported significance at 10% level as shown in Table 5.2, Panel B. The critical values considered for the analysis has also been reported in Table 5.2, Panel C. One of the pre-requisite for applying the ARDL model is that all

**Table 5.2** Unit root test results

| Variable | ADF test | | PP test | |
|---|---|---|---|---|
| | Intercept only | Intercept and trend | Intercept only | Intercept and trend |
| *Panel A: ADF test and PP test at levels* | | | | |
| Cottonseed | −0.68 | −2.53 | −0.94 | −2.7 |
| Castorseed | −1.47 | −2.1 | −1.27 | −1.87 |
| Soybeanseed | −1.85 | −2.13 | −2.1 | −2.55 |
| RMseed | −2.79 | −2.56 | −2.64 | −2.44 |
| Turmeric | −1.75 | −1.92 | −2 | −2.15 |
| Jeera | −2.48 | −3.27 | −2.36 | −3.04 |
| Coriander | −1.32 | −1.49 | −1.49 | −1.63 |
| Guarseed | −2.11 | −2.09 | −2.07 | −2.04 |
| Chana | −2.08 | −1.76 | −2.1 | −1.79 |
| BSE FMCG Index | −0.89 | −3.77 | −0.88 | −3.67 |
| *Panel B: ADF test and PP test at first difference* | | | | |
| Cottonseed | −40.39* | −40.40* | −41.75* | −41.73* |
| Castorseed | −20.81* | −20.80* | −20.63* | −20.61* |
| Soybeanseed | −43.00* | −43.00* | −44.63* | −44.63* |
| RMseed | −37.51* | −37.53* | −37.45* | −37.46* |
| Turmeric | −40.14* | −40.14* | −41.51* | −41.50* |
| Jeera | −21.04* | −21.04* | −49.48* | −49.47* |
| Coriander | −29.97* | −29.96* | −45.25* | −45.24* |
| Guarseed | −32.37* | −32.38* | −32.38* | −32.38* |
| Chana | −19.21* | −19.30* | −19.20* | −19.30* |
| BSE FMCG Index | −46.15* | −46.14* | -46.08* | −46.07* |
| *Panel C: Critical values at 1, 5, and 10% level of confidence* | | | | |
| | −3.44 | −3.97 | −3.44 | −3.97 |
| | −2.87 | −3.42 | −2.87 | −3.42 |
| | −2.57 | −3.13 | −2.57 | −3.13 |

*Note* The table lists the results of the ADF and PP test on the logarithm of spot and futures prices of indices
*Source* Author's own calculations using Accord Fintech data
*Indicates significance at 1% level of confidence

the series under study should be either I(0) or I(1). None of the series is integrated at order 2 or higher.

### 5.5.3 Cointegration Test Results

Before going ahead with the ARDL and Granger causality test, it is required to select the appropriate lag length of the variables under study. In order to select the optimal lag length, VAR lag selection criteria were applied. The optimal lag length as per Akaike Information Criteria (AIC) is given in Table 5.3.

The results of ARDL bound test presented in Table 5.4 exhibit the absence of cointegration relationship between the BSE FMCG index and agricultural commodities.

**Table 5.3** Optimal lag length for pairs of agricultural commodities and BSE FMCG index

| Pairs of variables | Lag length |
|---|---|
| Cottonseed-FMCG | 5 |
| Castorseed-FMCG | 2 |
| Soybeanseed-FMCG | 5 |
| RMseed-FMCG | 5 |
| Turmeric-FMCG | 2 |
| Jeera-FMCG | 7 |
| Coriander-FMCG | 5 |
| Guarseed-FMCG | 1 |
| Chana FMCG | 1 |

*Source* Author's own calculations using Accord Fintech data

**Table 5.4** ARDL bound results for agricultural commodities and BSE FMCG index

| Variables | F-statistics | Lower bound | Upper bound | Serial correlation | Ramsey RESET test |
|---|---|---|---|---|---|
| Cottonseed-FMCG | 1.88 | 3.02 | 3.51 | 0.92 (0.40) | 1.76 (0.17) |
| Castorseed-FMCG | 3.03 | 3.02 | 3.51 | 0.07 (0.93) | 0.55 (0.58) |
| Soybeanseed-FMCG | 3.01 | 3.02 | 3.51 | 2.30 (0.10) | 1.42 (0.24) |
| RMseed-FMCG | 2.20 | 3.02 | 3.51 | 0.16 (0.85) | 1.22 (0.30) |
| Turmeric-FMCG | 2.61 | 3.02 | 3.51 | 0.16 (0.85) | 0.99 (0.37) |
| Jeera-FMCG | 2.11 | 3.02 | 3.51 | 024 (0.78) | 1.52 (0.22) |
| Coriander-FMCG | 2.48 | 3.02 | 3.51 | 0.75 (0.47) | 2.04 (0.13) |
| Guarseed-FMCG | 1.56 | 3.02 | 3.51 | 3.71 (0.03) | 6.70 (0.01) |
| Chana-FMCG | 1.78 | 3.02 | 3.51 | 0.17 (0.84) | 0.27 (0.77) |

*Source* Author's own calculations using Accord Fintech data

The F-statistics is lower than the lower bound critical value except for castor seed. This shows the absence of any long-run cointegration between the individual agricultural commodities and FMCG index. The diagnostic results for ARDL model also show that there is an absence of serial correlation among the residuals. To further confirm the reliability and validity of the estimated model, the Ramsey RESET test has been done and found to indicate stability in the model.

In order to confirm the results of ARDL bound test, the robustness of ARDL model is investigated by using the Johansen cointegration test which is based on the maximum eigenvalue criteria. The cointegration tests are conducted on prices of the nine commodities and FMCG index using two methods: (i) Johansen trace test and (ii) Johansen maximum eigen test. As these tests are sensitive to lag selection, Vector Autoregression (VAR) is used to determine the appropriate lag length as per the Akaike Information Criterion (AIC) criteria. Table 5.5 reports the Johansen cointegration test results, which imply that there is no long-run relationship between the agricultural commodity prices and FMCG index. Panel A reveals that none of the price series is cointegrated at any significance level. Both the trace test and maximum eigen test indicate identical results and hence support no cointegration between the prices. Similarly, for the null hypothesis of one cointegrating vector ($r = 1$), trace and eigen statistics in the last column of Table 5.5 reveal that the null hypothesis can be rejected (except for castorseed and chana). The results corroborate the findings

**Table 5.5** Johansen cointegration test results

| Commodity | Cointegrating vector | r = 0 | r = 1 |
|---|---|---|---|
| | Trace | Max. Eigen | Trace and Max. Eigen |
| *Panel A: Cointegration results* | | | |
| Cottonseed-FMCG | 3.83 | 3.56 | 0.26 |
| Castorseed-FMCG | 7.57 | 4.23 | 3.35* |
| Soybeanseed-FMCG | 6.98 | 6.83 | 0.15 |
| RMseed-FMCG | 8.09 | 7.09 | 1.01 |
| Turmeric-FMCG | 5.22 | 5.01 | 0.22 |
| Jeera-FMCG | 9.63 | 9.35 | 0.28 |
| Coriander-FMCG | 3.03 | 2.57 | 0.46 |
| Guarseed-FMCG | 7.86 | 6.11 | 1.75 |
| Chana-FMCG | 10.83 | 7.01 | 3.82* |

| No. of cointegrating vectors | Trace statistics | | | Max eigenvalue statistics | | |
|---|---|---|---|---|---|---|
| | 10% | 5% | 1% | 10% | 5% | 1% |
| *Panel B: Trace test statistics and maximum eigenvalue test statistics critical values* | | | | | | |
| $r = 0$ | 13.43 | 15.49 | 19.94 | 12.3 | 14.26 | 18.52 |
| $r = 1$ | 2.71 | 3.84 | 6.63 | 2.71 | 3.84 | 6.63 |

*Note* significance at 10%, 5% and 1% level of confidence is indicated as *, ** and ***, respectively
*Source* Author's own calculations using Accord Fintech data

obtained from the ARDL bound test and can be concluded that there is an absence of long-run cointegration between the agricultural commodities and BSE FMCG index.

### 5.5.4 Causality Test Results

The Toda and Yamamoto approach of Granger causality test was applied to study the causal relationship between the agricultural commodities and BSE FMCG index. The results of ADF test in Table 5.2 suggest that the maximum order of integration is one. The optimal lag length (k) for each of the variable is given in Table 5.3. In addition, the test is estimated using VAR at level to specify the absence of feedback causal relationship between the agricultural commodities and BSE FMCG index except for cottonseed, rape mustard seed and jeera as shown in Table 5.6. These three commodities have a unidirectional causal relationship with BSE FMCG index. These results are in line with the findings of previous studies (Johnson and Soenen

**Table 5.6** Granger causality test results with Toda and Yamamoto approach

| Dependent variable | Independent variable | Chi-square | df | Prob |
|---|---|---|---|---|
| FMCG | Cottonseed | 5.78 | 5 | 0.33 |
| Cottonseed | FMCG | 10.82 | 5 | 0.06* |
| FMCG | Castorseed | 4.62 | 2 | 0.10 |
| Castorseed | FMCG | 2.95 | 2 | 0.23 |
| FMCG | Soybeanseed | 5.22 | 5 | 0.39 |
| Soybeanseed | FMCG | 6.85 | 5 | 0.23 |
| FMCG | RMseed | 3.64 | 5 | 0.6 |
| RMseed | FMCG | 11.36 | 5 | 0.04** |
| FMCG | Turmeric | 0.99 | 2 | 0.61 |
| Turmeric | FMCG | 0.77 | 2 | 0.68 |
| FMCG | Jeera | 2.85 | 7 | 0.9 |
| Jeera | FMCG | 13.01 | 7 | 0.07* |
| FMCG | Coriander | 2.76 | 5 | 0.74 |
| Coriander | FMCG | 5.84 | 5 | 0.32 |
| FMCG | Guarseed | 0.02 | 1 | 0.89 |
| Guarseed | FMCG | 0.69 | 1 | 0.41 |
| FMCG | Chana | 0.65 | 1 | 0.42 |
| Chana | FMCG | 0.32 | 1 | 0.58 |

*Note* *, ** and *** indicate significance at 10%, 5% and 1% level of confidence, respectively
*Source* Author's own calculations using Accord Fintech data
SR stands for Spot Price Returns and FR for Futures Price Returns

2014) where no evidence for the lead–lag relationship between stock market index and agricultural commodities index has been found.

## 5.6 Results Discussion

The empirical methodology consists of three steps. In the first, we examine the presence of unit roots in the data. The findings reveal that all the prices and index become stationary after first difference. The second step is to ponder on the existence of cointegration using the ARDL bound test and Johansen cointegration test. We infer the absence of cointegration between the agricultural commodity prices and FMCG index. The results recommend that all the agricultural commodities and FMCG index can be used as diversification tools in portfolio allocation due to the absence of long-run cointegration. Finally, we incorporate the lag using the VAR model to perform the Toda and Yamamoto Granger causality test to study the causal relationship between the prices and index. We found that there is no evidence for the lead–lag relationship between agricultural commodities index and stock market index.

Our findings are in line with Srinivasan and Prakasam (2014) and Hammoudeh and Aleisa (2004) in concluding that agricultural commodities do not contain enough information to forecast FMCG stock index prices. They also seem to not move together linearly in the long run and thus commodity market does not have any predictive power linked with stock market. As both the markets are independent or not cointegrated with each other in long run, investors can invest in both the markets to diversify their portfolio. There is no transmission of shocks from one market to another in case of turmoil in any one of the markets. This lack of dependence between both the markets can be exploited to make superior risk-adjusted returns by diversifying their risks and thus creating an efficient portfolio as suggested by Jain and Ghosh (2013). The same news affects both the commodity market and stock markets in a different manner. Ping et al. (2018) suggested that although there are numerous studies that analyse the relationship between stock and commodity markets, emerging markets like India may have different implications due to some unique characteristics imbibed in the financial markets, such as greater volatility and more speculative activities and thus differing from developed countries.

Markets are presumed to be independent of each other in the absence of causality in any of the direction, thereby providing an opportunity for investors to hedge the risk across different markets by diversifying their portfolio (Gormus 2013). We found that unidirectional causality runs from cottonseed, rape mustard seed and jeera to BSE FMCG index. It may be due to the fact that the domestic and global demand together has influenced the Indian commodity market for these three commodities. Also, broken mustard seed and cottonseed are exported from India in large amount along with jeera, whose bulk production is used for export purpose. When there is an insufficient supply of commodity as compared to demand then the price may be increased due to which the speculators or investors seeking large profits in the equity market are attracted towards commodity market and continue to buy while ignoring the commodity fundamentals. This can also be linked to the negative shock arising in one of the markets prompting the investors to cut down their investment in the other market in order to avoid more risk, due to which prices fall down in that market also (Nirmala and Deepthy 2015; Kaur and Dhiman 2019).

## 5.7 Conclusion and Implications

Agricultural commodity exchanges provide a centralized marketplace where the market participants and farmers can shift commodity price risk and help them discover the prices. For those who are interested to invest in agriculture futures, price movements in the agriculture market play a prominent role to hedge their risk. The variability in agricultural prices has widened the risk associated with these commodities. On the other hand, investors are keen to earn more returns from their risk-adjusted portfolio by understanding the relationship between the stock market and the commodity market. This study attempts to empirically assess the relationship between agricultural commodities and FMCG index in India by using the daily data. The absence of long-run cointegration between the BSE FMCG index and agricultural commodities is confirmed from the ARDL bound test. With respect to presence of any causal relationship between the BSE FMCG index and agricultural commodities, Toda and Yamamoto test do not provide evidence of supporting relationship except for cottonseed, rape mustard seed and jeera. Our conclusion for the above three commodities differs due to various reasons, such as change in traded spot market volume, speculative trading, seasonal production factors, government policies and different sample durations. These results also imply that the Indian agricultural commodity markets do not provide enough information to predict the movement in stock prices. This emphasizes the reforms that need to be carried out to make spot markets more liquid and efficient without getting affected by the speculative trading. The results convey that the effect of any shock or innovation in one market does not impact the other market in the same direction. This is crucial from the investors' point of view in building their portfolio. Hence, investors and traders can leverage this absence of cointegration and causality between agricultural commodities and BSE FMCG index to hedge their risk by diversifying their portfolio investments across both the markets. Explanation of possible determinants of the absence of the long-run relationship between the commodities and index might be a promising research direction. From the policy point of view, policymakers need to make regulatory and accounting changes to encourage deeper integration among these markets. Certain amendments to promote integration in the stock market and commodity market can build up confidence among the market participants.

## References


Ali, J., & Gupta, K. B. (2011). Efficiency in agricultural commodity futures markets in India: Evidence from cointegration and causality tests. *Agricultural Finance Review, 71*(2), 162–178.

Árendáš, M. (2005). Global growth of food commodity prices and the impact on inflation and monetary policy. *Chart, 100,* 1–5.

Baur, D. G., & McDermott, T. K. (2010). Is gold a safe haven? International evidence. *Journal of Banking & Finance, 34*(8), 1886–1898.

Bekiros, S., Nguyen, D. K., Uddin, G. S., & Sjö, B. (2016). On the time scale behavior of equity-commodity links: Implications for portfolio management. *Journal of International Financial Markets, Institutions and Money, 41,* 30–46.

Bouri, E., Jain, A., Biswal, P. C., & Roubaud, D. (2017). Cointegration and nonlinear causality among gold, oil, and the Indian stock market: Evidence from implied volatility indices. *Resources Policy, 52,* 201–206.

Broadstock, D. C., Cao, H., & Zhang, D. (2012). Oil shocks and their impact on energy related stocks in China. *Energy Economics, 34*(6), 1888–1895.

Chittedi, K. R. (2012). Do oil prices matters for Indian stock markets? An empirical analysis. *Journal of Applied Economics and Business Research, 2*(1), 2–10.

Ciner, C., Gurdgiev, C., & Lucey, B. M. (2013). Hedges and safe havens: An examination of stocks, bonds, gold, oil and exchange rates. *International Review of Financial Analysis, 29,* 202–211.

Dickey, D. A., & Fuller, W. A. (1981). Likelihood ratio statistics for autoregressive time series with a unit root. *Econometrica, 49*(4), 1057–1072.

Elder, J., Miao, H., & Ramchander, S. (2012). Impact of macroeconomic news on metal futures. *Journal of Banking & Finance, 36*(1), 51–65.

Gormus, N. A. (2013). *Causality and volatility spillover effects on sub-sector energy portfolios* (Published doctoral dissertation). Arlington, Texas: The University of Texas.

Gurgun, G., & Unalmis, I. (2014). Is gold a safe haven against equity market investment in emerging and developing countries? *Financial Research Letters, 11*(4), 341–348.

Hamilton, J. D. (1994). *Time series analysis* (Vol. 2). Princeton: Princeton University Press [online]. Retrieved May 16, 2015, from https://doc1.lbfl.li/aca/FLMF037168.pdf.

Hammoudeh, S., & Aleisa, E. (2004). Dynamic relationships among GCC stock markets and NYMEX oil futures. *Contemporary Economic Policy, 22*(2), 250–269.

Jain, A., & Ghosh, S. (2013). Dynamics of global oil prices, exchange rate and precious metal prices in India. *Resources Policy, 38*(1), 88–93.

Johansen, S. (1988). Statistical analysis of cointegration vectors. *Journal of Economic Dynamics and Control, 12*(2–3), 231–254.

Johnson, R., & Soenen, L. (2009). Commodity prices and stock market behavior in South American countries in the short run. *Emerging Markets Finance and Trade, 45*(4), 69–82.

Kang, J.-S., Hu, J.-L., & Chen, C.-W. (2013). Linkage between international food commodity prices and the Chinese stock markets. *International Journal of Economics and Finance, 5*(10), 147.

Kaur, G., & Dhiman, B. (2019). Agricultural commodities and FMCG stock prices in India: Evidence from the ARDL bound test and the Toda and Yamamoto causality analysis. *Global Business Review*. https://doi.org/10.1177/0972150919830803

Lehecka, G. V. (2014). The value of USDA crop progress and condition information: Reactions of corn and soybean futures markets. *Journal of Agricultural and Resource Economics, 39*(1), 88–105.

Memdani, L. A. (2014). Nexus between returns in commodity market and equity market: A case of Indian steel industry. *Acta Universitatis Danubius. ØEconomica, 10*(3), 59–72.

Nirmala, S., & Deepthy, K. (2015). An analysis of relationship between Sensex and selected agricultural commodity Indices in India. *International Journal of Science and Research, 5*(9), 368–371.

Pesaran, M. H., Shin, Y., & Smith, R. J. (2001). Bounds testing approaches to the analysis of level relationships. *Journal of Applied Econometrics, 16*(3), 289–326.

Phillips, P. C. B., & Perron, P. (1988). Testing for a unit root in time series regression. *Biometrika, 75*(2), 335–346.

Ping, L., Ziyi, Z., Tianna, Y., & Qingchao, Z. (2018). The relationship among China's fuel oil spot, futures and stock markets. *Finance Research Letters, 24,* 151–162.

Raza, N., Shahzad, S. J. H., Tiwari, A. K., & Shahbaz, M. (2016). Asymmetric impact of gold, oil prices and their volatilities on stock prices of emerging markets. *Resources Policy, 49,* 290–301.

Reddy, Y. V., & Sebastin, A. (2009). Are commodity and stock markets independent of each other? A case study in India. *The Journal of Alternative Investments, 11*(3), 85.

Manogna, R. L., & Mishra, A. K. (2020). Price discovery and volatility spillover: an empirical evidence from spot and futures agricultural commodity markets in India. *Journal of Agribusiness in Developing and Emerging Economies, 10*(4), 447–473. https://doi.org/10.1108/JADEE-10-2019-0175.

Souček, M. (2013). Crude oil, equity and gold futures open interest co-movements. *Energy Economics, 40*(C), 306–315.

Srinivasan, P., & Prakasam, K. (2014). Gold price, stock price and exchange rate nexus: The case of India. *IUP Journal of Financial Risk Management, 11*(3), 52.

Toda, H. Y., & Yamamoto, T. (1995). Statistical inference in vector autoregressions with possibly integrated processes. Journal of Econometrics, 66(1–2), 225–250.

Tursoy, T., & Faisal, F. (2017). The impact of gold and crude oil prices on stock market in Turkey: Empirical evidences from ARDL bounds test and combined cointegration. *Resources Policy, 55,* 49–54.

Urrutia, J., & Malliaris, A. G. (2005). *Equity and oil markets under external shocks* (pp. 121–134). London: Routledge.

# Chapter 6
# Exploring the Influence of Emotion in Investment Decision-Making: A Theoretical Perspective

**Abhijit Ranjan Das and Soma Panja**

**Abstract** The main purpose of this paper is to strengthen the theoretical underpinning of the relationship between emotion and investment decision-making. Since investment decisions are made both under the condition of risk and uncertainty, emotion acts as a crucial antecedent for making a better investment decision. Absence of emotion while making investment decisions can hinder for making better decisions. So, for being a successful investor, he/she should not only depend on the market fundamentals but also should be aware of their own emotion. This is because emotion is having a significant role in investment decision-making. However, a successful investor not only depends on their self-emotion but also to control and regulate their emotion carefully for making advantageous decisions.

**Keywords** Emotional finance · Emotional intelligence · Behavioral finance · Neuroscience

## 6.1 Introduction

The lifeline of any economic system is fund management, which is popularly known as wealth management but managing finance is the most difficult aspect of human life. So researchers put forward the different models and assumptions for efficient management of funds (Zahera and Bansal 2018). The underpinning of such a financial model started with Markowitz's Portfolio Theory of 1952. Markowitz's Portfolio Theory is focused on constructing the optimum portfolio which is based on a similar line of the Expected Utility Theory (Prosad et al. 2015a, b). Further in their study, they have advocated that a general perception to be a successful investor in the stock market is that investors should have the right kind of knowledge about the stock market and

A. R. Das · S. Panja (✉)
Department of Management Studies, National Institute of Technology Silchar, Silchar, India
e-mail: soma.panja2014@gmail.com

A. R. Das
e-mail: ndas5422@gmail.com

 
A. K. Mishra et al. (eds.), *The Financial Landscape of Emerging Economies*, Accounting, Finance, Sustainability, Governance & Fraud: Theory and Application,
https://doi.org/10.1007/978-3-030-60008-2_6

firm in which she/he wants to invest. For a general investor, to make large profits in the stock market one should have the correct prediction capability. This requires a rational analysis for a long time which makes use of the standard finance concepts.

The standard financial theories are based on the rationality of the individual (Prosad et al. 2015a, b). According to standard finance, rationality in it is assumed to be mainly of two ways: investors' decision-making is based on the expected utility theory and the investors' decision-making is not affected by the biases (Khresna Brahmana et al. 2012). A pioneering researcher Meir Statman stated that the "Standard finance is built on the pillars of the arbitrage principles of Miller and Modigliani, the portfolio principles of Markowitz, the Capital Asset Pricing Theory of Sharpe, Lintner, and Black, and the option pricing theory of Black, Scholes, and Merton" (Statman 1999). The basic assumptions of such standard finance theories are the rationality of investor, efficiency in the market, investors construct their portfolio based on mean–variance and the expected return is the function of risk (Statman 2008). Contradicting the assumptions of the standard finance theories, Prosad et al. (2015a, b) noted that standard finance theories could not explain the anomalies in the stock market. The anomalies formed in the stock market are caused by the irrationality behavior of the investor. This discards the basic assumption of the standard finance "investors are rational" (Khresna Brahmana et al. 2012).

Personal financial planning and the management of investment are the most crucial task for an individual, and decisions regarding personal finance are based on various beliefs and preferences which drive for taking investment decision and not solely driven by the rationality assumption (Kalra Sahi and Pratap Arora 2012). Lovric et al. (2010) pointed out that the "investment process is influenced by several independent variables and driven by dual mental systems, the interplay of which contributes to bounded rational behavior where investors use various heuristics and may exhibit behavioral biases". MacKenzie (2005) defined biases as "tendency towards a certain disposition or conclusion". Such biases hind an individual from taking rational decisions. Further criticizing the traditional finance, Daniel Kahneman, Amos Tversky, and Richard Thaler who are known as the father of behavioral finance first identified the psychological biases and their impact on the investment decision. Again Khresna Brahmana et al. (2012) identified eight psychological biases: bounded rationality, attribute substitution, salience, cognitive dissonance, heuristics, introspection illusion, adaptive bias, and misuse of statistics. While Sharma and Kumar (2019) combined the different factors and biases that influence the decision-making process are anchoring bias, conservatism bias, social bias, hindsight bias, ignorance of probability laws, emotional factors, disposition effect, confirmatory bias, overconfidence, certainty effect, endowment effect, house money effect, disappoint effect, and sunk cost. Tversky and Kahneman in the year 1981 identified sixteen additional psychological biases that affect investors in decision-making.

In behavioral finance, the irrationality behavior of investors can be explained by the Prospect Theory, Mental Account, Regret Theory, and Self Control (Khresna Brahmana et al. 2012). Daniel Kahneman in his book "Thinking Fast and Slow" first mentioned the prospect theory which is the backbone of the behavioral finance analyzed decision-making under the condition of risk. Another pioneering work in the field of behavioral finance by Shefrin and Statman which is an alternative to Markowitz's Portfolio Theory is the Behavioral Portfolio Theory (BPT). This theory deals with a different attitude towards risk.

Making investment decisions creates an investor both excited and anxious. Since the financial market is uncertain, complex, and is also unpredictable and so uncertainty in the financial market generates emotional response both at the psychological and neurological level, such emotions lead to anxiety and eventually stress. Anxiety is a prototypical emotion in investor behavior (Taffler and Tuckett 2011) and the unconscious emotional responses can provide an unbiased portrayal of an individual's initial emotional reactions when exposed to a stimulus (Michael et al. 2019). Unconscious processes operate at different levels and have an impact on decision-making hence Jarrett and Kellner (1996) stated that unconscious plays a significant role when teams or groups of people engage in core tasks, especially under risky conditions. The risk may be real or perceived but affects decision-making. Further by Jarrett and Kellner (1996) advocated that unconscious and irrational behavior becomes too pronounced when fulfilling under the condition of risk and anxiety.

## 6.2 Literature Survey

For being a successful investor, investors should have analytical capability, the general level of intelligence, and most importantly control of emotion. The reason is that emotions act as a bias in the cognitive processes when making any investment decision (Lerner et al. 2004; Lerner and Keltner 2001). For example excitement, fear, anger, and happiness have significant effects on the investment decision-making process as an investment involves risk (Vohra 2018) and emotion influences investors in the risk perceptions (George and Dane 2016). Behavioral finance theories also added the relevance of emotion in investment decision-making. This is because a financial decision is very complex and involves four steps, i.e., input, process, output, and feedback. In the process, emotion plays a significant role. The role of emotion in decision-making can be evidenced when Bechara and Damasio (2005) observed a patient who suffered damage in the area of the brain that is responsible for experiencing and expressing emotion, suffered largely with impaired decision.

Loewenstein et al. (2001), in the Risk-as-Feelings Model, advocated that people who experience emotions at the time of decision-making influences their subsequent decisions. Kuhnen and Knutson (2005) further advocated that positive emotions lead to a risk-seeker trader while negative emotions lead to a risk-averse trader. Emotion is not logical at all and a strong form of emotion even can lead to an impaired decision. In other words, emotional investors act irrationally and have poor judgment capability (Powell 2017). Russell (1980) in his a circumplex model has classified emotions into two components, i.e., arousal and valence. According to the model, arousal means the excitement level and valence means the state of emotion. Emotions help us to take superior decisions, and there is a reverse possibility, i.e., it can hinder to take a superior decision (Bontchev and Vassileva 2016). Managing emotion is very important as an individual/investor even can lose control of emotion while taking any decision (Jerčić and Sundstedt 2019).

According to the Somatic Marker Hypothesis (SMH) (Bechara and Damasio 2005), emotions are having a significant role in investment decision-making. El-Chaarani (2016) has advocated that decision-making processes in the financial market have two sequences. The first sequence is strategic. Investors may make the active, passive, or mixed investment strategy. In this strategy, their investment decisions or strategy is affected by their personality attributes, emotions, cognitive capability, financial strength, and social factors. The past positive investment events trigger to take any of the strategies. In the second sequence, investors make their investment strategy whether to sell or buy based on their emotional and mental intelligence. Emotion plays a central role in investors' thinking and behavior (Taffler and Tuckett 2011). Besides various biases, the investment decision is also affected by various psychological factors. These factors (include emotion and instinctive) have an indirect effect on investment decision-making under the condition of both uncertainty and risky situations (Sharma and Kumar 2019).

Emotion, mood, and feelings are all used interchangeably but there exist differences. Damasio (1994) described emotion as, "a combination of a simple and complex mental evaluative process resulting in an emotional state of the body as additional mental change". Further Damasio (1994) have classified emotion into three categories: primary emotions, secondary emotions, and background emotions. Lerner et al. (2004) again distinguished between two forms of emotions, i.e., expected emotions and immediate emotion. For making any decision, immediate emotion effects on the decision-making both directly and indirectly as immediate emotions are experienced at the time of making a decision.

The role of emotion in investment decision-making has been investigated by different scholars (Brighetti et al. 2014; Brundin and Gustafsson 2013; El-Chaarani 2016; Griffith et al. 2020; Kuzmina 2010; Lakomski and Evers 2010; Taffler and Tuckett 2011). Lively (2013) in his study found that emotions (positive and negative) are distant for individuals as the individuals grow. Brundin and Gustafsson (2013) in their study found that positive emotions (negative emotions) increases (decreases) the propensity to invest in any risky projects.

## 6.3 Objectives of the Study

To be a successful investor, apart from having analytical skills and intelligence levels, control of emotion is essential. Emotion is considered as a major determinant of decision-making. And an emotional mistake can also be responsible for the underperformance of the portfolio (El-Chaarani 2016). So, successful investors are those who are emotionally intelligent. Emotional intelligence is considered nowadays as a tool on the hand of the investor as well as for professional consultants for making a rational decision. Emotional responses relieve to sustain the performance of the portfolio even in the adverse market condition like market fluctuations, etc.

Keeping in view the importance of emotional intelligence, the study focuses on two objectives. Firstly, to explore the significance of emotion in investment decision-making. Secondly, to identify the extent to which the emotional influence in constructing an optimum portfolio.

So, besides the traditional finance theories, financial researchers perceived the importance of financial behavior. They have considered that financial decision-making is a complex phenomenon and in are in four sequences like input, process, output, and feedback, and the most important role is played by the emotion as under the condition of uncertainty the investor decision-making depends on the emotional intelligence as well as on the cognitive skills.

## 6.4 Research Methodology

The present research paper is conceptual in nature. For developing a theoretical foundation to justify the need for studying the emotion of individuals as well as of professional financial consultants and also to comprehend the prerequisite of emotion in the decision-making process. In order to achieve the objective of the study, different scholarly journals, working papers, thesis, a news bulletin from the public domain were collected for review purpose and also a cross-disciplinary review was done in the relevant natural and social sciences in order to give more comprehensive insights into the study of emotion which is essential for being a successful investor.

## 6.5 Discussion

The effects of emotion in investment decision-making is very wide (So et al. 2015). Researchers and psychologists raised the question that whether emotions help in making advantageous decisions? Bechara and Damasio (2005) in the Somatic Marker Hypothesis stated that emotion is one of the integral antecedents for making better decisions. They further advocated that better decision-making largely depends on the initial emotion processing. This is because emotion is a complex and multidimensional state of mind. This mental state at last impacts our behavior and more particularly towards our investment (So et al. 2015).

There are mainly three approaches to study emotion, i.e., the categories approach, the dimensional approach, and the cognitive appraisal approach (Watson and Spence 2007). The dimensional approach of emotion considers the valence and arousal aspect to distinguish emotion (So et al. 2015; Watson and Spence 2007). Further, they have also added that some emotional states can be predicted by valence and others by the appraisal dimension of emotion. However, Lerner and Keltner (2000) have shown that different emotional states specifically negative emotions like anger and fear have different risk-taking capabilities. For example, fearful investors take more pessimistic decisions while angry investors take more optimistic decisions. This is because of the level of certainty is underlying with different emotions. Fear being future-oriented is having more uncertainty compared to emotions (Tiedens and Linton 2001; Watson and Spence 2007).

Emotion is having a significant influence on investment decision-making. It is very important to properly handle the emotion when making an investment decision. For the first instance, psychologists and neurobiologists identified the influence of emotion in decision-making. This is because emotion always influences in decision-making. Ignoring emotion at the time decision-making can affect our rational economic behavior (Kuzmina 2010). For example, positive emotions (challenge, hope, self-confidence, etc.) help in making good investment decisions while negative emotions (embarrassment, frustration, strain, etc.) act as an obstacle in making a better investment decision. In other words, positive emotions enhance the value of the stocks and the negative emotions lead to a decrease in the value of the stock. Further confirming the role of emotion, Brundin and Gustafsson (2013) added that people rely on their own emotions when they face any difficulty in making decisions especially under the condition of risky and uncertainty. So, for being a successful investor, one needs to know not only self-emotion but also to control and regulate the emotion carefully. Lakomski and Evers (2010) pointed out the importance of emotion in making a rational decision. Absence of emotion in the decision-making acts as a hindrance to making a better investment decision.

## 6.6 Implications of the Study

Deciding optimum portfolio is not possible under the condition of a dynamic and complex environment taking the traditional finance theories as the basis. But traditional finance theories are being criticized due to incorrect assumptions and behavioral finance theories have overcome such limitations and given a practical reality of the market condition. As per behavioral finance theories, heuristics and behavioral biases affect investors in making investment decisions but the study of emotion will give detailed insights into the behavior of investors in choosing the investment options.

The result of the current study holds implications both for the investors and for the financial consultants. Firstly, the outcome of the study may be of interest for the investors as well as for financial consultant in order to understand the emotion which drives one's behavior while selecting a portfolio. The study holds good for both the categories of investors, i.e., those who are trying to form an optimum portfolio and also for those who are trying to enhance the portfolio performance effectively and efficiently. As the study revealed that emotion plays a significant role in decision-making. If the investor is able to understand the emotion and also able to control the emotion, it can make a better investment decision. Secondly, the study also holds good for the financial consultant. Understanding and managing emotion is not only essential for the investor but also essential for the financial consultant. The financial consultant guides the investor in selecting the portfolio. If the consultants are able to recognize their own emotions and also the emotion of their clients, they can suggest the best investment choices for their clients. Thirdly, policymakers in the stock market can apprehend the behavior of the investors.

## References


Bechara, A., & Damasio, A. R. (2005). The somatic marker hypothesis: A neural theory of economic decision. *Games and Economic Behavior, 52*(2), 336–372. https://doi.org/10.1016/j.geb.2004.06.010

Bontchev, B., & Vassileva, D. (2016). Assessing engagement in an emotionally-Adaptive applied game. In *ACM International Conference Proceeding Series, 02-04-Nove* (pp. 747–754). https://doi.org/10.1145/3012430.3012602.

Brighetti, G., Lucarelli, C., & Marinelli, N. (2014). Do emotions affect insurance demand? *Review of Behavioral Finance, 6*(2), 136–154. https://doi.org/10.1108/RBF-04-2014-0027

Brundin, E., & Gustafsson, V. (2013). Entrepreneurs' decision making under different levels of uncertainty: The role of emotions. *International Journal of Entrepreneurial Behaviour & Research, 19*(6), 568–591. https://doi.org/10.1108/IJEBR-07-2012-0074

Damasio, A. R. (1994). *Descartes error: Emotion, reason and the human brain.* London: Papermac.

El-Chaarani, H. (2016). Exploring the impact of emotional intelligence on portfolio performance. *Humanomics, 32*(4), 474–497. https://doi.org/10.1108/h-02-2016-0012

George, J. M., & Dane, E. (2016). Affect, emotion, and decision making. *Organizational Behavior and Human Decision Processes, 136,* 47–55. https://doi.org/10.1016/j.obhdp.2016.06.004

Griffith, J., Najand, M., & Shen, J. (2020). Emotions in the stock market. *Journal of Behavioral Finance, 21*(1), 42–56. https://doi.org/10.1080/15427560.2019.1588275

Jarrett, M., & Kellner, K. (1996). Coping with uncertainty: A psychodynamic perspective on the work of top teams. *Journal of Management Development, 15*(2), 54–68. https://doi.org/10.1108/02621719610147850

Jerčić, P., & Sundstedt, V. (2019). Practicing emotion-regulation through biofeedback on the decision-making performance in the context of serious games: A systematic review. *Entertainment Computing, 29,* 75–86. https://doi.org/10.1016/j.entcom.2019.01.001

Kalra Sahi, S., & Pratap Arora, A. (2012). Individual investor biases: A segmentation analysis. *Qualitative Research in Financial Markets, 4*(1), 6–25. https://doi.org/10.1108/17554171211213522

Khresna Brahmana, R., Hooy, C., & Ahmad, Z. (2012). Psychological factors on irrational financial decision making: Case of day-of-the-week anomaly. *Humanomics, 28*(4), 236–257. https://doi.org/10.1108/08288661211277317

Kuhnen, C. M., & Knutson, B. (2005). The neural basis of financial risk taking. *Neuron, 47*(5), 763–770. https://doi.org/10.1016/j.neuron.2005.08.008

Kuzmina, J. (2010). Emotion's component of expectations in financial decision making. *Baltic Journal of Management, 5*(3), 295–306. https://doi.org/10.1108/17465261011079721

Lakomski, G., & Evers, C. W. (2010). Passionate rationalism: The role of emotion in decision making. *Journal of Educational Administration, 48*(4), 438–450. https://doi.org/10.1108/09578231011054707

Lerner, J. S., & Keltner, D. (2000). Beyond valence: Toward a model of emotion-specific influences on judgement and choice. *Cognition and Emotion, 14*(4), 473–493. https://www.tandfonline.com/doi/abs/10.1080/026999300402763.

Lerner, J. S., & Keltner, D. (2001). Fear, anger, and risk. *Journal of Personality and Social Psychology, 81*(1), 146–159. https://doi.org/10.1037/0022-3514.81.1.146

Lerner, J. S., Small, D. A., & Loewenstein, G. (2004). Heart strings and purse strings: Carryover effects of emotions on economic decisions. *Psychological Science, 15*(5), 337–341. https://doi.org/10.1111/j.0956-7976.2004.00679.x

Lively, K. J. (2013). Age and the experience and management of emotion. *Advances in Group Processes*, 231–265. https://doi.org/10.1108/s0882-6145(2013)0000030012.

Loewenstein, H. C. K., Weber, E. U., & Welch, N. (2001). RiskAsFeelings.pdf. *Psychological Bulletin, 127*(2), 267–286. https://doi.org/10.1037//0033-29091272.267.

Lovric, M., Kaymak, U., & Spronk, J. (2010). A conceptual model of investor behavior. *Advances in Cognitive Systems*, 371–396. https://doi.org/10.1049/PBCE071E_ch13.

MacKenzie, D. (2005). Opening the black boxes of global finance. *Review of International Political Economy, 12*(4), 555–576. https://doi.org/10.1080/09692290500240222

Michael, I., Ramsoy, T., Stephens, M., & Kotsi, F. (2019). A study of unconscious emotional and cognitive responses to tourism images using a neuroscience method. *Journal of Islamic Marketing, 10*(2), 543–564. https://doi.org/10.1108/JIMA-09-2017-0098

Powell, S. M. (2017). Emotion and cognition. *The Impassioned Life*, 297–340. https://doi.org/10.2307/j.ctt17mcs8j.13.

Prosad, J. M., Kapoor, S., & Sengupta, J. (2015). Behavioral biases of Indian investors: A survey of Delhi-NCR region. *Qualitative Research in Financial Markets, 7*(3), 230–263. https://doi.org/10.1108/qrfm-04-2014-0012

Prosad, J. M., Kapoor, S., & Sengupta, J. (2015b, January). Theory of behavioral finance. *Handbook of Research on Behavioral Finance and Investment Strategies: Decision Making in the Financial Industry*, 1–24. https://doi.org/10.4018/978-1-4666-7484-4.ch001.

Russell, J. A. (1980). A circumplex model of affect. *Journal of Personality and Social Psychology, 39*(6), 1161–1178. https://doi.org/10.1037/h0077714

Sharma, A., & Kumar, A. (2019). A review paper on behavioral finance: Study of emerging trends. In *Qualitative Research in Financial Markets*. Emerald Group Publishing Ltd. https://doi.org/10.1108/QRFM-06-2017-0050.

So, J., Achar, C., Han, D. H., Agrawal, N., Duhachek, A., & Maheswaran, D. (2015). The psychology of appraisal: Specific emotions and decision-making. *Journal of Consumer Psychology, 25*(3), 359–371. https://doi.org/10.1016/j.jcps.2015.04.003

Statman, M. (1999). Behavioral finance: Past battles and future engagements. *Financial Analysts Journal, 55*(6), 18–27. https://doi.org/10.2469/faj.v55.n6.2311

Statman, M. (2008). What is behavioral finance? *Handbook of Finance*, May 2014. https://doi.org/10.1002/9780470404324.hof002009.

Taffler, R. J., & Tuckett, D. A. (2011). Emotional finance: The role of the unconscious in financial decisions. *Behavioral Finance: Investors, Corporations, and Markets*, 95–112. https://doi.org/10.1002/9781118258415.ch6.

Tiedens, L. Z., & Linton, S. (2001). Judgment under emotional certainty and uncertainty: The effects of specific emotions on information processing. *Journal of Personality and Social Psychology, 81*(6), 973–988. https://doi.org/10.1037/0022-3514.81.6.973

Vohra, S. (2018). Interpersonal emotion regulation in the work of financial traders. *Research on Emotion in Organizations*, 97–118. https://doi.org/10.1108/s1746-979120180000014013.

Watson, L., & Spence, M. T. (2007). Causes and consequences of emotions on consumer behaviour: A review and integrative cognitive appraisal theory. *European Journal of Marketing, 41*(5–6), 487–511. https://doi.org/10.1108/03090560710737570

Zahera, S. A., & Bansal, R. (2018). Do investors exhibit behavioral biases in investment decision making? A systematic review. *Qualitative Research in Financial Markets, 10*(2), 210–251. https://doi.org/10.1108/QRFM-04-2017-0028

# Chapter 7
# How Do Household and Spatial Factors Matter While Examining Inequality in Credit Availability? Evidence from an Emerging Economy

**Vedant Bhardwaj and Aswini Kumar Mishra**

**Abstract** Using a multi-level modelling approach, this paper analyzes the decomposition of the sources of inequality in credit availability from both informal and formal sources in India for the second half of the year 2002 and 2012. On decomposing inequality of credit availability in India at three nested levels—household, region and state. It is observed that around 80–87% of the variance in informal credit results from the variance between households, around 4.2–5.4% and the remaining 8.9–15.1% stems from variance at the regional level and at the state level, respectively. Whereas for formal credit, 80–87% of the variance stems from the variance between households, around 5.6–7.1% from the regional level and the remaining 8.3–14.9% comes from variance at the state level. The paper analyzes the effect of various household, regional and state-level characteristics on credit availability from both formal and informal sources in India.

**Keywords** Household debt · Institutional and non-institutional credit · Multi-level mixed-effects regression model · India

## 7.1 Introduction and Literature Review

Access to finance is considered a very crucial determinant of the development process in emerging market economies. Several recent studies have established a relationship between a country's financial system and the structure of the real economy. They further argue that financial development is not only an engine for economic growth, but it also promotes economic equality and social welfare. A significant strand of the literary works has shown that in order for financial development to be positively

V. Bhardwaj (✉)
Graduate, M.Sc. in Economics and B.E. in Electronics and Instrumentation, BITS Pilani-K.K. Birla Goa Campus, Pilani, India
e-mail: vedantbhardwaj.b3@gmail.com

A. K. Mishra
Head of Department, Economics Department, BITS Pilani-K.K. Birla Goa Campus, Pilani, India
e-mail: aswini@goa.bits-pilani.ac.in

 
A. K. Mishra et al. (eds.), *The Financial Landscape of Emerging Economies*, Accounting, Finance, Sustainability, Governance & Fraud: Theory and Application,
https://doi.org/10.1007/978-3-030-60008-2_7

associated with economic equality and decreasing poverty, the degree of access to financial services must increase (Honohan 2004; Clark et al. 2006; Demirgüç-Kunt et al. 2008; Allen et al. 2018). Therefore, the vital factor for reducing economic inequality or enhancing equality of opportunity is increased access to finance and not financial development. Financial access, or the household use of formal financial services, includes the ability to access transactions, credit and investment products and services from formal financial institutions. In this context, access to finance has positive effects in reducing income inequality and the poverty ratio (Bae et al. 2012). Moreover, access to formal credit is also an essential tool for upward economic and social mobility, especially for low-income households. Low income and less wealthy households need credit to invest in education or in creating enterprise to benefit from the growth of the economy. The high cost or simply unavailability of credit can hinder these prospects and create inefficiencies in the market economy.

The World Bank's "The Little Data Book on Financial Inclusion" (2018) figures out that in the world, around 68.5% of adults (age 15+ ) had an account in a financial institution while 22.5% of adults had borrowed from a financial institution or used a credit card. On the other hand, in lower middle countries, around 56.1% of adults (age 15+) had an account in account in a financial institution. In comparison, only 9.8% of adults had borrowed from a financial institution or used a credit card. Finally, when we look at these two figures in the context of India, almost 80% of adults had accounts in a financial institution. However, only 8.1% of adults have borrowed from a financial institution or used a credit card. These figures reveal the predominance of non-institutional or informal sources as far as access to credit is concerned. In general, we categorize financial markets into two forms: formal and informal financial markets. Formal financial markets as those financial market activities that are controlled by the government, whereas we define informal financial markets as activities of various financial intermediaries ranging from farmers, moneylenders, friends, relatives, shopkeepers, merchants, traders, and rotating savings and credit associations.

There are many works of literature, which looked into the issue of access to financial credit in the context of developing countries. Several studies focused on the reason for either not accessing credits or accessing credit from informal sector (see the following: Nigeria (Umoh 2006), Thailand (Giné (2011), Vietnam (Duy et al. 2012), South Africa (Biyase and Fisher 2017), Peru (Field and Torero 2006).

In India especially, various studies have emphasized the dynamism and diversity of Indian rural informal finance, highlighting both its strengths and weaknesses (Bouman, 1989; Harriss-White and Colatei 2004; Kochar 1997; Shah et al., 2007). A study by Swaminathan (2012) tried to find out who had access to formal credit in rural India and observed that manual workers and members of historically deprived social groups do not have much access to formal credit and are dependent on the informal sector. Similarly, Ghosh and Vinod (2017) tried to find whether gender mattered in financial inclusion and after taking into account other relevant household and state-level characteristics that are important in explaining financial access by households. Their results show that when compared to male-headed households, female-headed households were 8% less like to access formal finance, whereas were 6% more likely to access informal finance. Similarly, other studies (Guérin et al. 2013; Goedecke et al. 2018) examined the nature of debt in rural South India and observed that the social interactions shape the cost, use, and access to debt and found that caste, social class, and location affected the borrowing of individuals from distinct moneylenders. A study by Pal and Laha (2014) who tried to examine using quantile regression to find out the change in the distribution of credit off-take among borrowers of formal credit in rural areas.

This paper uses multi-level modelling to find out the variance in credit borrowed from formal and informal sources by a household across three different spatial levels, which are households, regions and states. It allows us to take into consideration level characteristics to explain the variance at each level and systematic sorting at a lower level to explain the variance at each level. Various studies have used multi-level modelling to answer questions related to spatial inequality. Gräb and Grimm (2011) use a multi-level mixed-effect regression model to nalyse the source of household income and its variance across different spatial units in Burkina Faso. Xi et al (2005) used a multi-level logistic regression model to associate income inequality at the public health unit level with the individual health status in Ontario.

## 7.2 Data and Methodology

### *7.2.1 Methodology*

This paper takes inspiration from the work of (Gräb and Grimm 2011) on income inequality in Burkina Faso and uses a multi-level regression model to analyze the determinants of credit availability from formal and informal sources and its variance across different spatial units. We choose a multi-level regression model as it allows us to decompose the variance of formal and informal credit availability measured by the natural log of credit borrowed by households from formal and informal sources across levels during June–December of 2002 and 2012. We have considered the household, region and the state as the levels of hierarchy in our analysis. We will start with random intercept null model M1 with no independent variables and informal/formal credit borrowed by households as a dependent variable, then we will consequently introduce household characteristics, regional level characteristics and state-level characteristics as an independent variable to form model M2, M3 and M4, respectively. This iterative process will allow us to identify which characteristics explain the formal and informal credit availability and allow us to understand how much the spatial variation at each level can be explained by these characteristics.

Our three-level full random effect model will be

$$Y_{ijk} = \beta_{000} + \sum_{h=1}^{H} \beta_{h00} X_{hijk} + \sum_{c=1}^{C} \beta_{0c0} R_{cjk} + \sum_{s=1}^{S} \beta_{00s} W_{sk} + U_k + V_{jk} + \epsilon_{ijk} \tag{7.1}$$

where i, j, k represent household, region and state, respectively, and X, R and W are vectors of household, regional and state characteristics, respectively, and $\beta s$ are fixed effect coefficient. $U_k$ represents regional random intercept while $V_{jk}$ represents the state's random intercept. We will further use the Variance Partition Coefficient (VPC) represented by $\rho$ to measure the contribution of variance at each level. VPC in the random intercept model measures the degree of clustering at each level. The multi-level model assumes error to be independently distributed at each level, so the variance of the dependent variable can be thought of as the sum of variance at each level. For our three-level random-intercept model decomposition of variance will be

$$var\left(Y_{ijk}|X_{ijk}\right) = var(U_k) + var\left(V_{kj}\right) + var\left(\epsilon_{jkl}\right) = \sigma_u^2 + \sigma_v^2 + \sigma_\epsilon^2 \quad (7.2)$$

And the VPC for a particular level can be written as

$$\rho_{level} = \frac{\sigma_{level}^2}{var\left(Yijk|X_{ijk}\right)} \quad (7.3)$$

So, for the regional level, it will be

$$\rho_V = \frac{\sigma_v^2}{\sigma_u^2 + \sigma_v^2 + \sigma_\epsilon^2} \quad (7.4)$$

The ability to decompose the error term allows us to compute the share of variance explained by the level-specific variables and by the sorting of observable lower level characteristics at that level. It will help us to answer the following question:

(1) How much of total variance in formal and informal credit availability between households can be attributed to differences between regions?
(2) What amount of variance between regions can be explained by differences in considered household variables?
(3) How much of the total variance in formal and informal credit can be attributed to the difference between states?
(4) What amount of variance between regions can be explained by the difference in considered regional characteristics?
(5) What amount of variance between states can be explained by the difference in considered state characteristics?

Question 1 and 3 can be answered by the VPC (Eq. 7.3), whereas the question 2, 4 and 5 can be answered by calculating the proportional change in variance when adding the level-specific characteristics. There are a few limitations in this method first that the variance that will be attributed to higher level characteristics would also have variation due to sorting of unobserved characteristics at lower levels, and secondly, the lower level characteristics may be driven by higher level characteristics. To answer question 2, we must calculate the proportional change in the variance at the regional level after the introduction of household variables. The change can be calculated by

$$\Delta\sigma^2_{\upsilon HH} = \frac{\{\sigma^2_{\upsilon M1} - \sigma^2_{\upsilon M2}\}}{\sigma^2_{\upsilon M1}} \tag{7.5}$$

Similarly, to answer question 4, we have to calculate the proportional change in variance observed at regional level on the introduction of regional variables, and it is given by

$$\Delta\sigma^2_{\upsilon R} = \frac{\{\sigma^2_{\upsilon M2} - \sigma^2_{\upsilon M3}\}}{\sigma^2_{\upsilon M1}} \tag{7.6}$$

In a similar fashion, we can calculate the change in the variance at the state level after considering the state variables.

### *7.2.2 Data*

The data used in this paper are from the two rounds of the All India Debt and Investment Survey (AIDIS) conducted in 2003 (59th round) for the year 2002 and in 2013 (70th round) for the year 2012 by National Sample Survey Organization, Ministry of Statistics and Programme Implementation, Government of India. The numbers of households surveyed were 143,285 and 110,800 for 59th round 70th round, respectively. Adding to this, the numbers of respondents were 709,291 and 519,595 in these two survey rounds, respectively.

The AIDIS collects information on assets and indebtedness of the household as well as source, purpose and interest rate of debt owned. According to the AIDIS, the agency from which a loan was taken treated as the credit agency. The credit agencies were either 'institutional agencies' or 'non-institutional agencies'. The various agencies which were treated as 'institutional agencies' were government, co-operative agencies, commercial banks including regional rural banks, insurance, provident fund, financial Corporation/institution, financial company and 'other institutional agencies'. The agencies which were treated as 'non-institutional agencies' were landlord, agriculturist money lender, professional moneylender, trader, relatives and friends, doctors, lawyers, and other professionals, and 'others'. The survey also collected data on household and individual characteristics like religion, caste, and the main occupation of the household and at individual level characteristics like education, age, gender, etc. Some changes to the survey have been made over the years, like information on religion followed by the household was introduced in the 59$^{th}$ round (2002). In the 70th round, the survey did not collect information on durables. In this analysis, we have excluded durables from assets for 2002 to make the values comparable with 2012.

Debt in our analysis defined as cash loans borrowed. Since there is a lack of a suitable asset price deflator, due to which one needs to use the Wholesale Price Index (WPI) or the Consumer Price Index (CPI) to deflate the nominal data. In this article, we use the former. In this analysis, we have considered debt and asset adjusted by household size that is in per capita terms.

## 7.3 Results

Figure 7.1 gives the share of average formal credit and informal credit borrowed by households during the period of July–December of 2002 and 2012. We observe that the share of informal credit to the total credit borrowed during the 2nd half of 2012 is just 3% less than its share in the 2nd half of 2002. Table 7.1 gives the summary statistics for the variables considered in our analysis.

Tables 7.2 and 7.4 give the fixed effect results for different models for informal credit for the 2002 and 2012, respectively, whereas Tables 7.3 and 7.5 give the fixed effect results for different models for formal credit for the year 2002 and 2012, respectively. Table 7.6 gives the variance effect for both formal and informal credit for the years 2002 and 2012. Finally, Table 7.7 gives the contribution of observed variables on the variance at each level for both types of credit for the years 2002 and 2012.

### *7.3.1 M1: Null Model*

In our first model, we only introduce the random intercept at the regional level and state level for all three rounds. To select the model, we use the likelihood ratio test to check whether the two-level model nested in the three-level model performs better than the three-level model. For this, we compare the two-level model to the three-level model, first by excluding the state level and then by removing the regional level. We find that the test shows significant variation at both state and regional levels.

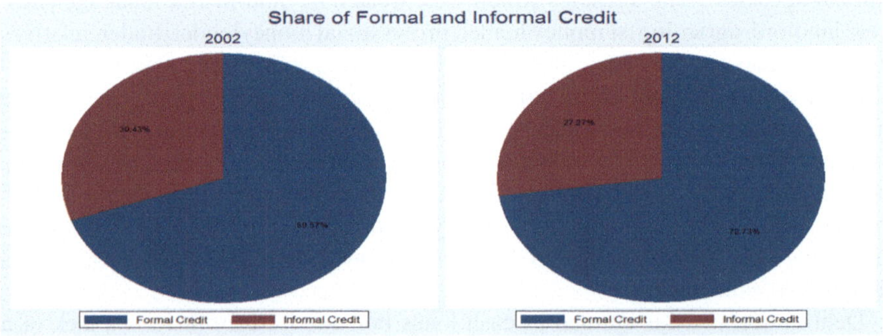


**Fig. 7.1** Share of average formal and informal credit borrowed (2nd half of 2002 and 2012). *Source* Calculation done by authors

**Table 7.1** Descriptive statistics for household characteristics

| Variable | Label | 2002 | | 2012 | |
|---|---|---|---|---|---|
| | | Mean | Std. Dev | Mean | Std. Dev |
| Household characteristics | | | | | |
| Formal credit | Formal credit borrowed by the household during second half of 2002 and 2012 | 2541.507 | 32,816.570 | 12,606.160 | 115,387.200 |
| Informal credit | Informal credit borrowed by the household during second half of 2002 and 2012 | 1111.033 | 9972.490 | 4726.025 | 34,299.710 |
| Gender of the household head | % of household | | | | |
| Male | | 88.340 | | 87.930 | |
| Female | | 11.660 | | 12.070 | |
| Household size | | 4.950 | 2.568 | 4.689 | 2.317 |
| Social group | % of the household belonging to the social group | | | | |
| ST | Household belongs to Scheduled Tribe | 10.960 | | 14.033 | |
| SC | Household belongs to Scheduled Caste | 18.400 | | 16.449 | |
| OBC | Household belongs to Other Backward Caste | 37.050 | | 38.812 | |
| Others | Household belongs to Other Caste | 33.590 | | 30.706 | |
| Household religion | % of the household following | | | | |
| Hinduism | | 78.290 | | 77.703 | |
| Islam | | 12.220 | | 12.366 | |
| Christianity | | 5.560 | | 6.308 | |
| Others | | 3.930 | | 3.624 | |
| Age of the head of household | % of household with the age of the head of household in category | | | | |
| 15–30 (Ref. Category) | | 14.718 | | 10.792 | |

(continued)

**Table 7.1** (continued)

| Variable | Label | 2002 | | 2012 | |
|---|---|---|---|---|---|
| | | Mean | Std. Dev | Mean | Std. Dev |
| 31–59 | | 67.053 | | 67.953 | |
| >59 | | 18.229 | | 21.254 | |
| Literate head | % of household heads who are literate | 64.321 | | 70.784 | |
| Household main occupations | % of the household involved in | | | | |
| Self-employed in agriculture | Self-employed in agriculture in the rural area | 23.560 | | 26.827 | |
| Self-employed in non-agriculture | Self-employed in non-agriculture in rural areas | 9.640 | | 6.208 | |
| Regular wage earner | Regular wage earner in rural areas | | | 6.497 | |
| Casual labour in agriculture | Casual labour in agriculture | 15.390 | | 7.190 | |
| Casual labour in non-agriculture | Casual labour in non-agriculture | 6.970 | | 6.834 | |
| Others | Other occupation in rural areas | 8.010 | | 2.523 | |
| Self-employed | Self-employed in urban areas | 13.950 | | 16.160 | |
| Regular wage earner | Regular wage earner in urban areas | 15.170 | | 17.544 | |
| Casual labour | Casual labour in urban areas | 4.370 | | 6.771 | |
| Others | Other occupation in urban areas | 2.840 | | 3.447 | |
| Household composition | | | | | |
| Adult share (Ref. Category) | | 0.651 | | 0.691 | |
| Elderly share | | 0.057 | | 0.064 | |
| Children share | | 0.291 | | 0.245 | |
| Max education of any adult in the household | % of household with maximum education as | | | | |

(continued)

**Table 7.1** (continued)

| Variable | Label | 2002 | | 2012 | |
|---|---|---|---|---|---|
| | | Mean | Std. Dev | Mean | Std. Dev |
| Not literate | | 19.740 | | 11.209 | |
| Till high school | | 66.240 | | 66.617 | |
| Above high school | | 14.020 | | 22.174 | |
| Regional characteristics | The average share of households in regions | | | | |
| Max education | The average regional share of household with max education as | | | | |
| Not literate | | 0.197 | 0.107 | 0.112 | 0.071 |
| Till high school | | 0.662 | 0.086 | 0.666 | 0.069 |
| Above high school | | 0.140 | 0.049 | 0.222 | 0.072 |
| Household main occupations | The average regional share of households involved in | | | | |
| Self-employed in agriculture | Self-employed in agriculture in rural area | 0.236 | 0.113 | 0.268 | 0.123 |
| Self-employed in non-agriculture | Self-employed in non-agriculture rural area | 0.096 | 0.038 | 0.062 | 0.033 |
| Regular wage earner | Regular wage earner rural area | | | 0.065 | 0.048 |
| Casual labour in agriculture | Casual labour in agriculture | 0.154 | 0.088 | 0.072 | 0.051 |
| Casual labour in non-agriculture | Casual labour in non-agriculture | 0.070 | 0.052 | 0.068 | 0.046 |
| Others | Other occupation in rural area | 0.080 | 0.034 | 0.025 | 0.017 |
| Self-employed | Self-employed in urban area | 0.140 | 0.056 | 0.162 | 0.055 |
| Regular wage earner | Regular wage earner in urban area | 0.152 | 0.104 | 0.175 | 0.087 |
| Casual labour | Casual labour in urban area | 0.044 | 0.027 | 0.068 | 0.032 |

(continued)

**Table 7.1** (continued)

| Variable | Label | 2002 | | 2012 | |
|---|---|---|---|---|---|
| | | Mean | Std. Dev | Mean | Std. Dev |
| Others | Other occupation in urban area | 0.028 | 0.013 | 0.034 | 0.019 |
| State-level characteristics | The average share of households in the state | | | | |
| Max education | State average share of household with max education as | | | | |
| Not literate | | 0.197 | 0.097 | 0.112 | 0.064 |
| Till high school | | 0.662 | 0.077 | 0.666 | 0.054 |
| Above high school | | 0.140 | 0.037 | 0.222 | 0.052 |
| Household main occupations | State average share of the household involved in | | | | |
| Self-employed in agriculture | Self-employed in agriculture in rural area | 0.236 | 0.093 | 0.268 | 0.101 |
| Self-employed in non-agriculture | Self-employed in non-agriculture rural area | 0.096 | 0.031 | 0.062 | 0.028 |
| Regular wage earner | Regular wage earner rural area | NA | NA | 0.065 | 0.044 |
| Casual labour in agriculture | Casual labour in agriculture | 0.154 | 0.074 | 0.072 | 0.041 |
| Casual labour in non-agriculture | Casual labour in non-agriculture | 0.070 | 0.041 | 0.068 | 0.035 |
| Others | Other occupation in rural area | 0.080 | 0.030 | 0.025 | 0.015 |
| Self-employed | Self-employed in urban area | 0.140 | 0.042 | 0.162 | 0.038 |
| Regular wage earner | Regular wage earner in urban area | 0.152 | 0.082 | 0.175 | 0.067 |
| Casual labour | Casual labour in urban area | 0.044 | 0.022 | 0.068 | 0.025 |
| Others | Other occupation in urban area | 0.028 | 0.009 | 0.034 | 0.016 |

*Source* Calculation done by authors

**Table 7.2** Fixed effect coefficient for informal credit availability in 2002

| | M1 | M2 | M3 | M4 |
|---|---|---|---|---|
| Debt | | | | |
| Gender of the household head | | | | |
| Male (Ref. Category) | | | | |
| Female | | −0.0829** | −0.0848** | −0.0849** |
| | | (0.0359) | (0.0359) | (0.0359) |
| Household size | | 0.0777*** | 0.0778*** | 0.0777*** |
| | | (0.00530) | (0.00530) | (0.00530) |
| Social group | | | | |
| Other social group (Reference) | | | | |
| ST | | −0.538*** | −0.540*** | −0.540*** |
| | | (0.0515) | (0.0517) | (0.0517) |
| SC | | −0.307*** | −0.307*** | −0.308*** |
| | | (0.0335) | (0.0335) | (0.0335) |
| OBC | | −0.0408 | −0.0383 | −0.0401 |
| | | (0.0288) | (0.0289) | (0.0289) |
| Age of household head | | | | |
| 15–30 (Ref. Category) | | | | |
| 31–59 | | 0.100*** | 0.102*** | 0.102*** |
| | | (0.0302) | (0.0302) | (0.0302) |
| >59 | | 0.0480 | 0.0490 | 0.0491 |
| | | (0.0443) | (0.0443) | (0.0443) |
| Religion | | | | |
| Hinduism (Ref. Category) | | | | |
| Islam | | −0.0772** | −0.0787** | −0.0802** |
| | | (0.0338) | (0.0338) | (0.0338) |
| Christianity | | 0.133** | 0.129** | 0.127** |
| | | (0.0606) | (0.0609) | (0.0611) |
| Others | | 0.346*** | 0.345*** | 0.349*** |
| | | (0.0797) | (0.0795) | (0.0797) |
| Literate head | | 0.0942*** | 0.0935*** | 0.0938*** |
| | | (0.0296) | (0.0296) | (0.0296) |
| Household composition | | | | |
| Adult share (Ref. Category) | | | | |
| Elderly dhare | | −0.488*** | −0.489*** | −0.489*** |
| | | (0.0938) | (0.0938) | (0.0938) |
| Children share | | −0.391*** | −0.391*** | −0.391*** |

(continued)

**Table 7.2** (continued)

| | M1 | M2 | M3 | M4 |
|---|---|---|---|---|
| | | (0.0533) | (0.0533) | (0.0533) |
| Education | | | | |
| Not literate | | | | |
| Till high school | | 0.193*** | 0.193*** | 0.193*** |
| | | (0.0354) | (0.0354) | (0.0354) |
| Above high school | | 0.653*** | 0.656*** | 0.656*** |
| | | (0.0532) | (0.0532) | (0.0532) |
| Household type | | | | |
| Self-employed in non-agriculture (Ref. Category) | | | | |
| Rural | | | | |
| Agricultural labour | | −0.389*** | −0.387*** | −0.388*** |
| | | (0.0413) | (0.0413) | (0.0413) |
| Other labour | | −0.263*** | −0.266*** | −0.266*** |
| | | (0.0494) | (0.0494) | (0.0494) |
| Self-employed in agriculture | | 0.104*** | 0.105*** | 0.104*** |
| | | (0.0386) | (0.0386) | (0.0386) |
| Others | | −0.0251 | −0.0265 | −0.0274 |
| | | (0.0561) | (0.0561) | (0.0561) |
| Urban | | | | |
| Self-employed | | 0.192*** | 0.187*** | 0.187*** |
| | | (0.0429) | (0.0429) | (0.0429) |
| Regular wage earner | | −0.00323 | −0.00866 | −0.00966 |
| | | (0.0465) | (0.0466) | (0.0466) |
| Casual labour | | −0.356*** | −0.359*** | −0.359*** |
| | | (0.0555) | (0.0555) | (0.0555) |
| Others | | 0.209** | 0.206** | 0.205** |
| | | (0.0910) | (0.0911) | (0.0911) |
| Regional level | | | | |
| (% of households at the regional level with) | | | | |
| Education | | | | |
| Not literate | (Reference) | | | |
| Mean till high school | | | −1.609** | −1.442 |
| | | | (0.772) | (0.882) |
| Mean high school | | | −3.354*** | −3.850*** |
| | | | (1.235) | (1.347) |

(continued)

**Table 7.2** (continued)

| | M1 | M2 | M3 | M4 |
|---|---|---|---|---|
| Household type | | | | |
| Self-employed in non-agriculture (Ref. Category) | | | | |
| Rural | | | | |
| Agricultural labour | | | −0.0233 | −0.896 |
| | | | (1.816) | (1.979) |
| Other labour | | | 1.864 | 0.239 |
| | | | (2.160) | (2.365) |
| Self-employed in agriculture | | | 0.436 | −0.502 |
| | | | (1.617) | (1.748) |
| Others | | | 5.780** | 4.465 |
| | | | (2.486) | (2.832) |
| Urban | | | | |
| self-employed | | | 4.057** | 3.011 |
| | | | (2.041) | (2.151) |
| Regular wage earner | | | 1.860 | 1.197 |
| | | | (1.493) | (1.638) |
| Casual labour | | | 1.672 | −0.153 |
| | | | (2.242) | (2.497) |
| Others | | | −5.581 | −5.663 |
| | | | (3.842) | (4.002) |
| State level | | | | |
| (% of households at state level with) | | | | |
| Education | | | | |
| Not literate | (Reference) | | | |
| Mean till high school | | | | −0.960 |
| | | | | (1.782) |
| Mean high school | | | | 5.321 |
| | | | | (5.457) |
| Household type | | | | |
| Self-employed in non-agriculture (Ref. Category) | | | | |
| Rural | | | | |
| Agricultural labour | | | | 5.501 |
| | | | | (6.178) |
| Other labour | | | | 8.666 |
| | | | | (7.591) |

(continued)

**Table 7.2** (continued)

| | M1 | M2 | M3 | M4 |
|---|---|---|---|---|
| Self-employed in agriculture | | | | 6.380 |
| | | | | (5.448) |
| Others | | | | 5.737 |
| | | | | (7.043) |
| Urban | | | | |
| Self-employed | | | | 8.242 |
| | | | | (7.813) |
| Regular wage earner | | | | 1.749 |
| | | | | (5.239) |
| Casual labour | | | | 13.58 |
| | | | | (10.05) |
| Others | | | | −10.75 |
| | | | | (18.89) |
| Constant | 8.567*** | 8.153*** | 8.193*** | 3.797 |
| | (0.117) | (0.119) | (1.538) | (4.840) |

Standard errors in parentheses
* $p < 0.10$, ** $p < 0.05$, *** $p < 0.01$
*Source* Calculation done by authors

Therefore, the average credit borrowed by a household from formal and informal sources vary significantly between state and regional level, so we go for a three-level model. Table 7.7 gives the VPC $\rho$ for each year at each level. We observe that VPC for State level for informal credit availability is around 15%, almost 80% higher than formal credit in the last six months of 2002. Whereas in the second half of 2012 VPC for State level for informal credit is 8.9% which is just 60% of formal credit (VPC:14.9%), so we see a reversal in the contribution of state-level factors in variance in credit availability by a household from informal and formal sources. When we look at VPC for the regional level, we observe that VPC $\rho$ at the regional level is less as compared to the state level. It can be due to the fact that the major policy decisions and economic factors do not vary much by region but by state. For the second half of both 2002 and 2012, it is higher for formal credit as compared to informal credit. We finally observe that around 80–86% of the variance in credit borrowed by a household from both informal and formal sources is not due to variance at the state and regional level.

**Table 7.3** Fixed effect coefficient for formal credit availability in 2002

| | M1 | M2 | M3 | M4 |
|---|---|---|---|---|
| Debt | | | | |
| Gender of the household head | | | | |
| Male (Ref. Category) | | | | |
| Female | | −0.0334 | −0.0370 | −0.0351 |
| | | (0.0541) | (0.0542) | (0.0542) |
| Household size | | 0.0364*** | 0.0361*** | 0.0366*** |
| | | (0.00621) | (0.00620) | (0.00620) |
| Social group | | | | |
| Other social group (Reference) | | | | |
| ST | | −0.313*** | −0.340*** | −0.310*** |
| | | (0.0661) | (0.0657) | (0.0660) |
| SC | | −0.421*** | −0.424*** | −0.422*** |
| | | (0.0460) | (0.0459) | (0.0459) |
| OBC | | −0.305*** | −0.305*** | −0.305*** |
| | | (0.0360) | (0.0358) | (0.0358) |
| Age of household head | | | | |
| 15–30 (Ref. Category) | | | | |
| 31–59 | | 0.134** | 0.135** | 0.135** |
| | | (0.0542) | (0.0542) | (0.0542) |
| > 59 | | 0.0946 | 0.0923 | 0.0915 |
| | | (0.0672) | (0.0672) | (0.0672) |
| Religion | | | | |
| Hinduism (Ref. Category) | | | | |
| Islam | | −0.0639 | −0.0704 | −0.0662 |
| | | (0.0508) | (0.0507) | (0.0508) |
| Christianity | | −0.111 | −0.123* | −0.120 |
| | | (0.0745) | (0.0737) | (0.0744) |
| Others | | 0.221*** | 0.209** | 0.199** |
| | | (0.0848) | (0.0825) | (0.0834) |
| Literate head | | 0.223*** | 0.219*** | 0.221*** |
| | | (0.0433) | (0.0433) | (0.0433) |
| Household composition | | | | |
| Adult share (Ref. Category) | | | | |
| Elderly share | | −0.0351 | −0.0278 | −0.0247 |
| | | (0.133) | (0.133) | (0.133) |
| Children share | | −0.242*** | −0.241*** | −0.244*** |

(continued)

**Table 7.3** (continued)

| | M1 | M2 | M3 | M4 |
|---|---|---|---|---|
| | | (0.0717) | (0.0717) | (0.0717) |
| Education | | | | |
| Not literate | | | | |
| Till high school | | 0.123* | 0.119* | 0.117* |
| | | (0.0642) | (0.0642) | (0.0642) |
| Above high school | | 0.774*** | 0.771*** | 0.770*** |
| | | (0.0744) | (0.0744) | (0.0744) |
| Household type | | | | |
| Self-employed in non-agriculture (Ref. Category) | | | | |
| Rural | | | | |
| Agricultural labour | | −0.657*** | −0.654*** | −0.649*** |
| | | (0.0701) | (0.0701) | (0.0701) |
| Other labour | | −0.417*** | −0.418*** | −0.419*** |
| | | (0.0751) | (0.0752) | (0.0752) |
| Self-employed in agriculture | | −0.149*** | −0.151*** | −0.148*** |
| | | (0.0549) | (0.0549) | (0.0549) |
| Others | | 0.102 | 0.0950 | 0.0931 |
| | | (0.0694) | (0.0694) | (0.0694) |
| Urban | | | | |
| Self-employed | | 0.616*** | 0.612*** | 0.610*** |
| | | (0.0632) | (0.0633) | (0.0633) |
| Regular wage earner | | 0.454*** | 0.446*** | 0.448*** |
| | | (0.0589) | (0.0590) | (0.0590) |
| Casual labour | | −0.273** | −0.273** | −0.273** |
| | | (0.109) | (0.110) | (0.110) |
| Others | | 0.296** | 0.299** | 0.301** |
| | | (0.124) | (0.124) | (0.124) |
| Regional level | | | | |
| (% of households at regional level with) | | | | |
| Education | | | | |
| Not literate | | | | |
| Mean till high school | | | 0.0267 | −0.00899 |
| | | | (0.523) | (0.898) |
| Mean high school | | | −0.413 | −1.937 |
| | | | (1.161) | (1.370) |

(continued)

**Table 7.3** (continued)

| | M1 | M2 | M3 | M4 |
|---|---|---|---|---|
| Household type | | | | |
| Self-employed in non-agriculture (Ref. Category) | | | | |
| Rural | | | | |
| Agricultural labour | | | 2.723* | 0.620 |
| | | | (1.521) | (1.935) |
| Other labour | | | 4.480** | −0.375 |
| | | | (1.795) | (2.263) |
| Self-employed in agriculture | | | 3.336** | 0.136 |
| | | | (1.369) | (1.698) |
| Others | | | 8.619*** | 0.967 |
| | | | (1.919) | (2.959) |
| Urban | | | | |
| Self-employed | | | 6.975*** | 4.772** |
| | | | (1.799) | (2.049) |
| Regular wage earner | | | 3.452*** | 1.020 |
| | | | (1.220) | (1.619) |
| Casual labour | | | 2.253 | −1.907 |
| | | | (1.861) | (2.431) |
| Others | | | −2.946 | −4.596 |
| | | | (3.672) | (3.819) |
| State level | | | | |
| (% of households at state level with) | | | | |
| Education | | | | |
| Not literate | | | | |
| Mean till high school | | | | −0.314 |
| | | | | (1.152) |
| Mean high school | | | | 3.332 |
| | | | | (3.003) |
| Household type | | | | |
| Self-employed in non-agriculture (Ref. Category) | | | | |
| Rural | | | | |
| Agricultural labour | | | | 3.399 |
| | | | | (3.323) |
| Other labour | | | | 7.089* |
| | | | | (4.081) |

(continued)

**Table 7.3** (continued)

| | M1 | M2 | M3 | M4 |
|---|---|---|---|---|
| Self-employed in agriculture | | | | 4.755 |
| | | | | (2.906) |
| Others | | | | 10.05** |
| | | | | (4.332) |
| Urban | | | | |
| Self-employed | | | | 4.487 |
| | | | | (4.045) |
| Regular wage earner | | | | 2.728 |
| | | | | (2.873) |
| Casual labour | | | | 3.287 |
| | | | | (5.338) |
| Others | | | | 4.983 |
| | | | | (9.273) |
| Constant | 9.863*** | 9.270*** | 5.524*** | 4.157* |
| | (0.100) | (0.118) | (1.289) | (2.224) |

Standard errors in parentheses
* $p < 0.10$, ** $p < 0.05$, *** $p < 0.01$
*Source* Calculation done by authors

## 7.3.2 *Model M2: Household Characteristics*

In this model, we add different household characteristics as the explanatory variables to observe their effect on credit borrowed by a household and to observe its contribution to variance at household, regional and state levels.

### 7.3.2.1 Household Characteristics

First thing, we observe from Tables 7.2, 7.3, 7.4 and 7.5 that having a female head as compared to the male head had a significant negative effect on credit availability from informal sources in the second half of 2002 and from formal sources in the second half of 2012, whereas having no significant impact credit availability from informal sources and formal sources in seconds half of 2002 and 2012, respectively. We also observe that household size has a significant positive impact on credit availability from both informal and formal credit in the 2nd half of 2002 and 2012. We then look at the impact of being part of a social group on credit availability with other social groups as the base and observe that being part of Scheduled Tribe (ST) and Scheduled Caste (SC) has a negative impact on credit availability from both informal and formal sources in the 2nd half of 2002 and 2012. We also observe that the negative impact of being part of the ST group is more pronounced in credit availability from informal

**Table 7.4** Fixed effect coefficient for informal credit availability in 2012

| | M1 | M2 | M3 | M4 |
|---|---|---|---|---|
| Debt | | | | |
| Gender of the household head | | | | |
| Male (Ref. Category) | | | | |
| Female | | −0.0397 | −0.0385 | −0.0372 |
| | | (0.0348) | (0.0348) | (0.0348) |
| Household size | | 0.0729*** | 0.0730*** | 0.0730*** |
| | | (0.00581) | (0.00581) | (0.00581) |
| Social group | | | | |
| Other social group (Reference) | | | | |
| ST | | −0.528*** | −0.536*** | −0.530*** |
| | | (0.0437) | (0.0439) | (0.0439) |
| SC | | −0.274*** | −0.275*** | −0.275*** |
| | | (0.0341) | (0.0341) | (0.0341) |
| OBC | | −0.0406 | −0.0443 | −0.0421 |
| | | (0.0289) | (0.0289) | (0.0289) |
| Age of household head | | | | |
| 15–30 (Ref. Category) | | | | |
| 31–59 | | 0.0931*** | 0.0925*** | 0.0937*** |
| | | (0.0338) | (0.0338) | (0.0338) |
| >59 | | 0.0726 | 0.0714 | 0.0722 |
| | | (0.0454) | (0.0455) | (0.0454) |
| Religion | | | | |
| Hinduism (Ref. Category) | | | | |
| Islam | | −0.0535 | −0.0564 | −0.0518 |
| | | (0.0344) | (0.0344) | (0.0344) |
| Christianity | | 0.145** | 0.134** | 0.142** |
| | | (0.0631) | (0.0632) | (0.0629) |
| Others | | 0.208*** | 0.202*** | 0.194*** |
| | | (0.0753) | (0.0751) | (0.0749) |
| Literate head | | 0.114*** | 0.116*** | 0.118*** |
| | | (0.0283) | (0.0283) | (0.0283) |
| Household composition | | | | |
| Adult share (Ref. Category) | | | | |
| Elderly share | | −0.412*** | −0.411*** | −0.411*** |
| | | (0.0866) | (0.0866) | (0.0866) |
| Children share | | −0.353*** | −0.352*** | −0.352*** |

(continued)

**Table 7.4** (continued)

| | M1 | M2 | M3 | M4 |
|---|---|---|---|---|
| | | (0.0534) | (0.0534) | (0.0533) |
| Education | | | | |
| Not literate | (Reference) | | | |
| Till high school | | 0.163*** | 0.163*** | 0.162*** |
| | | (0.0397) | (0.0397) | (0.0397) |
| Above high school | | 0.607*** | 0.605*** | 0.604*** |
| | | (0.0504) | (0.0504) | (0.0504) |
| Household type | | | | |
| Self-employed in non-agriculture (Ref. Category) | | | | |
| Rural | | | | |
| Self-employed in agriculture | | −0.0251 | −0.0266 | −0.0256 |
| | | (0.0429) | (0.0429) | (0.0429) |
| Regular wage earner | | −0.137** | −0.140** | −0.139** |
| | | (0.0568) | (0.0569) | (0.0568) |
| Casual labour in agriculture | | −0.398*** | −0.399*** | −0.398*** |
| | | (0.0526) | (0.0526) | (0.0526) |
| Casual labour in non-agriculture | | −0.330*** | −0.329*** | −0.329*** |
| | | (0.0522) | (0.0522) | (0.0522) |
| Others | | −0.00712 | −0.0109 | −0.0101 |
| | | (0.0877) | (0.0877) | (0.0877) |
| Urban | | | | |
| Self-employed | | 0.132*** | 0.128*** | 0.130*** |
| | | (0.0464) | (0.0464) | (0.0464) |
| Regular wage earner | | −0.0610 | −0.0629 | −0.0632 |
| | | (0.0483) | (0.0483) | (0.0483) |
| Casual labour | | −0.352*** | −0.358*** | −0.357*** |
| | | (0.0523) | (0.0523) | (0.0523) |
| Others | | −0.0515 | −0.0564 | −0.0567 |
| | | (0.0877) | (0.0877) | (0.0877) |
| Regional level | | | | |
| (% of households at regional level with) | | | | |
| Education | | | | |
| Not literate | (Reference) | | | |
| Mean till high school | | | −2.357*** | −2.438*** |
| | | | (0.842) | (0.930) |

(continued)

**Table 7.4** (continued)

| | M1 | M2 | M3 | M4 |
|---|---|---|---|---|
| Mean high school | | | 0.0740 | −0.262 |
| | | | (0.861) | (0.938) |
| Household type | | | | |
| Self-employed in non-agriculture (Ref. Category) | | | | |
| Rural | | | | |
| Self-employed in agriculture | | | 0.383 | −2.065 |
| | | | (1.834) | (1.969) |
| Regular wage earner | | | 2.117 | −1.273 |
| | | | (2.385) | (2.532) |
| Casual labour in agriculture | | | 0.0968 | −3.861* |
| | | | (2.050) | (2.269) |
| Casual labour in non-agriculture | | | −0.406 | −3.160 |
| | | | (2.272) | (2.423) |
| Others | | | −2.730 | −8.425* |
| | | | (4.668) | (5.075) |
| Urban | | | | |
| Self-employed | | | −0.0142 | −3.848 |
| | | | (2.384) | (2.580) |
| Regular wage earner | | | −0.856 | −3.820** |
| | | | (1.726) | (1.866) |
| Casual labour | | | 3.762* | 1.617 |
| | | | (1.957) | (2.092) |
| Others | | | 0.259 | −0.724 |
| | | | (2.938) | (3.070) |
| State level | | | | |
| (% of households at state level with) | | | | |
| Education | | | | |
| Not literate | (Reference) | | | |
| Mean till high school | | | | −0.981 |
| | | | | (1.650) |
| Mean high school | | | | 0.794 |
| | | | | (1.841) |
| Household type | | | | |
| Self-employed in non-agriculture (Ref. Category) | | | | |
| Rural | | | | |

(continued)

**Table 7.4** (continued)

| | M1 | M2 | M3 | M4 |
|---|---|---|---|---|
| Self-employed in agriculture | | | | 7.956** |
| | | | | (3.834) |
| Regular wage earner | | | | 14.60*** |
| | | | | (4.929) |
| Casual labour in agriculture | | | | 12.80*** |
| | | | | (4.695) |
| Casual labour in non-agriculture | | | | 12.14** |
| | | | | (5.321) |
| Others | | | | 19.41* |
| | | | | (9.964) |
| Urban | | | | |
| Self-employed | | | | 17.39*** |
| | | | | (4.951) |
| Regular wage earner | | | | 7.891* |
| | | | | (4.326) |
| Casual labour | | | | 6.304 |
| | | | | (4.919) |
| Others | | | | −0.773 |
| | | | | (7.984) |
| Constant | 9.673*** | 9.306*** | 10.59*** | 4.074 |
| | (0.0870) | (0.102) | (2.140) | (3.768) |

Standard errors in parentheses
* $p < 0.10$, ** $p < 0.05$, *** $p < 0.01$
*Source* Calculation done by authors

sources for both periods where for the SC group, it is more negative for formal sources as compared to informal sources. Similarly, when we look at the impact of being part of Other Backward caste, we observe that it is significantly negative on credit availability from formal sources while having no significant impact on credit availability from informal sources in both considered periods. Now we move on and observe the effect of age of household head on the credit availability to the household with households having a head in the age range of 15–30 years as the base. We observe that a household having a head in the age range of 31–59 years of age has a significant positive effect on credit availability from both formal and informal sources in the considered period of the second half of 2002 and 2012. We then look at the impact of religion followed by the household and their credit availability with households following Hinduism as the base, and we observe that being part of Islam seems to have a significant negative impact on credit availability from informal sources in the second half of 2002 and formal sources in the second half of 2002. Whereas being

**Table 7.5** Fixed effect coefficient for formal credit availability in 2012

| | M1 | M2 | M3 | M4 |
|---|---|---|---|---|
| Debt | | | | |
| Gender of household head | | | | |
| Male (Ref. Category) | | | | |
| Female | | −0.122*** | −0.120*** | −0.120*** |
| | | (0.0377) | (0.0377) | (0.0377) |
| Household size | | 0.0289*** | 0.0288*** | 0.0285*** |
| | | (0.00567) | (0.00567) | (0.00567) |
| Social group | | | | |
| Other social group (Reference) | | | | |
| ST | | −0.309*** | −0.329*** | −0.325*** |
| | | (0.0452) | (0.0454) | (0.0454) |
| SC | | −0.376*** | −0.378*** | −0.376*** |
| | | (0.0353) | (0.0353) | (0.0353) |
| OBC | | −0.188*** | −0.190*** | −0.189*** |
| | | (0.0281) | (0.0281) | (0.0281) |
| Age of household head | | | | |
| 15–30 (Ref. Category) | | | | |
| 31–59 | | 0.116*** | 0.117*** | 0.116*** |
| | | (0.0420) | (0.0420) | (0.0420) |
| >59 | | 0.170*** | 0.170*** | 0.169*** |
| | | (0.0513) | (0.0513) | (0.0513) |
| Religion | | | | |
| Hinduism (Ref. Category) | | | | |
| Islam | | −0.137*** | −0.140*** | −0.136*** |
| | | (0.0361) | (0.0361) | (0.0360) |
| Christianity | | 0.0588 | 0.0398 | 0.0438 |
| | | (0.0587) | (0.0586) | (0.0585) |
| Others | | 0.326*** | 0.315*** | 0.304*** |
| | | (0.0721) | (0.0717) | (0.0717) |
| Literate head | | 0.302*** | 0.302*** | 0.302*** |
| | | (0.0302) | (0.0302) | (0.0302) |
| Household composition | | | | |
| Adult Share (Ref. Category) | | | | |
| Elderly share | | −0.0921 | −0.0875 | −0.0885 |
| | | (0.0909) | (0.0909) | (0.0909) |
| Children share | | −0.133** | −0.130** | −0.132** |

(continued)

**Table 7.5** (continued)

| | M1 | M2 | M3 | M4 |
|---|---|---|---|---|
| | | (0.0557) | (0.0557) | (0.0557) |
| Education | | | | |
| Not literate | (Reference) | | | |
| Till high school | | 0.0108 | 0.0101 | 0.0104 |
| | | (0.0503) | (0.0503) | (0.0503) |
| Above high school | | 0.731*** | 0.729*** | 0.729*** |
| | | (0.0573) | (0.0573) | (0.0572) |
| Household type | | | | |
| Self-employed in non-agriculture (Ref. Category) | | | | |
| Rural | | | | |
| Self-employed in agriculture | | −0.0602 | −0.0580 | −0.0584 |
| | | (0.0452) | (0.0453) | (0.0453) |
| Regular wage earner | | −0.121** | −0.128** | −0.127** |
| | | (0.0575) | (0.0575) | (0.0575) |
| Casual labour in agriculture | | −0.473*** | −0.469*** | −0.470*** |
| | | (0.0613) | (0.0613) | (0.0613) |
| Casual labour in non-agriculture | | −0.480*** | −0.474*** | −0.474*** |
| | | (0.0598) | (0.0598) | (0.0598) |
| Others | | −0.117 | −0.117 | −0.116 |
| | | (0.103) | (0.103) | (0.103) |
| Urban | | | | |
| Self-employed | | 0.227*** | 0.225*** | 0.225*** |
| | | (0.0477) | (0.0477) | (0.0477) |
| Regular wage earner | | 0.319*** | 0.316*** | 0.316*** |
| | | (0.0489) | (0.0490) | (0.0490) |
| Casual labour | | −0.409*** | −0.411*** | −0.412*** |
| | | (0.0555) | (0.0555) | (0.0555) |
| Others | | 0.423*** | 0.423*** | 0.423*** |
| | | (0.0859) | (0.0859) | (0.0859) |
| Regional level | | | | |
| (% of households at regional level with) | | | | |
| Education | | | | |
| Not literate | (Reference) | | | |
| Mean till high school | | | −0.765 | −1.562* |
| | | | (0.825) | (0.935) |

(continued)

**Table 7.5** (continued)

| | M1 | M2 | M3 | M4 |
|---|---|---|---|---|
| Mean high school | | | 0.427 | −0.781 |
| | | | (0.857) | (0.954) |
| Household type | | | | |
| Self-employed in non-agriculture (Ref. Category) | | | | |
| Rural | | | | |
| Self-employed in agriculture | | | 1.807 | −0.257 |
| | | | (1.787) | (1.958) |
| Regular wage earner | | | 5.640** | 2.829 |
| | | | (2.322) | (2.509) |
| Casual labour in agriculture | | | −0.0694 | −1.904 |
| | | | (2.000) | (2.276) |
| Casual labour in non-agriculture | | | −0.714 | −3.682 |
| | | | (2.207) | (2.401) |
| Others | | | −1.215 | −4.295 |
| | | | (4.500) | (5.054) |
| Urban | | | | |
| Self-employed | | | 1.302 | −1.477 |
| | | | (2.322) | (2.565) |
| Regular wage earner | | | 1.021 | −0.710 |
| | | | (1.675) | (1.860) |
| Casual labour | | | 3.267* | 1.616 |
| | | | (1.903) | (2.081) |
| Others | | | 0.848 | −0.304 |
| | | | (2.939) | (3.121) |
| State-level | | | | |
| (% of households at the state level with) | | | | |
| Education | | | | |
| Not literate | (Reference) | | | |
| Mean till high school | | | | 0.977 |
| | | | | (1.722) |
| Mean high school | | | | 4.542** |
| | | | | (1.918) |
| Household type | | | | |
| Self-employed in non-agriculture (Ref. Category) | | | | |
| Rural | | | | |

(continued)

**Table 7.5** (continued)

| | M1 | M2 | M3 | M4 |
|---|---|---|---|---|
| Self-employed in agriculture | | | | 8.727** |
| | | | | (3.955) |
| Regular wage earner | | | | 12.43** |
| | | | | (5.108) |
| Casual labour in agriculture | | | | 9.241* |
| | | | | (4.911) |
| Casual labour in non-agriculture | | | | 14.13** |
| | | | | (5.555) |
| Others | | | | 17.56* |
| | | | | (9.526) |
| Urban | | | | |
| Self-employed | | | | 13.63*** |
| | | | | (5.160) |
| Regular wage earner | | | | 7.036 |
| | | | | (4.389) |
| Casual labour | | | | 6.636 |
| | | | | (5.077) |
| Others | | | | −0.229 |
| | | | | (8.374) |
| Constant | 10.81*** | 10.30*** | 9.238*** | 1.302 |
| | (0.116) | (0.117) | (2.075) | (3.951) |

Standard errors in parentheses
* $p < 0.10$, ** $p < 0.05$, *** $p < 0.01$
*Source* Calculation done by authors

a follower of Christianity as compared to being a follower of Hinduism seems to have a very significant positive impact on credit availability from informal sources in both periods. Similarly, being part of other than the considered religious group has a very significant positive effect on credit availability from both formal and informal sources in the considered period of the second half of both 2002 and 2012. Now let us move on to consider the impact of having a literate head on credit availability, and we observe that having a literate head has a very significant positive effect on credit availability from both formal and informal sources in both periods. Similarly, when we look at the impact of highest education attained by an adult in a household with households having no literate adults as the base, we observe that having at least an adult with an education level higher than high school level has a very significant positive impact on credit availability from both formal and informal sources in the considered periods. Whereas having at least an adult who is literate but does not have an education level higher than high school level has a very significant impact

**Table 7.6** Random effects for 59th (2002) and 70th round (2012)

| Variance | M1 | | M2 | | M3 | | M4 | |
|---|---|---|---|---|---|---|---|---|
| | Estimate | Std. Error | Estimate | Std. Error | Estimate | Std. Error | Estimate | Std. Error |
| Informal (2002) | | | | | | | | |
| State | 0.28360 | 0.09693 | 0.23651 | 0.07992 | 0.19370 | 0.06771 | 0.13731 | 0.04884 |
| Region | 0.10161 | 0.02526 | 0.07742 | 0.01936 | 0.04594 | 0.01284 | 0.04564 | 0.01263 |
| Household | 1.49540 | 0.01903 | 1.29245 | 0.01645 | 1.29256 | 0.01645 | 1.29248 | 0.01645 |
| formal (2002) | | | | | | | | |
| State | 0.17328 | 0.07931 | 0.09026 | 0.04612 | 0.00193 | 0.01201 | 0.01511 | 0.01184 |
| Region | 0.14825 | 0.03785 | 0.08504 | 0.02501 | 0.06146 | 0.02006 | 0.03098 | 0.01326 |
| Household | 1.76592 | 0.02942 | 1.37506 | 0.02292 | 1.37549 | 0.02293 | 1.37621 | 0.02297 |
| Informal (2012) | | | | | | | | |
| State | 0.15837 | 0.05388 | 0.13048 | 0.04437 | 0.09758 | 0.04088 | 0.03269 | 0.01434 |
| Region | 0.07508 | 0.01665 | 0.06310 | 0.01405 | 0.04809 | 0.01209 | 0.04147 | 0.00977 |
| Household | 1.54936 | 0.01889 | 1.39302 | 0.01699 | 1.39284 | 0.01698 | 1.39287 | 0.01699 |
| Formal (2012) | | | | | | | | |
| State | 0.29684 | 0.10252 | 0.17346 | 0.06097 | 0.08896 | 0.03531 | 0.03805 | 0.01559 |
| Region | 0.11201 | 0.02446 | 0.07693 | 0.01699 | 0.04858 | 0.01172 | 0.04334 | 0.01000 |
| Household | 1.58674 | 0.02056 | 1.28299 | 0.01662 | 1.28279 | 0.01661 | 1.28280 | 0.01662 |

*Source* Calculation done by authors

on informal credit availability in both periods. Now we move to look at the impact of household composition on credit availability with adults share in a household as the base, and we observe that having a higher share of children compared to adults has a very significant impact on credit from both formal and informal sources in both periods. Whereas having a higher share of the elderly has a negative impact only on informal credit in both periods. We finally look at the impact of the household's main occupation denoted by Household Type variable with self-employed in non-agriculture in the rural area as a base. We observe that households having agricultural labour, other labour in rural and casual labour in urban areas as the main occupation has a negative impact on credit availability from both informal and formal sources in both the periods. Whereas, being self-employed in urban areas has a very significant positive impact on credit availability from both formal and informal sources. When we look at the impact of having self-employed in agriculture as the main occupation, we observe that it has a significant negative impact on credit availability from formal sources, whereas it has a significant positive influence on credit availability from informal sources in the second half of 2002. Finally, when we look at the impact of

**Table 7.7** Contribution of observed variables on the variance at each level for both the rounds

| | | 2002 (informal) (%) | 2002 (formal) (%) | 2012 (informal) (%) | 2012 (formal) (%) |
|---|---|---|---|---|---|
| $\rho_s$ | State Level | 15.08 | 8.30 | 8.88 | 14.87 |
| $\Delta\sigma_u HH$ | Household variables | 16.60 | 47.91 | 17.61 | 41.56 |
| $\Delta\sigma_u R$ | Regional variables | 15.09 | 50.97 | 20.78 | 28.47 |
| $\Delta\sigma_u S$ | State level variables | 19.88 | −7.61 | 40.97 | 17.15 |
| $\rho R$ | Regional level | 5.40 | 7.10 | 4.21 | 5.61 |
| $\Delta\sigma_v HH$ | Household variables | 23.80 | 42.63 | 15.97 | 31.32 |
| $\Delta\sigma_v R$ | Regional variables | 30.99 | 15.91 | 19.99 | 25.31 |
| $\rho_{HH}$ | Household level | 79.52 | 84.60 | 86.91 | 79.51 |
| $\Delta\sigma_\varepsilon HH$ | Household variables | 13.57 | 22.13 | 10.09 | 19.14 |

*Source* Calculation done by authors

having regular wage earners in urban areas as the primary occupation in urban areas, we observe that it has a significant positive impact on credit availability from formal sources in both considered periods.

#### 7.3.2.2 Contribution of Household Characteristics

We now look into how the addition of household characteristics to the model affects the variance at the regional and state level. From Table 7.7, we observe that variance component at state and regional level decreases with the incorporation of household characteristics for credit from both formal and informal sources. We observe that the decrease in variance component for formal credit is much higher than informal credit at both the regional and state levels. This shows that the considered household characteristics explain much more variance in the formal credit than the informal one. At the state level, we notice that decrease in the variance of formal credit is around 47.9% and 41.6% for 2nd half of 2002 and 2012, respectively, which is more than double of decrease in the variance of informal credit, which stood at 16.6% and 17.6% in 2nd half of 2002 and 2012. When we look at the regional level, we notice that on comparing the same type of credit across the considered period, the decrease in variance after controlling for household characteristics was much higher in the second half of 2002 as compared to the second half of 2012. Considered household characteristics explain 23.8% and 16% of the variance in informal credit in the second half of 2002 and 2012, respectively. Whereas it explains 42.6% and 31.3% of the variance in the formal credit in the second half of 2002 and 2012, respectively.

### 7.3.3 *M3 & M4: Regional and State Characteristics*

Now we include some regional level and state-level variables in the model. We chose the proportion of households with the considered household type and max education of an adult at the regional and state level as our regional and state-level variables. We observe that the composition of max education of adults in households at regional and state levels does not have a very significant impact on formal credit in both periods. Whereas having a higher share of households with at least an adult with some schooling below high school level has a significant negative impact at informal credit as compared to a higher share of households with no literate adult at the regional level in the second half of 2002 and 2012. Similarly, at state level higher share of households with at least an adult having education higher than high school level has a significant positive impact on only formal credit availability as compared to a higher share of households with no literate adult in the second half of 2012. Now we look at the impact of the share of households with different household types in urban and rural with the share of households self-employed in non-agriculture as the base at regional and state levels for both periods. We observe that at the regional level, except for the share of regular wage earners in rural areas on formal credit, the share of no other household occupation has a significant impact on credit availability from both sources in the second half of 2012. Whereas for the second half of 2002, we see that a higher share of other occupations in rural areas and self-employed in urban areas have a significant positive impact on both informal and formal credit availability. When we look at the state level, we observe that for the second half of 2002, the share of occupational groups has a significant impact on credit availability from both sources. Whereas in the second half of 2012, the higher share of households having household type self-employed in agriculture, regular wage earner, agricultural labour and non-agricultural labour in rural areas and self-employed in urban areas have a significant positive impact on both formal and informal credit availability.

#### 7.3.3.1 Contribution of Regional and State Characteristics

Table 7.6 shows that the inclusion of regional level characters decreases the variance of formal and informal credit availability at regional and state levels for both periods. Whereas the inclusion of state-level variables decreases the variance of informal credit in both periods. It also decreases the variance of formal credit in the second half of 2012. Table 7.7 shows that after controlling for household characteristics, the inclusion of regional level variables causes a decrease in the variance of informal credit at the regional level by around 31 and 20% in the second half of 2002 and 2012, respectively. Whereas it decreases the variance of formal credit at the regional level by around 15.9 and 25.3% in the second half of 2002 and 2012, respectively. At state level inclusion of regional level, variable causes a decrease in the variance of informal credit at the regional level by around 15.1 and 20.8% in the second half of 2002 and 2012, respectively. Whereas in the case of formal credit decrease in the variance is 51 and 28.5% for the second half of 2002 and 2012, respectively.

## 7.4 Conclusion

We decomposed credit availability from formal and informal sources during the second half of 2002 and 2012 in Indian at three nested levels: household, region and state levels. We observed that around 79–87% of the variance in credit availability from informal sources stems from the variance between households, around 4–6% stems from variance at the regional level and the rest 8–16% comes from variance in the state level. While for credit availability from formal sources, 79–87% stem from the variance between households, 5–8% from the regional level and 8–15% from the state level. We then observed the role of various household characteristics in determining the credit availability from both formal and informal sources and explaining their variance at the regional and state level. We first observed that having a female head of household had a significant negative impact on credit availability from formal sources while having no significant impact on credit availability from informal sources in both considered periods. We then looked at the impact of being part of social groups on credit availability with other social groups as the base and observed that being part of the ST and SC group had a significant negative impact on credit availability from both informal and formal sources in the second half of 2002 and 2012. Whereas being part of the OBC group had a significant negative effect on formal credit in both periods while having no significant impact on informal credit. This shows that historically marginalized social groups have less access to credit than other social groups. Although the government of India has implemented policies for the economic and social progress of the marginalized group but as Mishra and Bhardwaj (2020) note, these policies do not provide equal opportunities to all households belonging to the disadvantaged group. Only a section of the marginalized community has access to it. So there is a need for a more equitable economic policy for the disadvantaged group. Similarly, we look at the impact of being part of a religious group on credit availability with followers of Hinduism as the base and observe that being a follower of Islam has a significant negative effect on formal credit in the second half of 2012 and informal credit in the second half of 2002, whereas being a follower of Christianity had a significant positive impact on only informal credit in both periods. When we looked at the impact of education by observing the impact of literate head and max education of any adult in the household with households having no literate as the base, we observed that having a literate adult had a significant positive impact on both informal and formal credit in both periods. In the case of the impact of max education of adults in the household, we observed that having an adult with education higher than high school level had a significant positive impact on credit from both formal and informal sources in the second half of 2002 and 2012. When we looked at the contribution of considered household variables in explaining the variance, we observe that at the state level in the variance of formal credit is around 47.9 and 41.6% for 2nd half of 2002 and 2012, respectively, which is more than double of decrease in the variance of informal credit, which stood at 16.6 and 17.6% in the second half of 2002 and 2012. While at the regional level, considered household variables explained 23.8 and 16% of the variance in informal credit in the second half of 2002 and 2012, respectively. In the case of formal credit explained 42.6 and 31.3% of the variance in the second half of 2002 and 2012, respectively. After controlling for household characteristics, the inclusion of considered regional level variables causes a decrease in the variance of informal credit at the regional level by around 31 and 20% in the second half of 2002 and 2012, respectively, whereas it decreases the variance of formal credit at the regional level by around 15.9 and 25.3% in the second half of 2002 and 2012, respectively. At state level inclusion of regional level, variable causes a decrease in the variance of informal credit at the regional level by around 15.1 and 20.8% in the second half of 2002 and 2012, respectively. Whereas in the case of formal credit decrease in the variance is 51 and 28.5% for the second half of 2002 and 2012, respectively. Finally, by including state-level variables, we observe a decrease in state-level variance for informal credit in both periods while only decreases variance in the formal credit in the second half of 2002.

## References


Allen, F., Bartilorob, L., Guc, X., & Kowalewski, O. (2018). Does economic structure determine financial structure? *Journal of International Economics, 114,* 389–409.

Bae, K., Han, D., & Sohn, H. (2012). Importance of access to finance in reducing income inequality and poverty level. *International Review of Public Administration, 17*(1), 55–77.

Biyase, M., & Fisher, B. (2017). Determinants of access to formal credit by the poor households. *Studia Universitatis Babes-Bolyai Oeconomica, 62*(1). Retrieved from https://content.sciendo.com/view/journals/subboec/62/1/article-p50.xml.

Bouman, F. J. A. (1989). *Small, short and unsecured: informal rural finance in India.* New Delhi and New York: Oxford University Press.

Clarke, G. R. G., Xu, L. C., & Zou, H. (2006). Finance and income inequality: What do the data tell us? *Southern Economic Journal, 72,* 578–596.

Demirgüç-Kunt, A., Beck, T., & Honohan, P. (2008). *Finance for all? Policies and pitfalls in expanding access.* Washington, DC: World Bank.

Duy, V. Q., D'Haese, M., Lemba, J., & D'Haese, L. (2012). Determinants of household access to formal credit in the rural areas of the mekong delta, Vietnam. *African and Asian Studies, 11*(3), 261–268.

Field, E., & Torero, M. (2006). Do property titles increase credit access among the urban poor? Evidence from a nationwide titling program. *Working paper, Department of Economics, Harvard University, Cambridge, MA.*

Ghosh, S., & Vinod, D. (2017). What constrains financial inclusion for women? Evidence from Indian micro data. *World Development, 92,* 60–81. https://doi.org/10.1016/j.worlddev.2016.11.011

Giné, X. (2011). Access to capital in rural Thailand: An estimated model of formal versus informal credit. *Journal of Development Economics, 96*(1), 16–29.

Goedecke, J., Guérin, I., D'Espallier, B., & Venkatasubramanian, G. (2018). Why do financial inclusion policies fail in mobilizing savings from the poor? Lessons from rural south India. *Development Policy Review, 36,* O201–O219.

Gräb, J., & Grimm, M. (2011). Inequality in Burkina Faso-to what extent do household, community and regional factors matter?: Inequality in burkina faso. *Journal of the Royal Statistical Society: Series A (Statistics in Society), 174*(3), 759–784. https://doi.org/10.1111/j.1467-985X.2010.00686.x

Guérin, I., D'Espallier, B., & Venkatasubramanian, G. (2013). Debt in rural South India: Fragmentation, social regulation and discrimination. *The Journal of Development Studies, 49*(9), 1155–1171. https://doi.org/10.1080/00220388.2012.720365.

Harriss-White B, Colatei D. (2004). Rural credit and the collateral question. In B. Harriss-White & S. Janakarajan (Eds.), *Rural India facing the 21st century: Essays on long term change and recent development policy* (pp. 252–283). London: Anthem South Asian Studies.

Honohan, P. (2004). Financial sector policy and the poor: Selected findings and issues. *Policy Research Working Paper 43.* Washington, D.C.: World Bank.

Kochar, A. (1997). Does lack of access to formal credit constrain agricultural production? Evidence from the land tenancy market in rural India. *American Journal of Agricultural Economics, 79*(3), 754–763.

Mishra, A. K., & Bhardwaj, V. (2020). Wealth distribution and accounting for changes in wealth inequality: Empirical evidence from India, 1991–2012. *Econ Change Restruct.* https://doi.org/10.1007/s10644-020-09290-9

Pal, D., & Laha, A. K. (2014). Credit off-take from formal financial institutions in rural India: Quantile regression results. *Agricultural and Food Economics, 2*(1), 9.

Swaminathan, M. (2012). Who has access to formal credit in rural India? Evidence from four villages. *Review of Agrarian Studies, 2*(1).

Umoh, G. S. (2006). Empirical investigation of access to micro-credit in an emerging economy. *Journal of African Business, 7*(1–2), 89–117.

World Bank. (2018). *The little data book on financial inclusion 2018.* Washington, DC: World Bank. Retrieved from https://data.worldbank.org/products/data-books/little-data-book-on-financial-inclusion.

Xi, G., McDowell, I., Nair, R., & Spasoff, R. (2005). Income inequality and health in ontario. *Canadian Journal of Public Health, 96*(3), 206–211. https://doi.org/10.1007/BF03403692

# Chapter 8
# Review of Corporate Governance in Emerging Economies from the Perspective of Principal–Principal Conflict

**Sumit Saurav**

**Abstract** The focus of the paper is on Principal–Principal (PP) conflicts which differ significantly from traditional Principal–Agent (PA) conflicts that dominate the corporate governance discourse in developed economies. In emerging economies, PP conflicts are the dominant form of governance conflicts. PP conflict is a term used to characterize the conflicts between controlling shareholders and minority shareholders. The genesis of this type of conflict is the weak institutional structure prevalent in the emerging economies that results in concentrated ownership in the form of family control and business group structure. Since PP conflicts are the result of completely different corporate dynamics, it requires remedies that differ considerably from the remedies of PA conflicts. This paper reviews the extant literature on PP conflicts with the aim to decipher its characteristics, institutional antecedents, and organizational consequences.

**Keywords** Agency cost · Principal–principal conflict · Emerging economies

## 8.1 Introduction

Corporate Governance in the last few decades has evolved from a topic of interest to none other than few scholars and shareholders to a topic regularly discussed in the boardrooms, policy-making circles, and popular press across the globe. The topic comes under the spotlight every now and then when some corporate scandal happens because of the lack of corporate governance and threaten the stability of the economic and financial systems. Very recently it was under the spotlight when the failure of corporate governance in financial institutions and corporations was cited as one of the reasons behind the 2008 financial crisis (Claessens and Yurtoglu 2013). Poor corporate governance manifests itself in the form of corporate scandals, which in turn engender situations that have the potential to endanger the stability of

S. Saurav (✉)
IIM-Ahmedabad, Vastrapur, Ahmedabad, Gujarat, India
e-mail: phd19sumits@iima.ac.in



A. K. Mishra et al. (eds.), *The Financial Landscape of Emerging Economies*, Accounting, Finance, Sustainability, Governance & Fraud: Theory and Application,
https://doi.org/10.1007/978-3-030-60008-2_8

economic and financial systems. The reason why poor corporate governance can lead to instability of the whole financial system is the way modern economic and financial systems are structured. In a free market-based investment process, good corporate governance forms its bedrock and any problem associated with it can be a threat to the stability of the whole process. Thus, good corporate governance is an important cog in the economic and financial machinery that ensures its proper functioning.

After establishing the importance of corporate governance let's see how it is defined. There are a wide variety of definitions proposed for corporate governance, I am quoting one proposed by Shleifer and Vishny in their 1997 review: "Corporate Governance deals with the ways in which suppliers of finance to corporations assure themselves of getting a return on their investment (Shleifer 1997)". In a more suave way, the same definition can be restated to define corporate governance as a field with the concern to reconcile collective action issues among the dispersed shareholders and resolve the conflict of interest among various corporate claim holders (Claessens and Yurtoglu 2013). The overall nature of the corporate governance challenges varies from country to country, and its form in a particular country is determined by the prevailing institutional environment, the ownership structure of firms in the country, and overall development level (Shleifer 1997). In the past, fair amount of research has been done to understand the factors that determine the nature of corporate governance challenges faced by different types of countries. As a result, over the period of time researchers increasingly realized that no single agency model is capable of explaining the corporate governance-related challenges of all the nations (Young et al. 2008).

In advance countries where the ownership is more dispersed, institutions are strong enough to protect the owner's right, and ownership and control of firms are often separated, the corporate governance challenge that takes the central stage is Principal–Agent (PA) conflict (Jensen and Meckling 1976). However, in emerging economies, institutions are not strong and therefore can't provide adequate protection to owners or the cost of seeking protection is high (North 1991). This idiosyncratic nature of emerging economies (for this paper they are the subject of interest) results in the more concentrated ownership structure of firms because it lowers the agency cost. The weak governance structure and limited protection to minority shareholders create a unique agency problem of expropriation of the firm's resources by controlling shareholders at the expense of minority shareholders (Dharwadkar et al. 2000). This perspective of corporate governance is known as Principal–Principal (PP) model, and it focuses specifically on the conflict between the controlling and minority shareholder of the firm.

Now that we know the dominant corporate governance challenge in emerging economies is PP conflict. It becomes easy to identify its characteristics like fewer publicly traded firms in the market, lower firm valuation, lower dividend payout, a weaker form of efficiency of the financial market, less investment in innovative ideas, concentrated ownership, etc. (Young et al. 2008). The research work of last decade in the field of corporate governance has convinced researchers in the field of finance and economics that the traditional PA model proposed by Jensen and Meckling (1976) doesn't explain the PP model of conflicts that dominates the emerging economies. This realization has invigorated the interest of many researchers from a variety of fields like strategy, psychology, economics, and finance to start exploring the topic of PP conflict. The convergence of various disciplines in the exploration of this topic has developed a rich literature pertaining to it. The endeavor of this paper is to review this rich literature with the focus to understand the nature, antecedents, consequences of PP conflict in the context of emerging economies.

The paper is structured as follows. In the next section, we have discussed the aspects in which governance issues in emerging economies differ from the developed world. The section next to it explains the characteristics of Principal–Principal conflict and on what parameters it differs from Principal–Agent conflict. In the next two sections, institutional antecedents of PP conflicts and its organizational implications are discussed, respectively. The last section is the concluding section.

## 8.2 Corporate Governance in Emerging Economies

In this section, we will discuss the corporate governance-related aspects in which emerging economies differ from the developed economies and try to decipher how these differences lead to the genesis of Principal–Principal (PP) conflict, which is fundamentally different then Principal–Agent (PA) conflict.

Emerging economies differ from developed economies in various aspects that are relevant to corporate governance. Let's first discuss the difference in economic and financial conditions. Emerging economies are "low per capita income, high growth rate countries that rely on economic liberalization as a primary source of growth". However, they still differ substantially from developed countries in terms of liberalization and openness of the economy (Filatotchev et al. 2003). This difference has huge repercussion on the mechanism of corporate governance that persists in the emerging economy. Internationalization and globalization of trade and finance that are complementing parts of liberalization provide substantial impetus to the corporate governance improvement. The absence or weak integration of emerging economies with the world's trade and financial system results in the absence of this very effective factor that has a positive impact on corporate governance from the economy (Claessens and Yurtoglu 2013).

One very crucial aspect of corporate governance is the state and origin of institutions of the country. The institutions that are relevant here are legal enforcement agencies, financial market watchdogs, the central bank, stock exchanges, etc. On parameters like legal origin, legal rights strength, creditor's rights, legal protection to minority shareholders, the efficiency of debt contract enforcement, anti-corruption, and disclosure requirements the performance of these institutions is much poorer in emerging markets vis-a-vis developed economies. The relatively unstable institutions of emerging economies adversely affect the corporate governance standard of the firms in the economy, because they fail to perform their intended job. Due to this, the standard corporate governance mechanisms find very little support from the institutions in emerging countries (Peng et al. 2005). Therefore, even the publicly traded firms that have an independent board of directors, professional management, and shareholders (which forms the troika of modern corporate governance mechanism) rarely function like their developed country counterparts.

Due to the failure of the corporate governance mechanisms that are prevalent in the developed countries in emerging economies, concentrated ownership and other informal mechanisms emerge to fill the vacuum. However, these mechanisms do solve some of the corporate governance issues but in the process also engender novel corporate governance challenges. And the dominant among those are Principal–Principal (PP) conflict the nitty–gritty of which we will discuss in the next section.

## 8.3 Characteristics of Principal–Principal Conflicts

In developed economies where dominant agency problem is the conflict between dispersed shareholders and Professional Management (PA), several corporate governance mechanisms work to align the interest of shareholders and managers. These mechanisms include internal mechanisms like the board of governors, concentrated ownership, carefully designed executive package, and external mechanisms such as product market competition, the factor market competition, and the threat of takeover (Fama and Jensen 1983). The effectiveness of a bundle of governance mechanism depends on the synergy between them and overall effectiveness depends on the particular combination. While research has shown that the efficient design of the governance bundle depends on the size of the firm or the industry in which it operates, it is argued that the efficiency varies systematically with the institutional structure at the country level (Young et al. 2008). In other words, it is highly likely that the effectiveness of firm-level external or internal corporate governance mechanism can vary depending on the institutional structure at the country level. Therefore, the institutional structure of emerging economies calls for a different bundle of governance mechanisms. Since the conflicts often happen between two categories of principals—controlling shareholders and minority shareholders. The diagram below shows the difference between the PP conflict and the PA conflict.

The top portion of the diagram shows a typical PA conflict, where conflict exists between the management of the firm and dispersed shareholders. The bottom portion of the diagram shows the typical PP conflict, where the dashed arrow shows the relation between the controlling shareholders and managers affiliated with them. These managers can be direct family members or associates of controlling shareholders. The solid arrow shows the conflict between the affiliated managers (who report to the controlling shareholders) and minority shareholders. Thus, the conflict is actually between the controlling shareholders at the one side and minority or dispersed shareholders at the other. This new dynamic has a huge impact on the effectiveness of the internal mechanisms of corporate governance. For example, due to a larger share in the firm the controlling shareholder can take a call about the appointment of the board of directors unilaterally. Thus, packing the board with his cronies and effectively making the board a rubber stamp (Young et al. 2008). Similarly, for other internal mechanisms, it can be logically shown that the controlling shareholder with

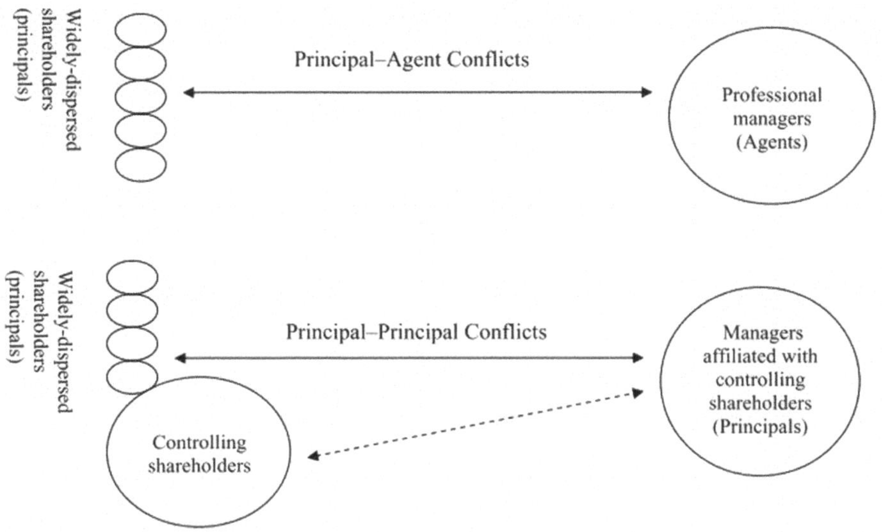


**Fig. 8.1** Principal–Principal conflicts versus Principal–Agent conflicts (Young et al. 2008)

his action can effectively nullify their impact on governance. So, concentrated ownership which is promoted as a solution for Principal–Agent problem is the root cause of Principal–Principal conflict (Faccio et al. 2001) (Fig. 8.1).

Similar to PA conflict, PP conflict also results in the expropriation of the value. Although in PP conflict the expropriator is controlling shareholders not managers and value is expropriated from minority shareholders. Expropriation can take many forms, "(1) installing inept family members, cronies or friends at important positions, (2) Purchasing supplies or raw materials at higher price from companies associated with controlling shareholders, or selling products, services or even assets at below market price to firms associated with controlling shareholder. (3) engaging in strategies that advance personal, family, or political agendas at the expense of firm performance such as excessive diversification" (Young et al. 2008). It clear from the above discussion that most of the differences between the PA and PP conflicts exist because of the differences in the institutional environment in developed and developing countries. All these factors make the PP conflict idiosyncratic in its own right.

## 8.4 Institutional Antecedents of PP Conflicts

Our discussion in the previous section helped us to understand the reasons behind the occurrence of the Principal–Principal (PP) conflicts, and dominant among them is the prevailing institutional environment in the emerging economies. The institutional condition makes the enforcement and monitoring of arm's length contract costly. In

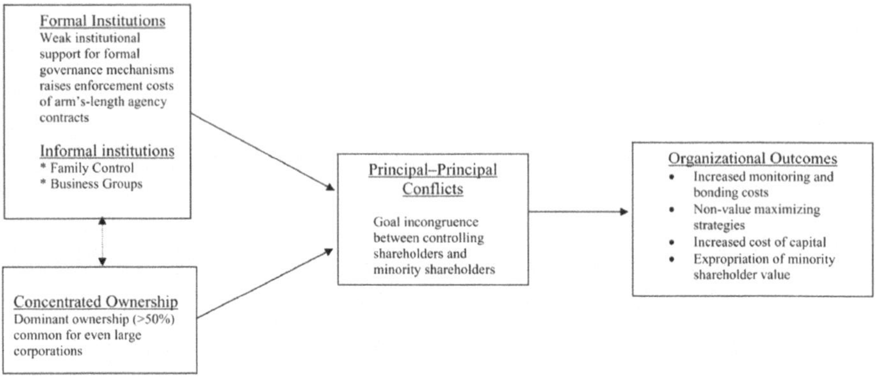


**Fig. 8.2** Principal–Principal conflicts antecedents and consequences in emerging economies (Young et al. 2008)

this scenario, the only viable governance mechanism is concentrated ownership, although it solves many issues but raises many others and PP conflict is one among them.

The controlling shareholders are mainly associated with either a family or a business group and have the means and motive to expropriate firm's value. Figure 8.2 shown demonstrates the antecedents and consequences (which we will discuss in the next section) of PP conflict. In the rest part of this section, we will discuss family owners and business groups.

### 8.4.1 Family Ownership

In emerging economies, one of the most dominant types of controlling ownership is "Family Ownership" (La Porta et al. 1999). Family control over a firm has both positive and negative impact on the performance of the firm. In the next paragraph, we will discuss the positive impact and then negative.

In their seminal paper, Jensen and Fama argued that family control over the firm reduces the agency cost by aligning the ownership with control (Fama and Jensen 1983). In the same vein, many researchers have found that "family control" helps in improving the performance of the firm through goal congruence (Habbershon and Williams 1999) of control and ownership, and through reducing the monitoring cost (Lubatkin et al. 2005). Similarly, there are studies that found family-controlled US "Fortune 500" firms do better than their counterparts (Anderson and Reeb 2003).

At the same time, family ownership has a negative impact also on the performance of the firms, as it may increase the possibility of expropriation of resources from the minority shareholders by the controlling family. The expropriation or firm's value destruction can happen because of the reasons like appoint of the unqualified family members on the key positions of the firm (Claessens and Yurtoglu 2013), decisions by the firm's management that favor the controlling family, sibling rivalry, generational envy, and "irrational" strategic decisions like excessive diversification (Gomez-Mejia et al. 2001). Some of the researchers have argued that PP conflicts in the family-based firms are difficult to solve because the relationship in the firm is not purely contractual in nature but is based on emotion, trust, sentiment, and other informal linkages (Young et al. 2008).

Now, the question arises under what conditions the family ownership will result in a net benefit for the firm and under what conditions it does not. Many researchers have concluded, based on their analysis, that when the external environment is characterized by the low level of munificence and complexity the family-controlled firms thrive and grow, but when the external environment is more complex and volatile they don't (Gedajlovic et al. 2004). This happens because under more complex and volatile environment firms require more formal and systematic control, so under such conditions, family-controlled businesses underperform. The firm's stage of development also determines the net impact of family control because as the firms become mature monitoring and ownership structure becomes much important (Zahra and Filatotchev 2004). In the next section, we will discuss business groups.

### *8.4.2 Business Groups*

Another corporate ownership trend that is quite ubiquitous in emerging economies is business groups. Yiu et al. in their paper have defined business groups as "a collection of legally independent firms connected by economic (such finance, ownership, or commercial) and social ties (such as family, kinship or friends)" (Yiu et al. 2005). In emerging economies, state-owned public sector firms also fall under this category, because legally they are independent but are connected by a common owner, the state. So, there are differences between family-owned, and state-owned family business groups, each has a different set of actors, agency cost, and strategy. Informal ties that characterize the business groups are—cross-holdings, coordinated actions, and board interlocks (Dieleman and Sachs 2006).

In emerging economies, same as family ownership, business groups too are the result of a weak institutional environment in factor markets and capital markets. In this scenario, business groups may provide a competitive advantage to the member firms (Young et al. 2008). While there are benefits of having business groups, they can be disadvantageous from the point of view of corporate governance. Some of the common governance issues that plague business groups are as follows:

- If the business group is loosely affiliated it becomes difficult for the minority shareholder to identify where actual control resides.
- It provides the opportunity for collusion or unethical transaction between the firms (that favors the business group not the minority shareholders of the individual firms) of the group by making it hard for the minority shareholders of the individual firms to identify them (Hoskisson et al. 2000).

- In the case when in a member firm the controlling owner has higher control rights than the cash flow rights, it has the incentive to tunnel resources from that firm to the firm where he has higher cash flow rights—a practice known as "pyramiding" (Bertrand et al. 2002). One example of how a typical pyramid works is as follows: Suppose there are three firms X, Y, and Z. A business group holds 50% shares of company X, i.e., has 50% cash flow right. Now, firm X holds 40% shares of firm Y and firm Y holds a 30% share of firm Z. The business group will end up having 6% cash flow rights in firm Z but 30% control rights. It happened because of cross-holding. This creates a situation of moral hazard, where the financial benefit of expropriation of resources from the firm Z far out weights the financial cost for the business group. Thus, providing an incentive to expropriate resources from firm Z to firm X where business group has higher cash flow rights.

In short, business group affiliation provides opportunities for controlling shareholders to expropriate resources from minority shareholders of the member firms, thus causing PP conflict. The next section will discuss the consequences of PP conflict.

## 8.5 Organizational Consequences

The Principal–Principal conflicts have a multi-level impact. At the highest level, i.e., country level, it impacts the efficiency of financial markets, scuttles the growth of firms, and lowers the standards of living (Morck et al. 2005). At the intermediate level, it results in a large number of nominally independent firms in the economy organized in an informal way and controlled by business groups. And at the lowest level, i.e., "firm-level", it results in the adoption of strategy by firms that is sub-optimal for them and expropriation of resources form minority shareholders (Claessens and Yurtoglu 2013). In this section, we will focus on the firm-level impact of Principal–Principal conflicts. These impacts are mainly two-fold—Agency cost (it encompasses monitoring costs, bonding costs) and the impact of organizational strategy and competitiveness. We will discuss both in the same sequence.

### *8.5.1 Agency Cost of Principal–Principal Conflict*

In their seminal paper, Jensen and Meckling defined agency cost as the sum of monitoring cost, bonding cost, and residual loss (Jensen and Meckling 1976). The same framework is used here to analyze the agency cost incurred due to PP conflict.

We will start our discussion with the nature of monitoring cost under PP conflict. In emerging countries, under PP conflict monitoring cost is higher than the traditional PA conflict. The following are the reasons to believe this.

- The weaker institutional environment prevalent in the emerging economies makes the monitoring of arm's length contract expensive (North 1991).
- Because top management of firms has informal relations with the controlling shareholder (and in some cases both are same). It becomes easy for them to evade traditional governance mechanisms like the board of directors (Dharwadkar et al. 2000).
- It impairs the monitoring power of the capital market because concentrated ownership decreases the liquidity of the firm's stock and in turn information contained in share price (Holmstrom and Tirole 1993).

The second part of agency cost is bonding cost. In PP conflict, it is incurred by controlling shareholders to attract the minority shareholders. It is incurred in the form of bonding cost as an implicit or explicit guarantee against expropriation. The type of bonding that can happen between the controlling and minority shareholders are as follows:

- Over the period of time, the controlling shareholders sometimes develop the reputation of treating the minority shareholders well. It does so because if it expropriates a large amount of minority shareholders' resources then the market would discount the value of remaining shares, causing a loss of wealth to controlling shareholders (Gomes 2000). However, this type of bonding is implicit in nature and there is always a suspicion that in the bad times controlling shareholders may renege its commitment.
- Sometimes reputation is not enough to attract the minority shareholders. In that case many firms issue instruments like American Depository Receipts (ADRs) to signal to the market that they will expropriate the minority shareholder's wealth. Because these listings are time-consuming and costly, at the same time it invites the scrutiny of the US SEC thus removing the information asymmetry (Young et al. 2008).

### *8.5.2 Impact on Strategy and Competitiveness of Firms*

Principal–Principal (PP) conflicts also affect the performance and competitiveness of the firms. The example of actions that can affect the performance of the firm are (1) appointing less qualified family members, or cronies at the key positions and neglecting the qualified candidate. (2) Purchasing material at above market price from suppliers associated with the controlling shareholder or selling goods and services to firms (associated with controlling shareholders) at below market price. (3) Excessive diversification, and (4) low expenditure on innovation. These actions are relatively easy for controlling shareholder to take in the emerging market setting where institutions are weak.

PP conflicts also affect the competitiveness of the firm because firms having PP conflict has a higher cost of capital. They have to provide a higher dividend to attract minority shareholders which in turn leaves them with less money available for investing.

## 8.6 Conclusion

Based on the research done on corporate governance, researchers realized that the traditional model of PA conflicts does not explain the governance issues in the emerging economies. In emerging economies, it is costly to monitor and enforce arm's-length agency contracts and it impairs the effectiveness of traditional mechanisms of governance (both external mechanism and internal mechanisms). The reduced effectiveness of most of the traditional mechanisms (in emerging economies) leads to concentrated ownership structure of the firms. It helps in addressing many of the governance conflicts but by doing so give rise to a new kind of conflict that is known as PP conflict which exists between controlling shareholders and minority shareholders. The dynamics of PP conflicts differ substantially from PA conflicts, and it impacts both agency cost and competitiveness of the firms. That is why resolving it requires a completely new approach because traditional approaches would not solve it and individual emerging countries have to devise solutions suited to their own institutional environment (Young et al. 2004).

## References

Anderson, R. C., & Reeb, D. M. (2003). Founding-family ownership and firm performance: Evidence from the S&P 500. *The Journal of Finance, 58*(3), 1301–1328.

Bertrand, M., Mehta, P., & Mullainathan, S. (2002). Ferreting out tunneling: An application to Indian business groups. *The Quarterly Journal of Economics, 117*(1), 121–148.

Claessens, S., & Yurtoglu, B. B. (2013). Corporate governance in emerging markets: A survey.

Dharwadkar, B., George, G., & Brandes, P. (2000). Privatization in emerging economies: An agency theory perspective. *Academy of Management Review, 25*(3), 650–669.

Dieleman, M., & Sachs, W. (2006). Oscillating between a relationship-based and a market-based model: The Salim group. *Asia Pacific Journal of Management, 23*(4), 521–536.

Faccio, M., Lang, L. H., & Young, L. (2001). Debt and corporate governance. In *Meetings of Association of Financial Economics in New Orleans.*

Fama, E. F., & Jensen, M. C. (1983). Separation of ownership and control. *The Journal of Law and Economics, 26*(2), 301–325.

Filatotchev, I., Wright, M., Uhlenbruck, K., Tihanyi, L., & Hoskisson, R. E. (2003). Governance, organizational capabilities, and restructuring in transition economies. *Journal of World Business, 38*(4), 331–347.

Gedajlovic, E., Lubatkin, M. H., & Schulze, W. S. (2004). Crossing the threshold from founder management to professional management: A governance perspective. *Journal of Management Studies, 41*(5), 899–912.

Gomes, A. (2000). Going public without governance: Managerial reputation effects. *The Journal of Finance, 55*(2), 615–646.

Gomez-Mejia, L. R., Nunez-Nickel, M., & Gutierrez, I. (2001). The role of family ties in agency contracts. *Academy of Management Journal, 44*(1), 81–95.
Habbershon, T. G., & Williams, M. L. (1999). A resource-based framework for assessing the strategic advantages of family firms. *Family Business Review, 12*(1), 1–25.
Holmstrom, B., & Tirole, J. (1993). Market liquidity and performance monitoring. *Journal of Political Economy, 101*(4), 678–709.
Hoskisson, R. E., Eden, L., Lau, C. M., & Wright, M. (2000). Strategy in emerging economies. *Academy of Management Journal, 43*(3), 249–267.
Jensen, M. C., & Meckling, W. H. (1976). Theory of the firm: Managerial behavior, agency costs and ownership structure. *Journal of Financial Economics, 3*(4), 305–360.
La Porta, R., Lopez-de Silanes, F., & Shleifer, A. (1999). Corporate ownership around the world. *The Journal of Finance, 54*(2), 471–517.
Lubatkin, M. H., Schulze, W. S., Ling, Y., & Dino, R. N. (2005). The effects of parental altruism on the governance of family-managed firms. *Journal of Organizational Behavior: The International Journal of Industrial, Occupational and Organizational Psychology and Behavior, 26*(3), 313–330.
Morck, R., Wolfenzon, D., & Yeung, B. (2005). Corporate governance, economic entrenchment, and growth. *Journal of Economic Literature, 43*(3), 655–720.
North, D. C. (1991). Institutions. *Journal of Economic Perspectives, 5*(1), 97–112.
Peng, M. W., Lee, S.-H., & Wang, D. Y. (2005). What determines the scope of the firm over time? A focus on institutional relatedness. *Academy of Management Review, 30*(3), 622–633.
Shleifer, V. (1997). A survey of corporate governance. *The Journal of Finance* (5), 450–459.
Yiu, D., Bruton, G. D., & Lu, Y. (2005). Understanding business group performance in an emerging economy: Acquiring resources and capabilities in order to prosper. *Journal of Management Studies, 42*(1), 183–206.
Young, M. N., Ahlstrom, D., & Bruton, G. D. (2004). The globalization of corporate governance in East Asia: The "transnational" solution. *Management and International Review,* 31–50. Springer.
Young, M. N., Peng, M. W., Ahlstrom, D., Bruton, G. D., Jiang, Y. (2008). Corporate governance in emerging economies: A review of the principal-principal perspective: Review paper. *Journal of Management Studies, 45*(1), 196–220.
Zahra, S. A., & Filatotchev, I. (2004). Governance of the entrepreneurial threshold firm: A knowledge-based perspective. *Journal of Management Studies, 41*(5), 885–897.

# Chapter 9
# Influence of Board Composition on Agency Cost and Its Governance Outcomes

**Riyanka Baral and Debasis Patnaik**

**Abstract** This paper explores the impact of board composition on agency costs of large and small commercial banks in India. Asset turnover ratio and leverage ratio are taken to measure agency costs. Board composition is measured under three categories, i.e., board structure, board independence, and board committee. Board size and employee representative on board were taken as a proxy of board structure. CEO duality and independent chairperson represent board independence. Audit committee meetings and board meetings per year have been taken as a proxy for the board committee. Multiple linear regression analysis was used to assess the relationship between the dependent and independent variables. The sample consists of 35 Indian commercial banks from the year 2008–2018. The finding of the study reveals that in large banks board structure, board independence, and board committee influence agency costs. While in the case of small banks, board structure and board committee impact agency cost.

**Keywords** Agency costs · Governance · Banks

## 9.1 Introduction

The control of a firm rests with shareholders. They always intend to have a better return from their investment. Shareholders elect the board of directors who in turn hires managers having managerial skills to manage the firms in an ethical way to bring out the profit. The board of directors act as the shareholders' monitoring tool within the firm. The stability of a firm depends majorly on the foresight of management in handling the limited resources wisely as there exist cutthroat competition in businesses. However, shareholders have an informational disadvantage because

R. Baral (✉) · D. Patnaik
Department of Economics, BITS Pilani, KK Birla Goa Campus, NH-17 B Bypass Road, Zuarinagar 403726, Goa, India
e-mail: riya.s14@gmail.com

D. Patnaik
e-mail: marikesh@goa.bits-pilani.ac.in



A. K. Mishra et al. (eds.), *The Financial Landscape of Emerging Economies*, Accounting, Finance, Sustainability, Governance & Fraud: Theory and Application,
https://doi.org/10.1007/978-3-030-60008-2_9

the managers not only have the required skills to work in that environment, but also they know things better than shareholders. They are in everyday contact with the activity of the firm. Thus, shareholders can rely only on the information provided by the managers. Shareholders also do not have immediate information about the manager. Mangers have short-term goals, whereas shareholder aims at long-term perspectives. This difference in goals among both leads to a clash thereby landing in agency problem. The agency problem arises due to the conflict between shareholders and managers. Agency cost emerges from an agency problem. The concept of agency cost was introduced by Jensen, citing that managers have more power on the resources of the firm. They tend to avoid providing information to shareholders. Instead, they reinvest for their profit thereby leading to agency cost (Jensen, 1986).

Under the contemporary corporate system, reducing agency cost is a major challenge that the internal governance structure is facing. Against this backdrop, the objective of this study is to examine the impact of the board composition of banks on agency costs it incurs. The data set comprises 35 banks in a balanced panel from 2008 to 2018. This paper throws insight into the theoretical and empirical aspects of agency cost using secondary data from the Reserve Bank of India and Bloomberg database. The paper is organized into five sections. The first section deals with the literature review on agency cost and board compositions. The second section deals with the theoretical framework. The third section outlines the research design. The fourth section deals with empirical results. The fifth section discusses the finding of the study and conclusion.

## 9.2 Literature Review

Studies have been conducted on factors affecting agency cost and its impact of corporate governance in developed countries like US, UK, Australia (Doukas, Kim, & Pantzalis, 2000; Ang, Cole, & Lin, 2000; Fleming, Heaney, & Mccosker, 2005; Florackis & Ozkan, 2008; Henry, 2010; Singh & Davidson, 2003). But in a developing country like India, very few studies have been conducted as the corporate governance mechanism is still at a nascent stage. The relationship between a principal and an agent is established through an explicit or implicit contract. The contract included the transfer of all decision-making powers to the agents. The overall cost incurred for structuring, implementation, and compliance of the contract shall be the agency cost. Therefore, agency costs include all contractual expenditures often referred to as transaction costs, cost of moral hazard, and cost of information. All banks may be similarly susceptible to agency costs, or differences can occur. Some banks will consistently have lower agency costs than others. This paper employs the asset turnover ratio and leverage ratio to measure agency costs (dependent variable).

### 9.2.1 Asset Turnover Ratio

ATR is one of the management efficiency ratios. ATR is considered in this study to show how good a firm is at generating revenue from its assets. Higher ATR is favorable for firms' showing that firms are utilizing their asset efficiently to create revenue. On the other hand, lower ATR shows firms need to relook into its business to maximize its efficiency. This variable is identical to the variable used by (Ang et al., 2000; Singh & Davidson, 2003; Mcknight & Weir, 2009). High ATR leads to low agency costs and vice versa.

### 9.2.2 Leverage Ratio

The leverage ratio was introduced by the Basel Committee on banking supervision (BCBS) in 2010. If the leverage ratio is more, it means the firm has taken many loans and is in debt. In India, the leverage ratio for domestic systematically important banks is 4% and 3.5% for other banks. The outcomes of a few studies reveal a negative relationship between LR and agency costs (Byrd, 2010; Davidson, Bouresli, & Singh, 2006). While the study by (Hirth & Uhrig-homburg, 2010) suggested that high LR leads to an increase in agency costs. This is because the debt holder is keen to participate and inevitably distorts investment policies adopted by the management.

The role of the board in disciplining the management of the firm is discussed extensively in the literature. The capacity of the board to execute the management role depends on a variety of board attributes such as board size, CEO duality, employee representative on board, independent chairperson, and board meeting per year.

### 9.2.3 CEO Duality

CEO duality is when the CEO also serves as the chairman of the board. Historically, this is the case in the United States of America where the same person is CEO and the chairman. However, many countries have moved toward separating these two roles. In this situation, the chairman of the board should be an independent director. The case of CEO duality does not arise in the case of a two-tier board structure. In the case of a two-tier board, the CEO is in charge of the management board and an independent director will be the head of the supervisory board. When there is a blend of both positions it will generate a conflict of interest (Mcgrath, 2009).The CEO will have the chance to take advantage of the profits at the expense of shareholder's value. According to agency theory, CEO duality increases the CEO's dominance over the board, leading to higher agency costs. Spilled in both roles will lead to low agency costs. On the other hand, as per resource dependency (Pfeffer, 2020) and stewardship theories (Donaldson & Davis, 1991), CEOs behave according to the interests of shareholders by making use of the bigger, more cohesive, and double leadership role. Studies conducted by (Dalton & Rechner, 1989; Pi & Timme, 1993) concluded that CEO duality has an inverse impact on a firm's performance.

### 9.2.4 Board Size

Board size is an important factor in influencing the agency costs. From the viewpoint of agency theory, it may be argued that in the case of large boards too many directors will be assessing the action of the management. They may be mismonitoring which can lead to higher agency costs (Kiel & Nicholson, 2003). The larger board creates agency costs and harms the performance of a firm (Yermack, 1996; Eisenberg, Sundgren, & Wells, 1998). Board size and composition affect the functioning of the board in terms of effectiveness and efficiency (Ii & Zahra, 1991; Zahra & Pearce, 1989). Large board sizes are less efficient in their asset turnover (Florackis & Ozkan, 2008). While some other studies reveal that the efficiency of smaller boards is better than larger boards as they have high values and there is less conflict which in turn lowers the agency costs (Shaw & College, 2007; Lipton & Lorsch, 1992; Sajid, Ahmad, Haris Khursheed Saita, & Muhammad Musarrat Nawaz, 2012; Majeed, Aziz, & Saleem, 2015).

### 9.2.5 Bank Size

Each firm is of different sizes. The size of the bank is determined by its total assets. Large banks enjoy the benefit of economies of scale. However, the board of large firms' sometimes are struck between lack of coordination and the conflict of management which produces high agency costs. Small firms are more agile than large firms, this has been revealed by some studies (Moeller & Schlingemann, 2005). On the other hand, few pieces of research showed small firms operate at high agency costs than large firms. Agency costs are considered to be a big barrier for these firms when they seek to get external funding (Guillen, 2000).

### 9.2.6 Bank Age

Bage age indicates how long the bank has maintained its identity and gained a more detailed understanding of the business that helps to position it in the market. Consequently, large banks are considered better than small banks. Agency costs can be influenced by a firm's age. When firms become efficient and mature with age they generate more revenue from its operation which increases the growth of the firm.

Due to the learning curve, as the age increases agency costs decreases (Moeller & Schlingemann, 2005; Arikan, 2016; Jensen, 1986).

### 9.2.7 Employee Representative on Board

There have been debates on employees being allocated control rights in the firm for which they work for effective corporate governance. In Europe, the employee representation on the corporate board is common, while in the US it is a recent development. The employee representative on board has the same responsibility as shareholder-elected board members. The employee representative serves as "the voice" for employees and hopefully protecting corporate culture, values, and better information transfer from board to the employees (Freeman & Lazear, 2014). The employee representative knows the atmosphere among employees, issues, brings detailed firm-specific knowledge to the boardroom, and try to avoid any friction between management and employees. If there is an employee representative on board, there is less agency problem which may lead to low agency costs. Few studies have predicted employees representation on board will pressure the management to pay higher wages or other benefits as they will get advantage from this at the detriment of shareholders which would increase the agency costs (Fauver & Fuerst, 2006; Acharya, Myers, & Rajan, 2011).

### 9.2.8 Independent Chairperson

The role of an independent chairperson shows that there is a bifurcation between the role of board and management. An independent director has the sole authority to supervise. Agency theory proposes for the separate role of independent chairperson. Studies reveal that due to the clash in both the leadership position agency costs becomes high (Palmon & Wald, 2002; Majeed et al., 2015).

### 9.2.9 Audit Committee Meeting

One of the effective mechanisms of corporate governance is the audit committee. The board establishes audit committees to focus on specific functions as they are answerable to the shareholders. Several authors (Pincus, Rusbarsky, & Jilnaught, 1989) argue that audit committees meeting can reduce agency costs as the flow of information from the shareholders and managers gets refined. During audit committee meetings, there is more reporting interaction with the internal auditors which also helps to lower agency costs. However, few studies concluded that the existence of an audit committee does not necessarily show that the committee is efficient in executing its oversight role (Defond, Hann, & Hu, 2005; Karamanou & Nikos, 2005; Krishnan, 2005; Vafeas, 2005).

### *9.2.10 Board Meeting Per Year*

There has been a consistent argument in literature as regards the purpose of board meetings. The board meeting is designed to bring together board members to explore and resolve critical concerns concerning their experience, current problems, and forward-looking concerns related to firms' sustainability. Every resolution adopted during this process is legal and is operational in the firm. The frequency of board meetings is determined by the number of meetings held by senior managers over one year. The exercise is an excellent tool for successful consensus harmonization to achieve the overall objectives of firms. Through board meetings, the performance and the monitoring capacity of the board directors are assessed. Few types of research reveal that the board meeting has a significant impact on banks' performance in Nigeria and China. Through board meetings, the directors get the information and the progress of the firm which can be presented to shareholders (Gafoor, Mariappan, & Thyagarajan, 2018).

## 9.3 Theoretical and Conceptual Framework

The scope of the study is to explore the relation between board composition and agency costs. The board should safeguard every stakeholder's interest. This study used agency theory as a theoretical framework. The literature explains the relationship between board composition and agency costs. Agency theory is considered to be the oldest theory on corporate governance. The person to believe the presence of agency theory in organizations is Adam Smith in 1937 when he suggested that an organization is managed by people who are not the owners of the organization then they are less likely to act in an unbiased way that would entirely have principal's interests at heart. The concept was developed further by contributions from (Ross, 1973; Jensen & Meckling, 1976).

The conceptual framework shown in Fig. 9.1 presents a pictorial view of the relationship between the variables. The dependent variable is the agency costs which is influenced by the independent variables board composition (CEO duality, board meeting per year, employee representative on board, audit committee, independent chairperson, and board size) and bank-specific characteristics (Bank size and bank age).

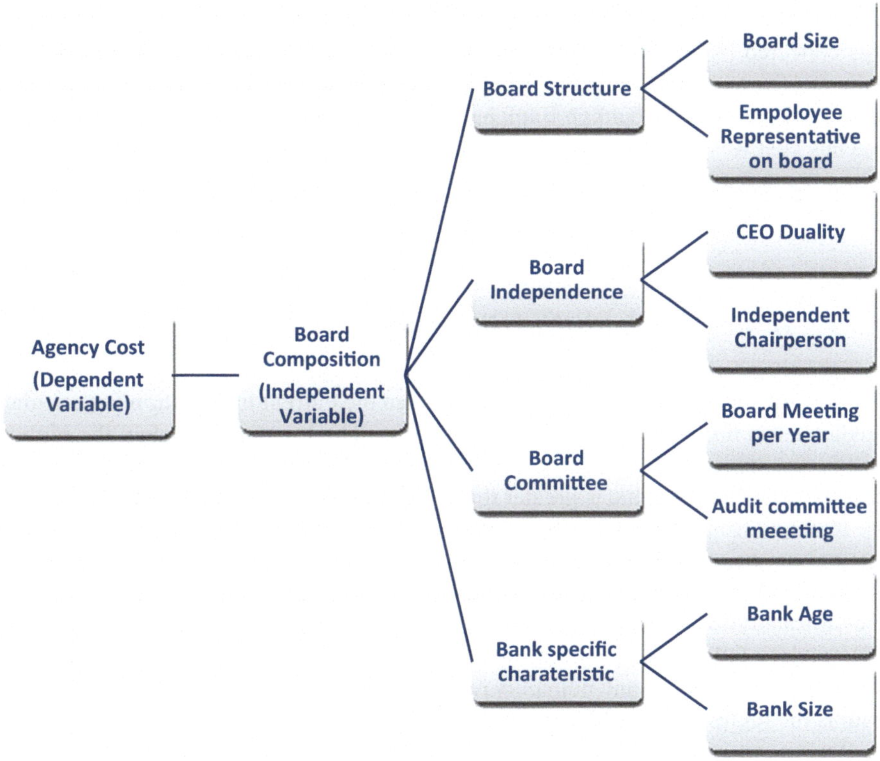


**Fig. 9.1** Pictorial representation of dependent and independent variables

## 9.4 Objective

a. To evaluate the board structure of large and small bank and its influence on agency cost.
b. To assess the board independence of large and small banks and its effect on agency cost.
c. To assess the variability of the board committee and its impact on agency cost of large and small banks.

## 9.5 Data and Methodology

The sample of the study considered 35 commercial banks operating in India. They were further divided under the large bank and small bank category based on market capitalization. Banks having market capitalization above Rs 13,000 crores fall under a large bank category. A descriptive research design was used so that it sheds more insight into the relationship. The study used secondary data to perform quantitative analysis for the period 2008–2018. Data on agency cost and board composition was collected from the Bloomberg database. The data on the size of the bank was collected from the RBI database (Time-series publications on liabilities and assets of scheduled commercial banks). Bank age was calculated from the year of inception. Agency cost was measured using annual data on ATR and LR. Asset turnover is the ratio of revenue and average assets. Leverage ratio is calculated by dividing average assets with average equity.

### 9.5.1 *Testing for Statistical Significance*

The *p* value measures the probability that given the current information a particular predictor has no relationship with the response. The lower the *p* value, the higher will be the statistical importance of the predictor. Typically, we consider a variable as if the associated *p* value is greater than 0.05. Statistically unimportant parameters are removed from the model which will result in a better fit of data. The confidence interval on the slope helps us to measure the practical importance of the model so created. 95% confidence interval on the slope was calculated in this study. Multiregression analysis was used to assess the relationship between the Dependent Variable (DV) and the Independent Variable (IV). This is one of the most commonly used techniques in social science and humanity research. The basic concept that has been dealt with is the regression coefficient (β), $R^2$, and adjusted $R^2$.

Regression coefficient (β) measures how strongly each of the IV predicts DV. There are two types of regression coefficient such as unstandardized coefficients and standardized coefficients. Unstandardized coefficients are used in the equation as the coefficient of different IV's along with the constant term predicts the value of DV. The standardized coefficients are, however, measured in standard deviation. $R^2$ represents the correlation between the observed value and the predicted value. $R^2$ gives the proportion of variance in the DV account for the set of IV chosen for the model. $R^2$ is used to find out how well the IVs can forecast the DV. Adjusted $R^2$ takes into account the fact when the number of IVs is more $R^2$ value trends to be bit inflated. It gives more accruable information about the fitness of our model. High discrepancy between the values of $R^2$ and adjusted $R^2$ indicated a poor fit of the model. A meaningless addition of variable to the model will lower the adjusted $R^2$. Adjusted $R^2$ will always be less than or equal to $R^2$. The standard error of a model fit is a measure of the precision of the model. It is the standard deviation of the residuals. Standard error is used to get a confidence interval for the predicted values.

Frost (2017) states that low $R^2$ is not always a concern, and high $R^2$ values are not necessarily good. For example, outcome variables such as extremely complicated human behavior. A high $R^2$ value is almost impossible to predict. A good model can have a low $R^2$ value. On the other hand, a biased model can have a high $R^2$ value. Artificial inflate of $R^2$ may occur in several other circumstances. Multicollinearity is a problem that needs to be addressed in every research study to obtain accurate results (Kothari, 1990). It is a phenomenon where a predictor variable highly correlates with

**Table 9.1** Definition of variables

| Variable | Type | Description | Notation |
|---|---|---|---|
| *Dependent variable* | | | |
| Asset turnover ratio | Continuous | Revenue/average assets | ATR |
| Leverage ratio | Continuous | Average assets/average equity | LR |
| *Explanatory variables* | | | |
| Bank size | Continuous | Natural log of the book value of the total asset | BNKSIZE |
| Bank age | Continuous | Total year of operation | BNKAGE |
| Board size | Continuous | Number of Directors on the bank's board | BS |
| CEO duality | Binary | Dummy variable that takes the value of 1 if the CEO is also the chair of the board; 0 otherwise | CEODUAL |
| Independent Chairperson | Binary | Dummy variable that takes the value of 1 if the bank has independent chairperson on the board; 0 otherwise | INDCHAIR |
| Audit committee meeting | Continuous | Number of meetings of the Board's Audit Committee during the reporting period | ACM |
| Board meeting per year | Continuous | Total number of corporate board meetings held in the past year | BMPY |
| Employee representative on board | Continuous | Number of employee representatives on the board | ERB |

*Source* Compiled by Author

another predictor variable in a redundant way that does not add value to the entire model. Variance Inflation Factor (VIF) was used to test multicollinearity. Durbin Watson test is used to detect the presence of autocorrelation in the data (Table 9.1).

## 9.6 Analytical Model

The study used a multilinear regression model to estimate the linear relationship between agency costs and board composition of large and small banks in India.

**Model 1**

The dependent variable in this analysis is ATR of a banks "i" in year "t". The model employed to explain the variation in the banks-level ATR (large and small banks) is defined as below

$$
\begin{aligned}
\mathrm{ATR}_{it} = {} & \beta_0 + \beta_1 * \mathrm{BNKSIZE}_{it} + \beta_2 * \mathrm{BNKAGE}_{it} + \beta_3 * \mathrm{BS}_{it} \\
& + \beta_4 * \mathrm{ERB}_{it} + \beta_5 * \mathrm{INDCHAIR}_{it} + \beta_6 * \mathrm{CEODUAL}_{it} \\
& + \beta_7 * \mathrm{BMPY}_{it} + \beta_8 * \mathrm{ACM}_{it} + \varepsilon_{it}
\end{aligned} \tag{9.1}
$$

**Model 2**
The dependent variable in the second model is LR of a banks "i" in year "t". The model employed to explain the variation in the bank-level LR (large and small banks) is defined as below

$$
\begin{aligned}
LR_{it} = {} & \beta_0 + \beta_1 * \mathrm{BNKSIZE}_{it} + \beta_2 * \mathrm{BNKAGE}_{it} + \beta_3 * \mathrm{BS}_{it} \\
& + \beta_4 * \mathrm{ERB}_{it} + \beta_5 * \mathrm{INDCHAIR}_{it} + \beta_6 * \mathrm{CEODUAL}_{it} \\
& + \beta_7 * \mathrm{BMPY}_{it} + \beta_8 * \mathrm{ACM}_{it} + \varepsilon_{it}
\end{aligned} \tag{9.2}
$$

$\beta_1$, $\beta_2$ $\beta_3$, and $\beta_4$ are the parameters being estimated by the regression; while $\varepsilon$ is the random error or residuals from the regression estimates.

## 9.7 Large Banks

### *9.7.1 Descriptive Statistics*

Table 9.2 represents the descriptive statistics of large banks. In the entire period from 2008 to 2018, large banks recorded the highest ATR of 0.14 while the minimum ATR was 0.06. The mean was 0.09 with a standard deviation at 0.01. Kurtosis shows the data on ATR is leptokurtic. The maximum and minimum leverage ratio of large banks is 41.67 and 8.39, respectively. This shows that agency cost is not uniform across banks and varies from year to year. CEO duality is 0.37 implying 37% of banks have the same person holding the position of CEO as well chairperson in large banks.

### *9.7.2 Correlation Analysis*

Pearson correlation analysis of the independent and dependent variables is shown in Table 9.3 There exists a positive and strongest correlation between the age of the banks and the number of board meetings per year of 0.73 in large banks. CEO Duality and the number of an employee representative on board of large banks also show a strong correlation of 0.53.

**Table 9.2** Descriptive statistics of large banks

| | ACM | BNK AGE | ATR | BMPY | BS | BNK SIZE | CEO DUAL | ERB | IND CHAIR | LR |
|---|---|---|---|---|---|---|---|---|---|---|
| Mean | 9.98 | 69.29 | 0.10 | 12.20 | 10.95 | 12.87 | 0.37 | 0.49 | 0.18 | 15.31 |
| Median | 10.00 | 76.00 | 0.10 | 12.00 | 11.00 | 13.04 | 0.00 | 0.00 | 0.00 | 15.05 |
| Maximum | 24.00 | 124.00 | 0.14 | 27.00 | 18.00 | 15.06 | 1.00 | 2.00 | 1.00 | 41.67 |
| Minimum | 4.00 | 4.00 | 0.06 | 4.00 | 6.00 | 8.90 | 0.00 | 0.00 | 0.00 | 8.39 |
| Std. dev. | 2.66 | 38.81 | 0.01 | 4.93 | 2.11 | 1.23 | 0.48 | 0.80 | 0.38 | 5.23 |
| Skewness | 0.71 | −0.28 | 0.33 | 0.73 | 0.33 | −0.84 | 0.54 | 1.17 | 1.70 | 1.73 |
| Kurtosis | 5.79 | 1.55 | 3.14 | 3.57 | 3.30 | 3.84 | 1.29 | 2.59 | 3.88 | 7.61 |
| Jarque-Bera | 76.53 | 18.90 | 3.51 | 19.16 | 4.10 | 27.32 | 31.84 | 43.81 | 95.84 | 258.05 |
| Probability | 0.00 | 0.00 | 0.17 | 0.00 | 0.13 | 0.00 | 0.00 | 0.00 | 0.00 | 0.00 |
| Sum | 1866.0 | 12,958.0 | 18.12 | 2281.00 | 2047.0 | 2406.6 | 69.00 | 92.00 | 33.00 | 2863.9 |
| Sum sq. dev. | 1319.91 | 280,142.8 | 0.04 | 4525.68 | 831.47 | 280.72 | 43.54 | 118.74 | 27.18 | 5081.4 |
| Observations | 187.00 | 187.00 | 187.00 | 187.00 | 187.00 | 187.00 | 187.00 | 187.00 | 187.0 | 187.00 |

*Source* Compiled by Author

**Table 9.3** Correlation analysis of large banks

| | ACM | BNK AGE | ATR | BMPY | BS | BNK SIZE | CEO DUAL | ERB | IND CHAIR | LR |
|---|---|---|---|---|---|---|---|---|---|---|
| ACM | 1 | | | | | | | | | |
| BNKAGE | 0.51 | 1 | | | | | | | | |
| ATR | −0.26 | −0.40 | 1 | | | | | | | |
| BMPY | 0.45 | 0.73 | −0.21 | 1 | | | | | | |
| BS | 0.26 | 0.10 | −0.15 | 0.09 | 1 | | | | | |
| BNKSIZE | −0.14 | −0.07 | −0.27 | 0.02 | 0.12 | 1 | | | | |
| CEODUAL | 0.16 | 0.36 | −0.36 | 0.20 | 0.11 | −0.10 | 1 | | | |
| ERB | 0.20 | 0.36 | −0.24 | 0.30 | 0.32 | 0.28 | 0.53 | 1 | | |
| INDCHAIR | −0.29 | −0.22 | 0.23 | −0.14 | −0.03 | 0.15 | −0.35 | −0.29 | 1 | |
| LR | 0.19 | 0.45 | −0.57 | 0.33 | 0.05 | 0.21 | 0.46 | 0.35 | −0.38 | 1 |

*Source* Compiled by Author

### 9.7.3 Regression Summary

All models were estimated from the data. In the interpretation of the regression line, the estimated coefficient (intercept and the slope) has an important role. The quality of the regression model was evaluated using the concept of $R^2$. It measures the percentage of total uncertainty in the data that is explained by the regression line. A higher value of $R^2$ denotes a better model. A better way of comparing the regression model has been used, i.e., the adjusted $R^2$. Adjusted *R*-squared penalize a model for the variable that does not affect output.

**Model 1 (ATR)**
Table 9.4 represents the regression variable estimate for ATR in large banks. Given that, the *t*-value and corresponding *p*-value are in the "t" and "sig" column, respectively. It was observed from the table that board structure (ERB), board independence (CEODUAL, INDCHAIR), and board committee (BMPY) have a significant relationship with agency cost (ATR). The bank-specific variables (BNKAGE and BNKSIZE) also influence agency cost negatively. BMPY, ERB, and INDCHAIR have a positive relationship with ATR while CEODUAL has a negative relationship. The standardized coefficient is called beta weights. In this model, CEODUAL is the highest contributing (0.341) predictor to explain ATR. The figures under VIF suggest that the model is free from the multicollinearity problem. Table 9.5 shows the model summary and tells how well the regression model fits the data. The value of 0.382 shows that independent variables explain 38% of the variability of the dependent variable (ATR). 61.8% of the variable is caused by factors other than the predictors included in this model. $R^2$ appears to be, at first glance, an easy-to-understand figure showing how a regression model matches a data set. However, it does not reveal the whole story. To get a better picture, we looked at $R^2$ in conjunction with residual charts, other statistics, and detailed subject matter information. Adjusted $R^2$ is also an important factor. A value of 0.355 indicates 35.5% of the variation in the outcome variable is explained by the predictors which are to be kept in the model. The F-ratio in the ANOVA (Table 9.6) tests whether the overall regression model is a good fit for the data. The table shows that the independent variables statistically significantly predict the dependent variable, $F\ (8{,}178) = 13.772$, $p\ (0.000) < 0.05$. Thus, it is evidence that the model is significant.

**Model 2 (LR)**
Table 9.7 represents the regression variable estimate for LR in large banks. It was observed that only board independence (CEODUAL, INDCHAIR) has a significant relationship with agency cost (LR). The bank-specific variables (BNKAGE and BNKSIZE) influence the agency cost positively. CEODUAL has a positive relationship with LR while INDCHAIR has a negative relationship. In this model, CEODUAL is the highest contributing (0.341) predictor to explain LR. Multicollinerity problem does not exist in this model as VIF for all variables is less than 5 (or tolerance >0.01). In Table 9.8, the value of 0.444 shows that independent variables explain 44.4% of the variability of the dependent variable (LR). 55.6% of the

**Table 9.4** Coefficients for large banks (ATR)

| | Unstandardized coefficients | | Standardized coefficients | *t* | Sig. | 95.0% confidence interval for B | | Collinearity statistics | |
|---|---|---|---|---|---|---|---|---|---|
| | B | Std. error | Beta | | | Lower Bound | Upper Bound | Tolerance | VIF |
| (Constant) | 0.180 | 0.012 | | 15.493 | 0.000 | 0.157 | 0.203 | | |
| BNKAGE | 0.000 | 0.000 | −0.431 | −4.479 | 0.000 | 0.000 | 0.000 | 0.375 | 2.664 |
| BNKSIZE | −0.005 | 0.001 | −0.432 | −6.474 | 0.000 | −0.007 | −0.004 | 0.781 | 1.280 |
| CEODUAL | −0.010 | 0.002 | −0.337 | −4.434 | 0.000 | −0.015 | −0.006 | 0.601 | 1.665 |
| BMPY | 0.001 | 0.000 | 0.192 | 2.171 | 0.031 | 0.000 | 0.001 | 0.445 | 2.246 |
| ACM | −0.001 | 0.000 | −0.123 | −1.658 | 0.099 | −0.001 | 0.000 | 0.627 | 1.595 |
| BS | −0.001 | 0.000 | −0.077 | −1.196 | 0.233 | −0.001 | 0.000 | 0.826 | 1.210 |
| ERB | 0.004 | 0.001 | 0.240 | 2.910 | 0.004 | 0.001 | 0.007 | 0.510 | 1.961 |
| INDCHAIR | 0.005 | 0.003 | 0.133 | 2.001 | 0.047 | 0.000 | 0.010 | 0.781 | 1.281 |

**Table 9.5** Multiple linear regression goodness of fit for large bank (ATR)

Model summary[b]

| Model | $R$ | $R$ square | Adjusted $R$ square | Std. error of the estimate | Durbin-watson |
|---|---|---|---|---|---|
| 1 | 0.618[a] | 0.382 | 0.355 | 0.01163 | 0.696 |

[a]Predictors: (constant), INDCHAIR, BS, BMPY, BNKSIZE, CEODUAL, ACM, ERB, ERB, BNKAGE
[b]Dependent variable: ATR

**Table 9.6** Analysis of variance (ATR)

ANOVA[a]

| Model | | Sum of squares | df | Mean square | $F$ | Sig. |
|---|---|---|---|---|---|---|
| 1 | Regression | 0.015 | 8 | 0.002 | 13.772 | 0.000[b] |
| | Residual | 0.024 | 178 | 0.000 | | |
| | Total | 0.039 | 186 | | | |

[a]Dependent variable: ATR
[b]Predictors: (constant), INDCHAIR, BS, BMPY, BNKSIZE, CEODUAL, ACM, ERB, ERB, BNKAGE

variable is caused by factors other than the predictors included in this model. The F-ratio in the ANOVA (Table 9.9) tests whether the overall regression model is a good fit for the data. The table shows that the independent variables statistically significantly predict the dependent variable, $F\ (8,178) = 17.782$, $p(0.000) < 0.05$. Thus, it is evidence that the model is significant.

## 9.8 Small Banks

### *9.8.1 Descriptive Statistics*

Table 9.10 represents the descriptive statistics of small banks. The highest ATR of 0.12 while the minimum ATR was 0.04. The mean was 0.09 with a standard deviation at 0.01. The maximum and minimum leverage ratios of large banks are 28.20 and 1.95, respectively. CEO duality is 0.62 implying 62% of banks have the same person holding the position of CEO as well chairperson in small banks, whereas in large banks it was observed 37% of banks have CEO duality.

**Table 9.7** Coefficients for large banks (LR)

| | Unstandardized coefficients | | Standardized coefficients | t | Sig. | 95.0% confidence interval for B | | Collinearity statistics | |
|---|---|---|---|---|---|---|---|---|---|
| | B | Std. error | Beta | | | Lower bound | Upper bound | Tolerance | VIF |
| (Constant) | −5.167 | 3.974 | | −1.300 | 0.195 | −13.009 | 2.676 | | |
| BNKAGE | 0.045 | 0.012 | 0.337 | 3.690 | 0.000 | 0.021 | 0.070 | 0.375 | 2.664 |
| BNKSIZE | 1.438 | 0.269 | 0.338 | 5.345 | 0.000 | 0.907 | 1.969 | 0.781 | 1.280 |
| CEODUAL | 3.683 | 0.779 | 0.341 | 4.729 | 0.000 | 2.146 | 5.220 | 0.601 | 1.665 |
| BMPY | 0.036 | 0.089 | 0.034 | 0.403 | 0.688 | −0.139 | 0.211 | 0.445 | 2.246 |
| ACM | −0.119 | 0.138 | −0.061 | −0.860 | 0.391 | −0.392 | 0.154 | 0.627 | 1.595 |
| BS | −0.065 | 0.152 | −0.026 | −0.429 | 0.669 | −0.365 | 0.235 | 0.826 | 1.210 |
| ERB | −0.761 | 0.512 | −0.116 | −1.487 | 0.139 | −1.771 | 0.249 | 0.510 | 1.961 |
| INDCHAIR | −3.873 | 0.865 | −0.283 | −4.479 | 0.000 | −5.579 | −2.166 | 0.781 | 1.281 |

**Table 9.8** Multiple linear regression goodness of fit for large bank (LR)

| Model summary[b] | | | | | |
|---|---|---|---|---|---|
| Model | *R* | *R* Square | Adjusted *R* square | Std. error of the estimate | Durbin-Watson |
| 2 | 0.666[a] | 0.444 | 0.419 | 3.98332 | 0.553 |

[a]Predictors: (constant), INDCHAIR, BS, BMPY, BNKSIZE, CEODUAL, ACM, ERB, ERB, BNKAGE
[b]Dependent variable: LR

**Table 9.9** Analysis of Variance (LR)

| ANOVA[a] | | | | | | |
|---|---|---|---|---|---|---|
| Model | | Sum of squares | df | Mean square | *F* | Sig. |
| 2 | Regression | 2257.124 | 8 | 282.141 | 17.782 | 0.000[b] |
| | Residual | 2824.298 | 178 | 15.867 | | |
| | Total | 5081.422 | 186 | | | |

[a]Dependent variable: LR
[b]Predictors: (constant), INDCHAIR, BS, BMPY, BNKSIZE, CEODUAL, ACM, ERB, ERB, BNKAGE

### *9.8.2 Correlation Analysis*

Table 9.11 shows the Pearson correlation between variables in small banks. There exist a negative and strongest correlation between CEODUAL and INDCHAIR. ERB and CEODUAL reflect a strong positive correlation of 0.54.

### *9.8.3 Regression Summary*

**Model 1 (ATR)**
Table 9.12 represents the regression variable estimate for ATR in small banks. It was observed that Board Structure (BS) and board committee (BMPY) have a significant relationship with agency cost (ATR). The bank-specific variables that influence agency cost are BNKSIZE. BMPY and BS have a positive relationship with ATR. In this model, BS is the highest contributing (0.274) predictor to explain ATR. Multicollinearity problem also does not exist in this model (tolerance > 0.01). In Table 9.13, the value of 0.234 shows that independent variables explain 23.4% of the variability of the dependent variable (ATR). 76.6% of the variable is caused by factors other than the predictors included in this model. The F-ratio in the ANOVA (Table 9.14) tests whether the overall regression model is a good fit for the data. The table shows that the independent variables statistically significantly predict the dependent variable, F (8,189) = 7.198, $p$ (0.000) < 0.05. It is evident that the model is significant.

**Table 9.10** Descriptive statistic for small banks

| | ACM | BNKAGE | ATR | BNKSIZE | BMPY | BS | CEODUAL | ERB | INDCHAIR | LR |
|---|---|---|---|---|---|---|---|---|---|---|
| Mean | 9.36 | 92.01 | 0.09 | 12.85 | 13.30 | 10.60 | 0.62 | 0.67 | 0.17 | 17.14 |
| Median | 9.00 | 87.50 | 0.09 | 13.07 | 13.00 | 10.00 | 1.00 | 0.00 | 0.00 | 17.08 |
| Maximum | 16.00 | 153.00 | 0.12 | 15.02 | 27.00 | 14.00 | 1.00 | 3.00 | 1.00 | 28.20 |
| Minimum | 4.00 | 65.00 | 0.04 | 9.87 | 5.00 | 5.00 | 0.00 | 0.00 | 0.00 | 1.95 |
| Std. dev. | 2.31 | 17.73 | 0.01 | 1.48 | 4.00 | 1.64 | 0.49 | 0.84 | 0.38 | 4.06 |
| Skewness | 0.29 | 1.60 | −0.42 | −0.12 | 1.05 | −0.26 | −0.48 | 0.73 | 1.74 | −0.15 |
| Kurtosis | 2.68 | 6.11 | 6.49 | 1.56 | 5.37 | 3.05 | 1.23 | 1.96 | 4.03 | 4.03 |
| Jarque-Bera | 3.57 | 164.04 | 106.29 | 17.50 | 83.09 | 2.33 | 33.43 | 26.54 | 108.78 | 9.42 |
| Probability | 0.17 | 0.00 | 0.00 | 0.00 | 0.00 | 0.31 | 0.00 | 0.00 | 0.00 | 0.01 |
| Sum | 1853.50 | 18,217.00 | 18.74 | 2543.57 | 2633.50 | 2098.00 | 122.00 | 133.00 | 34.00 | 3394.53 |
| Sum Sq. dev. | 1048.43 | 61,908.99 | 0.02 | 431.59 | 3151.37 | 529.68 | 46.83 | 139.66 | 28.16 | 3253.12 |
| Observations | 198 | 198 | 198 | 198 | 198 | 198 | 198 | 198 | 198 | 198 |

*Source* Compiled by Author

**Table 9.11** Correlation analysis of small banks

| | ACM | BNKAGE | ATR | BNKSIZE | BMPY | BS | CEODUAL | ERB | INDCHAIR | LR |
|---|---|---|---|---|---|---|---|---|---|---|
| ACM | 1 | | | | | | | | | |
| BNKAGE | 0.05 | 1 | | | | | | | | |
| ATR | −0.13 | −0.13 | 1 | | | | | | | |
| BNKSIZE | 0.29 | 0.40 | −0.25 | 1 | | | | | | |
| BMPY | 0.26 | 0.09 | 0.15 | 0.19 | 1 | | | | | |
| BS | 0.00 | 0.12 | 0.17 | 0.10 | 0.01 | 1 | | | | |
| CEODUAL | 0.30 | 0.12 | −0.36 | 0.30 | −0.18 | 0.18 | 1 | | | |
| ERB | 0.24 | 0.18 | −0.26 | 0.33 | 0.02 | 0.33 | 0.54 | 1 | | |
| INDCHAIR | −0.14 | −0.07 | 0.23 | −0.22 | 0.00 | −0.18 | −0.55 | −0.33 | 1 | |
| LR | 0.04 | −0.03 | −0.35 | 0.14 | 0.03 | −0.08 | 0.28 | 0.43 | −0.26 | 1 |

*Source* Compiled by Author

**Table 9.12** Coefficients for small banks (ATR)

| | Unstandardized coefficients | | Standardized coefficients | $t$ | Sig. | Collinearity statistics | |
|---|---|---|---|---|---|---|---|
| | B | Std. error | Beta | | | Tolerance | VIF |
| (Constant) | 0.093 | 0.008 | | 11.723 | 0.000 | | |
| BNKAGE | −3.266E-05 | 0.000 | −0.056 | −0.798 | 0.426 | 0.826 | 1.210 |
| BNKSIZE | −0.001 | 0.001 | −0.164 | −2.152 | 0.033 | 0.697 | 1.434 |
| CEODUAL | −0.004 | 0.002 | −0.177 | −1.891 | 0.060 | 0.464 | 2.156 |
| BMPY | 0.000 | 0.000 | 0.152 | 2.142 | 0.033 | 0.804 | 1.245 |
| ACM | −6.629E-05 | 0.000 | −0.015 | −0.203 | 0.839 | 0.769 | 1.301 |
| BS | 0.002 | 0.000 | 0.274 | 4.010 | 0.000 | 0.871 | 1.149 |
| ERB | −0.002 | 0.001 | −0.138 | −1.699 | 0.091 | 0.611 | 1.636 |
| INDCHAIR | 0.003 | 0.002 | 0.098 | 1.262 | 0.208 | 0.675 | 1.482 |

**Table 9.13** Multiple linear regression goodness of fit for the small bank (LR)

Model summary[b]

| Model | $R$ | $R$ square | Adjusted $R$ square | Std. error of the estimate | Durbin-Watson |
|---|---|---|---|---|---|
| 1 | 0.483[a] | 0.234 | 0.201 | 0.00926 | 1.296 |

[a]Predictors: (constant), INDCHAIR, BS, BMPY, BNKSIZE, CEODUAL, ACM, ERB, ERB, BNKAGE
[b]Dependent variable: ATR

**Table 9.14** Analysis of variance (ATR)

ANOVA[a]

| Model | | Sum of squares | df | Mean square | $F$ | Sig. |
|---|---|---|---|---|---|---|
| 1 | Regression | 0.005 | 8 | 0.001 | 7.198 | 0.000[b] |
| | Residual | 0.016 | 189 | 0.000 | | |
| | Total | 0.021 | 197 | | | |

[a]Predictors: (constant), INDCHAIR, BS, BMPY, BNKSIZE, CEODUAL, ACM, ERB, ERB, BNKAGE
[b]Dependent variable: ATR

### Model 2 (LR)

Table 9.15 represents the regression variable estimate for LR in small banks. It was observed that only the board structure (ERB, BS) has a significant relationship with agency cost (LR). The bank-specific variables do not have any impact on agency costs. BS has a negative relation with LR while ERB shares a positive relationship with LR. In this model, ERB is the highest contributing (0.491) predictor to explain LR. This model is free from the multicollinearity problem as VIF for all variables is

**Table 9.15** Coefficients for small banks (LR)

| | Unstandardized coefficients | | Standardized coefficients | *t* | Sig. | Collinearity statistics | |
|---|---|---|---|---|---|---|---|
| | *B* | Std. error | Beta | | | Tolerance | VIF |
| (Constant) | 25.297 | 2.989 | | 8.463 | 0.000 | | |
| BNKAGE | −0.027 | 0.016 | −0.119 | −1.762 | 0.080 | 0.826 | 1.210 |
| BNKSIZE | 0.078 | 0.202 | 0.028 | 0.386 | 0.700 | 0.697 | 1.434 |
| CEODUAL | 0.381 | 0.752 | 0.046 | 0.506 | 0.613 | 0.464 | 2.156 |
| BMPY | 0.068 | 0.070 | 0.067 | 0.975 | 0.331 | 0.804 | 1.245 |
| ACM | −0.222 | 0.124 | −0.126 | −1.800 | 0.073 | 0.769 | 1.301 |
| BS | −0.664 | 0.163 | −0.268 | −4.065 | 0.000 | 0.871 | 1.149 |
| ERB | 2.367 | 0.380 | 0.491 | 6.237 | 0.000 | 0.611 | 1.636 |
| INDCHAIR | −1.488 | 0.804 | −0.138 | −1.850 | 0.066 | 0.675 | 1.482 |

**Table 9.16** Multiple linear regression goodness of fit for the small bank (LR)

Model summary[b]

| Model | *R* | *R* square | Adjusted *R* square | Std. error of the estimate | Durbin-Watson |
|---|---|---|---|---|---|
| 2 | 0.534[a] | 0.286 | 0.255 | 3.50668 | 0.679 |

[a]Predictors: (constant), INDCHAIR, BS, BMPY, BNKSIZE, CEODUAL, ACM, ERB, ERB, BNKAGE

[b]Dependent variable: LR

<5. In Table 9.16, the value of 0.286 shows that independent variables explain 28.6% of the variability of the dependent variable (LR). 71.4% of the variable is caused by factors other than the predictors included in this model. The *F*-ratio in the ANOVA (Table 9.17) tests whether the overall regression model is a good fit for the data. The table shows that the independent variables statistically significantly predict the dependent variable, F (8,189) = 9.444, *p* (0.000) < 0.05. It is evident that the model is significant.

## 9.9 Model Quality and Summary

A multilinear regression was run to predict ATR and LR from CEODUAL, BMPY, ACM, ERB, INDCHAIR, BNKSIZE, BNKAGE. The below models appear to be of reasonable quality. The value of $R^2$ in large banks suggests 38% and 44% total uncertainty in ATR and LR is explained by the model. Whereas in small banks $R^2$ of 23 and 28% in ATR and LR is explained by the model. The model 1 for large banks statistically significantly predicted ATR (8,178) = 13.772, $p$ (0.000), $R^2 = 0.382$. Out of seven variables, six variables are added statistically significantly to the predictor.

**Table 9.17** Analysis of variance (LR)

| ANOVA[a] | | | | | | |
|---|---|---|---|---|---|---|
| Model | | Sum of squares | df | Mean square | *F* | Sig. |
| 2 | Regression | 929.031 | 8 | 116.129 | 9.444 | 0.000[b] |
| | Residual | 2324.096 | 189 | 12.297 | | |
| | Total | 3253.127 | 197 | | | |

[a]Dependent variable: leverage ratio
[b]Predictors: (constant), INDCHAIR, BS, BMPY, BNKSIZE, CEODUAL, ACM, ERB, ERB, BNKAGE
Dependent variable: LR

Model 2 for large banks statistically significantly predicted LR (8,178) = 17.782, $p$ (0.000), $R^2 = 0.444$. Out of seven variables, four variables are added statistically significantly to the predictor. The highest contributing predictor is CEODUAL in both the models. The model 1 for small banks statistically significantly predicted ATR, $F$ (8,189) = 7.198, $p$ (0.000), $R^2 = 0.234$. Out of seven variables, only three variables are added statistically significantly to the predictor. In this model, the highest contributing predictor is BS. Model 2 for small banks statistically significantly predicted LR, $F$ (8,189) = 9.444, $R^2 = 0.286$. The highest contributing predictor is ERB. Only two variables are added statistically significantly to the predictor (Table 9.18).

**Table 9.18** Comparison of both model of large and small banks

| | Large banks | | | | Small Banks | | | |
|---|---|---|---|---|---|---|---|---|
| | Model 1 | | Model 2 | | Model 1 | | Model 2 | |
| | *t* | Sig. | *t* | Sig. | *t* | Sig. | *t* | Sig. |
| BNKAGE | −4.479 | 0.000 | 3.690 | 0.000 | −0.798 | 0.426 | −1.762 | 0.080 |
| BNKSIZE | −6.474 | 0.000 | 5.345 | 0.000 | −2.152 | 0.033 | 0.386 | 0.700 |
| CEODUAL | −4.434 | 0.000 | 4.729 | 0.000 | −1.891 | 0.060 | 0.506 | 0.613 |
| BMPY | 2.171 | 0.031 | 0.403 | 0.688 | 2.142 | 0.033 | 0.975 | 0.331 |
| ACM | −1.658 | 0.099 | −0.860 | 0.391 | −0.203 | 0.839 | −1.800 | 0.073 |
| BS | −1.196 | 0.233 | −0.429 | 0.669 | 4.010 | 0.000 | −4.065 | 0.000 |
| ERB | 2.910 | 0.004 | −1.487 | 0.139 | −1.699 | 0.091 | 6.237 | 0.000 |
| INDCHAIR | 2.001 | 0.047 | −4.479 | 0.000 | 1.262 | 0.208 | −1.850 | 0.066 |
| (Constant) | 15.493 | 0.000 | −1.300 | 0.195 | 11.723 | 0.000 | 8.463 | 0.000 |
| Observation | 187 | 187 | 187 | 187 | 198 | 198 | 198 | 198 |
| R-squared | 0.382 | | 0.444 | | 0.234 | | 0.286 | |

*Source* Compiled by Author

## 9.10 Conclusion

This study found the vital role of board composition in impacting the agency cost of large and small banks. Agency cost arises due to the agency problem between shareholders and managers. In large banks, it was found that board meetings per year, employee representative on board, and independent chairperson increase agency cost. While CEO duality decreases agency cost. With the increase in the board meeting per year, there will be a new agenda each time in front of the board of directors. There are chances of undue and unfavorable proposals which the board members would not agree to, this in turn increases agency cost. Employee representative on board increases the chances of the employee to defend workers against shareholder control. The employee representative on the board feels like a part of the management. They try to protest their interest and urge for a new benefit at the cost of shareholders' interest and thus agency cost increases. When the chairman is independent there is no check and balance and he can oversee the views of directors. This conflict between the chairman and the board of directors leads to an increase in agency costs. Due to the presence of CEO duality in large banks, there is a concentration of power on business activity and the board decision process. This highlights the benefit of active stewardship in the bank which reduces agency cost.

Small bank scenario depicts a different picture. Board structure and board committee impact agency costs in small banks. Board size which is a proxy for board structure has a dual impact on agency cost. It has a positive impact on model 1. As the size of the board increases there will many independent views as well as issues that give rise to conflict and hence increase in agency cost. It was also observed board size has a negative impact on agency cost in model 2. When there is an increase in the size of the board, there are high values added to the decision-making process and there is less conflict which in turn lowers the agency cost. However, board meetings per year and employee representative on board increase agency cost in small banks which synchronizes with the findings of large banks.

## References

Acharya, V. V., Myers, S. C., & Rajan, R. G. (2011). The internal governance of firms. *The Journal of Finance, 66*(3), 689–720.

Ang, J. S., Cole, R. A., & Lin, J. W. U. H. (2000). Agency costs and ownership structure. *The Journal of Finance, 55*(1), 1–26.

Arikan, A. M. (2016). Corporate acquisitions, diversification, and the firm' s life cycle. *The Journal of Finance, 72I*(1), 139–194. https://doi.org/10.1111/jofi.12362.

Byrd, J. W. (2010). Financial policies and the agency costs of free cash flow: Evidence from the oil industry. *International Review of Accounting, Banking and Finance, 2*, 23–50.

Dalton, D. R., & Rechner, P. L. (1989). On the antecedents of corporate severance agreements: An empirical assessment. *Journal of Business Ethics, 8*, 455–462.

Davidson, W. N., Bouresli, A. K., & Singh, M. (2006). Agency costs, ownership structure, and corporate governance in pre-and post-IPO firms. *Corporate Ownership & Control, 3*(3), 88–95.

Defond, M. L., Hann, R. N., & Hu, X. (2005). Does the market value financial expertise on audit committees of boards of directors? *Journal of Accounting Research, 43*(2), 153–193. https://doi.org/10.1111/j.1475-679x.2005.00166.x.

Donaldson, L., & Davis, J. H. (1991). Stewardship theory or agency theory: CEO governance and shareholder returns. *Australian Journal of Management, 16*(1), 49–64. https://doi.org/10.1177/031289629101600103.

Doukas, J. A., Kim, C., & Pantzalis, C. (2000). Security analysis, agency costs, and company characteristics. *Financial Analysts Journal, 56*(6), 54–63.

Eisenberg, T., Sundgren, S., & Wells, M. T. (1998). Larger board size and decreasing firm value in small firms. *Journal of Financial Economics, 48,* 35–54.

Fauver, L., & Fuerst, M. E. (2006). Does good corporate governance include employee representation? Evidence from German corporate boards $. *Journal of Financial Economics, 82,* 673–710. https://doi.org/10.1016/j.jfineco.2005.10.005.

Fleming, G., Heaney, R., & Mccosker, R. (2005). Agency costs and ownership structure in Australia. *Pacific-Basin Finance Journal, 13,* 29–52. https://doi.org/10.1016/j.pacfin.2004.04.001.

Florackis, C., & Ozkan, A. (2008). Agency costs and corporate governance mechanisms: Evidence for UK firms. *International Journal of Managerial Finance, 4,* 37–59.

Freeman, R., & Lazear, E. (2014). *An economic analysis of works councils.*

Gafoor, C. P. A., Mariappan, V., & Thyagarajan, S. (2018). Board characteristics and bank performance in India. *IIMB Management Review, 30*(2), 160–167. https://doi.org/10.1016/j.iimb.2018.01.007.

Guillen, M. F. (2000). Business groups in emerging economies: A resource-based view. *Academy of Management Journal, 43*(3), 362–380.

Henry, D. (2010). Paci fi c-basin finance journal agency costs, ownership structure and corporate governance compliance: A private contracting perspective. *Pacific-Basin Finance Journal, 18*(1), 24–46. https://doi.org/10.1016/j.pacfin.2009.05.004.

Hirth, S., & Uhrig-homburg, M. (2010). Investment timing, liquidity, and agency costs of debt. *Journal of Corporate Finance, 16*(2), 243–258. https://doi.org/10.1016/j.jcorpfin.2010.01.002.

Ii, J. A. P., & Zahra, S. A. (1991). The relative power of CEOs and boards of directors: Associations with corporate performance. *Strategic Management Journal, 12,* 135–153.

Jensen, C., & Meckling, H. (1976). Theory of the firm: Managerial behavior, agency costs and ownership structure. *Journal of Financial Economics, 3,* 305–360.

Jensen, M. C. (1986). American economic association agency costs of free cash flow, corporate finance, and takeovers. *The American Economic Review, 76*(2), 323–329.

Karamanou, I., & Nikos, V. (2005). The association between corporate boards, audit committees, and management earnings forecasts: An empirical analysis. *Journal of Accounting Research, 43*(3), 453–486. https://doi.org/10.1111/j.1475-679X.2005.00177.x.

Kiel, G. C., & Nicholson, G. J. (2003). Board composition and corporate performance: how the Australian experience informs contrasting theories of corporate governance. *Corporate Governance, 11*(3), 189–205.

Kothari, C. R. (1990). *Research methodology.*

Krishnan, J. (2005). Audit committee quality and internal control: An empirical analysis. *The Accounting Review, 80*(2), 649–675.

Lipton, M., & Lorsch, J. W. (1992). A modest proposal for improved corporate governance. *The Business Lawyer, 48*(1), 59–77.

Majeed, S., Aziz, T., & Saleem, S. (2015). The effect of corporate governance elements on corporate social responsibility (CSR) disclosure: An empirical evidence from listed companies at KSE Pakistan. *International Journal of Financial Studies, 3,* 530–556. https://doi.org/10.3390/ijfs3040530.

Mcgrath, S. (2009). The puzzle of pure moral deference1 Sarah. *Philosophical Perspectives, 23,* 321–344.

Mcknight, P. J., & Weir, C. (2009). Agency costs, corporate governance mechanisms and ownership structure in large UK publicly quoted companies: A panel data analysis. *The Quarterly Review of Economics and Finance, 49,* 139–158. https://doi.org/10.1016/j.qref.2007.09.008.

Moeller, S. B., & Schlingemann, F. P. (2005). Wealth destruction on a massive scale ? A study of acquiring-firm returns in the recent merger wave. *The Journal of Finance, 60*(2), 577–582.

Palmon, O., & Wald, J. K. (2002). Are two heads better than one? The impact of changes in management structure on performance by firm size. *Journal of Corporate Finance, 8,* 213–226.

Pfeffer, J. (2020). Size and composition of corporate boards of directors: The organization and its environment. *Administrative Science Quarterly, 17*(2), 218–228.

Pi, L., & Timme, S. (1993). Corporate control and bank efficiency. *Journal of Banking & Finance, 17,* 515–530.

Pincus, K., Rusbarsky, M., & Jilnaught, W. (1989). Voluntary formation of corporate audit committees among NASDAQ firms. *Lwmal of Accounting and Public Policy, 8,* 239–265.

Ross, S. A. (1973). The economic theory of agency: The Principal's problem. *The American Economic Review, 63*(2), 134–139.

Sajid, M. N., Ahmad, I., Saita, Haris Khursheed, & Nawaz, Muhammad Musarrat. (2012). How leverage affects agency cost: Investigating a non-linear relationship in Pakistani Firms. *Innova Ciencia, 4*(9), 2–19.

Shaw, L., & College, T. C. (2007). *Overview of corporate governance issues for*. (November 2006).

Singh, M., & Davidson, W. N. (2003). Agency costs, ownership structure and corporate governance mechanisms. *Journal of Banking & Finance, 27,* 793–816. https://doi.org/10.1016/S0378-4266(01)00260-6.

Vafeas, N. (2005). Audit committees, boards, and the quality of reported earnings. *Contemporary Accounting Research, 22*(4), 1093–1122.

Yermack, D. (1996). Higher market valuation of companies with a small board of directors. *Journal of Financial Economics, 40,* 185–211.

Zahra, S., & Pearce, J. (1989). Boards of directors and corporate financial performance: A review and integrative model. *Journal of Management, 15*(2), 291–334.

# Chapter 10
# Assessing Airline Bankruptcy in India

**Sushma Verma and Samik Shome**

**Abstract** The Indian aviation sector has been experiencing substantial growth in recent years. This remarkable growth, however, has not been reflecting in the financial statement of majority of the leading air carriers. In 2019, Jet Airways has been grounded due to severe financial crisis. Considering the dynamic and competitive environment in which airline companies operate, early warning signal of financial distress is extremely important. This study attempts to analyse the financial situation of selected airline companies in India using various bankruptcy predicting models viz. Altman Model, Pilarski Model, Fuzzy Logic Model and Kroeze Model. This paper examined financial data of four major national carriers viz. Indigo, Jet Airways, Air India and Spice Jet between 2014 and 2019. The scores calculated from various models have indicated that there exists financial distress among the Indian air carriers. It is observed that different models have given more or less similar predictions and grades for different air carriers in India. This study is of great relevance considering the contribution of aviation sector to the national growth and series of bankruptcy instances in this sector.

**Keywords** Indian aviation sector · Competitive environment · Financial distress · Bankruptcy predicting models

## 10.1 Introduction

Air transportation sector plays a very significant role in fuelling the economic growth of any nation (Baker et al. 2015). Aviation sector has become a major economic and financial force today considering its contribution towards global supply

---

S. Verma
VES Institute of Management Studies and Research, Mumbai, India

S. Shome (✉)
Institute of Management, Nirma University, Ahmedabad, India
e-mail: samik@nirmauni.ac.in



A. K. Mishra et al. (eds.), *The Financial Landscape of Emerging Economies*, Accounting, Finance, Sustainability, Governance & Fraud: Theory and Application,
https://doi.org/10.1007/978-3-030-60008-2_10

chain, tourism and hospitality sector, among others. This sector generates substantial employment opportunities and provides tremendous socio–economic benefits (Fung et al. 2006). Globally, the sector has shown considerable growth with revenue reaching USD 754 billion in 2017 showing a Compound Annual Growth Rate (CAGR) of 5.9% from 2007 to 2017.[1] By 2021, it is expected to reach USD 872 billion.[2] However, this industry is highly vulnerable to geopolitical and economic volatility. This includes currency fluctuation, instability in commodity prices, protectionism, infrastructure challenges, weather fluctuations and natural disasters.[3] Moreover, dynamics of this sector is also changing very fast due to technological advancements. These issues lead to unpredictable fluctuations in the airline or air carrier profitability making them highly susceptible to financial distress. Warren Buffett had once stated that the aviation sector is the death trap for investors.[4]

The Indian aviation sector has been showing very encouraging growth prospects in terms of domestic passenger traffic in recent years. India, currently the third-largest civil aviation market globally, is expected to surpass the United Kingdom and become the third-largest air passenger market in the world by 2024.[5] Despite this encouraging statistics, financials of this sector is in red. In the year 2018–19, combined operating profit for all scheduled air carriers in India was negative. Aviation sector has lost more than USD 10 billion since the year 2009.[6] As the aviation sector in India is highly competitive, this leads to an unfavourable pricing of air tickets. Many a time, tickets are priced even lower than the cost leading to a reduction in revenue. Companies are often found resorting to new strategies and experimenting with new business models in an attempt to survive and also to maintain profit margins.

Volatile jet fuel prices, fare war, weak rupee, significantly high parking charges and high finance cost for debt-laden scheduled Indian air carriers increase pressure on them. Peculiarities of this sector coupled with complexities of a developing nation make this sector more vulnerable to financial distress. In the last decade, many instances of financial distress have been observed in the Indian aviation sector. Kingfisher stopped its operations in 2012. Spice Jet faced severe cash crunch in 2014 and had to cancel more than 2000 flights because it had to return the aircrafts back to lessor as it could not pay them. In December 2016, Air Asia suffered huge loss and severe cash crunch forcing it to put on hold all its expansion plans. In February 2017, Air Costa suspended its services due to cash crunch and by the end of 2017, Director General of Civil Aviation (DGCA) suspended its air operating permit. In July 2018, regional airline Air Pegasus ceased its operations due to severe fund crunch. Latest

---

[1] https://www.statista.com/statistics/278372/revenue-of-commercial-airlines-worldwide/, accessed on 20 May 2020.

[2] https://www.lucintel.com/airline-market-2020.aspx, accessed on 20 May 2020.

[3] Airlines for America (A4A), Airline Handbook, Available at: http://airlines.org/Pages/Airline-HandbookChapter-1-Brief-History-of-Aviation.aspx, accessed on 22 January 2020.

[4] https://www.forbes.com/sites/tedreed/2013/05/13/buffett-decries-airline-investing-even-though-at-worst-he-broke-even/#51554ecb3b5e, accessed on 27 January 2020.

[5] https://www.ibef.org/industry/indian-aviation.aspx. Accessed on 28 February 2020.

[6] https://centreforaviation.com/analysis/reports/india-aviation-outlook-traffic-up-losses-down-but-operating-environment-remains-challenging-228991, accessed on 20 May 2020.

in the row is the case of Jet Airways, suspending its operation completely in April 2019 due to severe financial issues. Moreover, for Kingfisher and Jet Airways, it was a shift from enviable second position in terms of market share to suspension of operations just in a matter of few months. This highlights the turbulent and uncertain pattern of operating performance of Indian air carriers.

Seeing the susceptibility to financial distress among Indian carriers, it is only prudent to have an early warning signal in place for predicting bankruptcy which can be considered to be a natural successor of financial distress if left unaddressed. Bankruptcy has several disastrous macro as well as microeconomic consequences for various stakeholders. It is extremely important to identify the models which can accurately identify the firms before they actually start showing the symptoms of bankruptcy. If the situation can be identified much earlier, the firm might get sufficient lead time to take appropriate corrective actions to bail themselves out of this situation. As per Altman (1983), it is possible to predict financial distress much before its actual occurrence using financial ratios and appropriate statistical analysis.

In this backdrop, the primary objective of this study is to do a financial analysis for four major national air carriers of India using select models of bankruptcy. Of the chosen national carriers, three are operational and one has recently stopped operations due to severe financial crisis. The study also attempts to assess the suitability of chosen bankruptcy prediction models in the Indian scenario. The models differ in their choice of ratios, weightage allotted to different ratios and also in terms of statistical method employed. The study contributes to the existing body of knowledge on bankruptcy in aviation sector in India. Since bankruptcy precedes insolvency, it may be of great interest to various stakeholders such as lenders, government and common people in addition to management of air carriers. This paper is structured as follows. Section 10.2 provides the brief overview of the Indian aviation sector followed by a short survey of the existing literature presented in Sect. 10.3. In Sect. 10.4, the research methodology of the study is explained. Section 10.5 summarises the research findings. Section 10.6 highlights the implications of the study and certain concluding observations including limitations and future scope is stated in Sect. 10.7.

## 10.2 Indian Aviation Industry: An Overview

The Indian aviation industry at present contributes USD 72 billion[7] to the country's GDP. Aviation sector has been continuously on a rising spree post-2012. The demand for air travel has increased significantly. This is visible in the increasing growth rate of passenger traffic. There are several reasons for this growth including, growing middle class and their rising income coupled with size and unique topological feature

[7] https://www.investindia.gov.in/sector/aviation, accessed on 22 May 2020.

of the country; lower air fares (sometimes at par with railway fares); and also limited capacity of alternative mode of travel such as railways, road transport, among others.[8]

As per DGCA, overall passenger traffic grew at the rate of 18.1% in 2017–18 as compared to 2016–17. In the same year, domestic traffic grew at the rate of 18.9% and international traffic at the rate of 14.4%.

From Table 10.1, it can be observed that the total number of travellers (both domestic as well as international) has doubled in past seven years. The only year of negative growth is 2012–13. This might be due to grounding of Kingfisher Airlines in the same year and also relatively higher air fare due to sudden decline in the competition among the air carriers. As per the latest data of DGCA, in the year 2019, there was a sharp fall in growth rate of domestic air traffic which stood at 3.7% as compared to the preceding 2018 showing a growth of 18%. This is lowest since 2012–13. Prima facie reason for this is believed to be grounding of Jet Airways and weak consumer sentiments.[9] Till January 2020, total passenger traffic was 293.99 million comprising of 235.44 million domestic travellers and 58.55 million international travellers.[10] The Indian air carriers also use a very high proportion of leased air crafts. As per Data from Centre for Asia Pacific Aviation (CAPA), approximately 81% of total commercial air crafts in India are leased as on October 2018.[11] This percentage is much higher as compared to the global figure of 53% of leased aircrafts. This is also an indicator of financial fragility.

Considering the market share of different air carriers until January 2019, Low-Cost Carriers[12] (LCC) viz. Indigo, Spice Jet and Go Air, dominated the domestic market in India with more than 60% share. Indigo is the market leader with 42.5% market share. It is followed by Spice Jet (13.3%), Air India (12.2%), Jet Airways (11.9%), Go Air (8.7%), Air Asia (5.3%) and Vistara (3.8%). Jet Airways has suspended its operations from April 2019 due to severe financial crunch.[13] Post-grounding of Jet Airways, data of December 2019[14] showed an increase in market shares of other remaining operational airlines, i.e. Indigo (47.1%), Spice Jet (14.9%), Air India (12.7%), Go Air (10.6%), Air Asia (6.2%) and Vistara (5.2%).

---

[8]http://www.careratings.com/upload/NewsFiles/Studies/Airlines%20and%20Airports.pdf accessed on 27 May 2020.

[9]https://www.businesstoday.in/current/slowdown-blues/the-worst-year-for-indian-aviation-in-six-years/story/375927.html, accessed on 23 April 2020.

[10]https://www.ibef.org/industry/indian-aviation.aspx, accessed on 03 May 2020.

[11]https://centreforaviation.com/analysis/reports/aircraft-leasing-in-india-opportunity-knocks-for-an-indian-lessor-443995, accessed on 8 June 2020.

[12]A low-cost carrier is an airline that offers generally low fares in exchange for eliminating many traditional passenger services.

[13]https://economictimes.indiatimes.com/industry/transportation/airlines-/-aviation/jet-airways-stares-at-shutdown-as-lenders-reject-appeal-for-funds-report/articleshow/68923128.cms, accessed on 8 June 2020.

[14]https://data.gov.in › catalog › monthly-air-traffic-statistics on 27 January 2020.

**Table 10.1** Domestic and international passenger traffic in India

| Year | Scheduled domestic passengers (in million) | Scheduled international passengers (in million) | Yearly growth in domestic passengers | CAGR domestic passengers | Yearly growth in international passengers | CAGR international passengers | Yearly growth in total passengers |
|---|---|---|---|---|---|---|---|
| 2010–11 | 53.84 | 13.16 | 18.8 | 6.7 | 13.3 | 13 | 17.7 |
| 2011–12 | 60.84 | 14.38 | 13.0 | 8.2 | 9.3 | 12.1 | 12.3 |
| 2012–13 | 57.87 | 13.73 | −4.9 | 5.4 | −4.5 | 8.5 | −4.8 |
| 2013–14 | 60.67 | 15.77 | 4.8 | 5.3 | 14.8 | 9.6 | 6.8 |
| 2014–15 | 70.08 | 17.33 | 15.5 | 6.7 | 9.9 | 9.6 | 14.4 |
| 2015–16 | 85.20 | 18.63 | 21.6 | 8.5 | 7.5 | 9.4 | 18.8 |
| 2016–17 | 103.75 | 20.81 | 21.8 | 9.9 | 11.8 | 9.6 | 20.0 |
| 2017–18 | 123.32 | 23.80 | 18.8 | 10.8 | 14.4 | 10.1 | 18.1 |

*Source* http://dgca.gov.in/reports/stat-ind.htm, accessed on 25 May 2020

## 10.3 Literature Survey

Business failure has been widely discussed in academic literature for more than seven decades (Balcaen and Ooghe 2006). There are four commonly discussed approaches on forecasting bankruptcy viz. economic, strategic, organisational and financial (Cultrera and Brédart 2016). This study is based exclusively on the financial approach. The other aspects of bankruptcy are not considered here. The objective of any bankruptcy prediction model is to identify the companies which are probable candidate for bankruptcy and that too several years before actual filing. One of the earliest work in this field was conducted by Patrick (1932) who compared successful firms with failed firms using ratio analysis. Beaver (1966) used cash flows for bankruptcy prediction. He used a univariate model and tried to assess the relationship between each chosen financial ratio and bankruptcy individually. Beaver after examining 29 ratios over a period of five years identified six ratios having discriminating power between bankrupt and non-bankrupt firms. Post-1960s, multivariate approach was widely used involving Multiple Discriminant Analysis (MDA), Logit and Probit models.

The first bankruptcy prediction model was developed by Altman in 1968 which is commonly known as Z score Model. It was a five variable generic model using MDA. This model was succeeded by ZETA model (Altman et al. 1977) which was successfully applied by Altman and Gritta (1984) to the US aviation sector. In 1993, the five variable model was reduced to a four variable model which became popular as Altman $Z''$ score model. This model is believed to be fairly accurate for non-manufacturing sector. This model was also used by Hanson (2003) for assessing bankruptcy in services companies. Different researchers from time to time attempted to apply different statistical techniques to develop new models. Ohlson (1980) used logistic regression to develop bankruptcy prediction model. Gepp and Kumar (2008) created a new model by combining discriminant and logit analysis.

Chow et al. (1991) came up with AIRSCORE model specifically for aviation sector. Pilarski and Dinh (1999) developed P-Score model exclusively for aviation sector. Neural Network Model was developed by Davalos et al. (1999) for major US air carriers and by Gritta et al. (2000) for small carriers for predicting financial distress. Though these models forecasted bankruptcy with great degree of accuracy, no evidence is available to prove that they have greater predictive capability as compared to models using MDA or logistic regression (Gudmundsson 2002). Timmermans (2014) attempted to understand the forecasting accuracy of Altman (1968), Ohlson (1980) and Zmijewski (1984) models. However, from the extensive review of literature, it is evident that Z score model and/or modified $Z''$ score model have been the most popular models for predicting airline bankruptcy and is widely used in several studies (Wang et al. 2013; Vasigh et al. 2014; Lu et al. 2015; Majid et al. 2016) even after development of aviation-specific models. However, most of these studies are confined to developed countries.

There are several studies done in the Indian context also for predicting bankruptcy across sectors using Z score or modified $Z''$ score model. Kumar and Anand (2013),

Vasantha et al. (2013), Barki and Halageri (2014), Safiuddin (2017), Kulkarni (2018) and Panigrahi (2019) have applied Z score and modified Z″ score to various Indian companies belonging to different sectors including aviation for bankruptcy prediction. Barki and Halageri (2014) applied Z score model to companies belonging to textile sector, whereas Panigrahi (2019) applied it to the pharmaceutical sector in India to analyse their financial strength. Kumar and Anand (2013) and Vasantha et al. (2013) applied both Z score and modified Z″ score to assess the financial health of Kingfisher Airlines. Both the studies accurately identified the poor financial condition of this particular air carrier. Kulkarni (2018) also assessed the prevailing situation of financial distress in airline sector using Z score model.

In this paper, to predict the bankruptcy in Indian airlines industry, four bankruptcy predicting models viz. Altman Z″ score, P-score model, Fuzzy Logic model and Kroeze model are applied together for a combined analysis and to find out their predictive capability and suitability by relating their conclusions with the prevailing situation in this sector. With a specific focus on Indian aviation sector, following objectives have been set for this study: (a) to assess the financial condition of chosen Indian air carriers using various bankruptcy predicting models; (b) to examine the existence of financial distress in the Indian aviation sector and (c) to evaluate the suitability of the chosen models in the Indian context.

## 10.4 Research Methodology

For this study, four national air carriers of India viz. Indigo, Jet Airways, Air India and Spice Jet are chosen based on their market share and also on the basis of availability of the data. This study used secondary data for quantitative analysis. The financial data has been obtained from the annual reports of the chosen air carriers. Financial statements from 2014 to 2019 have been considered for calculating various financial ratios for chosen models. However, for Jet Airways, data for Financial Year (FY) 2018–19 is not available. Four models viz. Altman Z″ score model, P-score model, Fuzzy Logic model and Kroeze model are used to examine the existence of financial distress in Indian aviation sector. Of these chosen models, Z″ score is a non-industry specific generic model and the remaining three models are specifically designed for aviation sector. The models were chosen on the basis of their predictive capabilities as specified in the literature. Also, another criterion for choosing models is that it should be non-proprietary. A brief about all these four models are discussed in the subsequent section.

### *10.4.1 Altman Model (Z″ score)*

The calculation equation of original model of Altman known as Z score model is represented as

$$Z = 0.012X_1 + 0.014X_2 + 0.033X_3 + 0.006X_4 + 0.999X_5 \quad (10.1)$$

where $X_1$ = liquidity ratio which is calculated as net working capital/total assets;
$X_2$ = profitability ratio measured as retained earnings/total assets;
$X_3$ = profitability ratio measured as operating profit/total assets;
$X_4$ = leverage ratio measured as the market value of equity/book value of debt and
$X_5$ = turnover ratio measured as operating revenues/total assets.

Thus, $X_1$ to $X_5$ ratios measure different aspects of financial strength. Altman (1968) developed this model using Multiple Discriminant Regression (MDR). However, because of the significantly high use of operating lease in aviation sector, there is a strong viewpoint that $X_5$ ratio can give misleading results (Gritta et al. 1995). Altman (1983) also recommended the modified $Z''$ model for non-manufacturing firms.

$$Z'' = 6.56X_1 + 3.26X_2 + 6.72X_3 + 1.05X_4 \quad (10.2)$$

where $X_1$ = net working capital/total assets;
$X_2$ = retained earnings/total assets;
$X_3$ = operating profit/total assets and
$X_4$ = book value of equity/book value of debt.

The $X_4$ ratio in modified model is calculated using book value of equity.

Based on the value of $Z''$, the companies have been segregated into three groups:

1. $Z'' \leq 1.10$ indicates higher level of financial distress which can lead to high probability of bankruptcy.
2. $1.10 \leq Z'' \leq 2.60$ is treated as a grey zone which is unpredictable. In this range, profiling seems to be difficult as here some firms may fail and some may survive.
3. $Z'' \geq 2.60$ denotes lower level of financial distress and reduced probability of bankruptcy.

Considering that there is a significant use of lease of fleets in the Indian aviation industry, modified $Z''$ score model has been used in this study.

### *10.4.2 The Pilarski or P-score Model*

Pilarski and Dinh (1999) developed a logit model known as P-score model. This model calculates P-scores which is technically the probability of bankruptcy. It is believed that this model gives superior results in comparison to other models (Goodfriend et al. 2004). Probability of bankruptcy 'P' is calculated as follows:

$$W = -1.98X_1 - 4.95X_2 - 1.96X_3 - 0.14X_4 - 2.38X_5 \quad (10.3)$$

$$P = 1/\left[1 + e^{-w}\right] \tag{10.4}$$

where $X_1$ = operating revenues/total assets;
$X_2$ = retained earnings/total assets;
$X_3$ = equity/total debt;
$X_4$ = liquid assets/current maturities of total debt;
$X_5$ = Earnings Before Interest and Taxes (EBIT)/operating revenues.
Here, 'e' is mathematical constant with value equal to 2.718.

Higher the P-value greater is the probability of bankruptcy and vice versa. The P-score model is considered to be appropriate for this study because it is specific to aviation sector with a high prediction rate of around 85.1% (Gritta et al. 2006).

### *10.4.3 Fuzzy Logic Model*

Fuzzy Logic is another approach developed by Silva et al. (2005), for estimating airlines insolvency. Following is the equation for calculation:

$$Z = 2.637 - 0.879X_1 + 0.466X_2 - 0.268X_3 - 0.28X_4 \tag{10.5}$$

where $X_1$ = shareholder funds/total assets;
$X_2$ = (current liabilities +long term liabilities)/total asset;
$X_3$ = net operating revenue/total assets and
$X_4$ = fixed assets/total asset.

Based on Z scores, companies have been classified into the following five categories:

1. $Z \leq 1.862$ implies healthy
2. $1.862 \leq Z \leq 2.2$ denotes low risk
3. $2.2 \leq Z \leq 2.515$ indicates moderate risk
4. $2.515 \leq Z \leq 2.73$ specifies high risk
5. $Z \geq 2.73$ suggests insolvent

Several researchers including Chen et al. (2009) and Korol (2012) have used fuzzy logic model and expressed that results of this model are superior as compared to the traditional classical models.

### *10.4.4 Kroeze Model*

Kroeze (2005) used the following equation for predicting air carriers insolvency:

$$Y_a = 0.268X_1 + 0.838X_2 + 0.111X_3 + \acute{\epsilon} \tag{10.6}$$

where $Y_a$ = overall index;

$X_1$ = working capital/total assets;

$X_2$ = retained earnings/total assets;

$X_3$ = book value of equity/total liabilities and

$\acute{\varepsilon}$ = error term.

This model uses MDA. Positive value of $Y_a$ indicates a situation of non-bankruptcy and the negative value of $Y_a$ indicates a high probability of bankruptcy. Kroeze used this model to successfully forecast the bankruptcy of Air Canada, US Airways and Hawaiian four years before their actual filing and that of Trans World Airlines and American Trans Air, three and two years before their actual filing of bankruptcies, respectively.

## 10.5 Findings and Discussion

In this section, all the four models have been analysed for the chosen airline companies. Next, the paper attempts to relate the results with the prevailing situation. This is done to assess the suitability of chosen models in the Indian context.

### *10.5.1 Altman Model (Z″ score)*

The Z″ score values for all the four chosen airlines are depicted in Table 10.2. Subsequently, in Table 10.3, the risk profile of the chosen carriers is assessed. The financial statement of Jet Airways for the year 2019 is not available as this particular airline was grounded in April 2019. It can be observed that all the air carriers other than Indigo have negative net worth and reported operating loss for all the six years selected for the study (Table 10.2). Another significant observation is the negative $X_4$ ratio. Except for Indigo, this particular ratio which indicates relative proportion of debt and equity is negative. This is due to negative equity because of accumulated losses over the years.

It can be clearly observed from Table 10.3 that all the airlines except Indigo are in zone of distress for all the years under study. Indigo from being in distress zone in 2014, moved to the healthy zone in 2019 as depicted by its Z″ score which has increased significantly from 0.863 in 2014 to 2.626 in 2019. Z″ scores for other three air carriers are continuously in negative zone. The analysis of individual X variable shows that all the air carriers are operating with negative working capital.

**Table 10.2** Altman Z″ score of selected air carriers

| Air carrier | Year | Net working capital/Total asset | Retained earnings/Total asset | Operating profit/Total asset | Book value of equity/Book value of debt | Z″ score |
|---|---|---|---|---|---|---|
| | | $X_1$ | $X_2$ | $X_3$ | $X_4$ | |
| Indigo | 2014 | −0.221 | 0.004 | 0.065 | 0.137 | −0.853 |
| | 2015 | −0.134 | 0.218 | 0.182 | 0.117 | 1.197 |
| | 2016 | −0.003 | 0.181 | 0.268 | 0.906 | 3.324 |
| | 2017 | −0.117 | 0.182 | 0.186 | 1.578 | 2.732 |
| | 2018 | −0.109 | 0.193 | 0.201 | 3.158 | 4.567 |
| | 2019 | −0.166 | 0.146 | −0.011 | 3.154 | 2.626 |
| Jet Airways | 2014 | −0.299 | −0.162 | −0.091 | −0.296 | −3.412 |
| | 2015 | −0.212 | −0.254 | −0.007 | −0.430 | −2.716 |
| | 2016 | −0.215 | −0.195 | 0.125 | −0.361 | −1.579 |
| | 2017 | −0.569 | −0.615 | 0.141 | −0.897 | −5.728 |
| | 2018 | −0.533 | −0.624 | 0.002 | −1.368 | −6.953 |
| | 2019 | NA | NA | NA | NA | NA |
| Air India | 2014 | −6.581 | −0.082 | −0.053 | −0.466 | −44.278 |
| | 2015 | −0.588 | −0.151 | −0.018 | −0.555 | −5.058 |
| | 2016 | −0.433 | −0.105 | 0.053 | −0.533 | −3.384 |
| | 2017 | −0.686 | −0.160 | 0.053 | −0.561 | −5.254 |
| | 2018 | −1.184 | −0.165 | −0.003 | −0.759 | −9.128 |
| | 2019 | −0.177 | −0.165 | −0.051 | −0.759 | −17.86 |
| Spice Jet | 2014 | −0.471 | −0.101 | −0.290 | −0.672 | −6.072 |
| | 2015 | −0.598 | −1.231 | −0.253 | 0.892 | −10.572 |
| | 2016 | −0.584 | −0.923 | 0.189 | −1.013 | −6.631 |
| | 2017 | −0.471 | −0.773 | 0.191 | −0.593 | −4.940 |
| | 2018 | −0.182 | −0.043 | 0.187 | −0.040 | −1.317 |
| | 2019 | −0.204 | −0.407 | −0.002 | 0.359 | −2.305 |

*Source* Calculated from Annual Reports of different Airline companies

### *10.5.2 The Pilarski or P-score Model*

The ‘P’ in P-score Model indicates the probability of any particular entity becoming bankrupt. This happens because of high degree of financial distress. From P-score of Jet Airways, it is evident that probability of bankruptcy increased from 70.8% in 2014 to 98.1% in 2018 (Table 10.4). This air carrier is grounded since April 2019 due to financial crunch. Therefore, the result is consistent with the actual scenario.

For Spice Jet, the probability of bankruptcy has shown volatility. It has gone down significantly from 10.4% in 2014 to 2.1% in 2018. However, this increased again to

**Table 10.3** Assessment of selected air carriers based on Z″ score

| Air carrier | Year | Z″ score | Z ≤ 1.10 | 1.1 ≤ Z ≤ 2.60 | Z ≥ 2.60 | Assessment |
|---|---|---|---|---|---|---|
| Indigo | 2014 | −0.853 | ✓ | | | Distress |
| | 2015 | 1.197 | | ✓ | | Grey zone |
| | 2016 | 3.324 | | | ✓ | Stable |
| | 2017 | 2.732 | | | ✓ | Stable |
| | 2018 | 4.567 | | | ✓ | Stable |
| | 2019 | 2.626 | | | ✓ | Stable |
| Jet Airways | 2014 | −3.412 | ✓ | | | Distress |
| | 2015 | −2.716 | ✓ | | | Distress |
| | 2016 | −1.579 | ✓ | | | Distress |
| | 2017 | −5.728 | ✓ | | | Distress |
| | 2018 | −6.953 | ✓ | | | Distress |
| | 2019 | NA | | | | |
| Air India | 2014 | −44.278 | ✓ | | | Distress |
| | 2015 | −5.058 | ✓ | | | Distress |
| | 2016 | −3.384 | ✓ | | | Distress |
| | 2017 | −5.254 | ✓ | | | Distress |
| | 2018 | −9.128 | ✓ | | | Distress |
| | 2019 | −17.860 | ✓ | | | Distress |
| Spice Jet | 2014 | −6.072 | ✓ | | | Distress |
| | 2015 | −10.572 | ✓ | | | Distress |
| | 2016 | −6.631 | ✓ | | | Distress |
| | 2017 | −4.940 | ✓ | | | Distress |
| | 2018 | −1.317 | ✓ | | | Distress |
| | 2019 | −2.305 | ✓ | | | Distress |

approximately 25% in 2019. It should be noted that FY 2019 has been a stressful year for entire aviation sector in India. Indigo is clearly out of danger zone with very low P score. Air India is also showing more than 50% probability of going bankrupt for all the years. This particular airline is sponsored by Government of India. For Jet Airways, probability increased up to 98% in 2018.

From Table 10.5, it can be clearly seen that Indigo and Spice Jet have shown relatively low probability of bankruptcy for all the six years, whereas this is significantly on a higher side for Jet Airways and Air India.

**Table 10.4** P-score of selected air carriers

| Air carriers | Year | Operating revenue/Total assets | Retained earnings/Total assets | Equity/Debt | Liquid asset/Current liability | EBIT/Operating revenues | W | P | % |
|---|---|---|---|---|---|---|---|---|---|
| | | $X_1$ | $X_2$ | $X_3$ | $X_4$ | $X_5$ | | | |
| Indigo | 2014 | 1.427 | 0.004 | 0.137 | 1.022 | 0.054 | −3.385 | 0.03276 | 3.276 |
| | 2015 | 1.731 | 0.218 | 0.117 | 1.074 | 0.141 | −5.564 | 0.00382 | 0.382 |
| | 2016 | 1.554 | 0.181 | 0.906 | 1.524 | 0.194 | −6.522 | 0.00147 | 0.147 |
| | 2017 | 1.401 | 0.182 | 1.577 | 1.974 | 0.133 | −7.242 | 0.000715 | 0.0715 |
| | 2018 | 1.196 | 0.193 | 3.158 | 2.389 | 0.151 | −9.987 | 0.000046 | 0.0046 |
| | 2019 | 1.198 | 0.146 | 3.154 | 2.263 | 0.013 | −9.481 | 0.000076 | 0.0076 |
| Jet Airways | 2014 | 1.050 | −0.162 | −0.296 | 0.591 | −0.113 | 0.886 | 0.708 | 70.80 |
| | 2015 | 0.619 | −0.254 | −0.430 | 0.691 | −0.011 | 3.691 | 0.979 | 97.90 |
| | 2016 | 0.779 | −0.195 | −0.361 | 0.699 | 0.139 | 2.617 | 0.929 | 92.91 |
| | 2017 | 1.569 | −0.615 | −0.897 | 0.479 | 0.139 | 3.029 | 0.949 | 94.90 |
| | 2018 | 1.669 | −0.624 | −1.368 | 0.559 | 0.039 | 4.069 | 0.981 | 98.10 |
| Air India | 2014 | 0.469 | −0.082 | −0.466 | 0.242 | −0.156 | 4.365 | 0.980 | 98.00 |
| | 2015 | 0.509 | −0.151 | −0.555 | 0.191 | −0.089 | 1.009 | 0.729 | 72.90 |
| | 2016 | 0.551 | −0.105 | −0.533 | 0.398 | 0.020 | 0.339 | 0.5801 | 58.01 |
| | 2017 | 0.610 | −0.160 | −0.561 | 0.210 | 0.149 | 0.270 | 0.570 | 57.00 |
| | 2018 | 0.699 | −0.165 | −0.759 | 0.131 | −0.037 | 0.950 | 0.711 | 71.10 |
| | 2019 | 0.820 | −0.165 | −0.759 | 0.076 | −0.014 | 1.313 | 0.789 | 78.90 |
| Spice Jet | 2014 | 2.140 | −0.101 | −0.672 | 0.434 | −0.144 | −2.150 | 0.104 | 10.40 |
| | 2015 | 1.989 | −1.231 | −0.892 | 0.359 | −0.109 | −1.359 | 0.210 | 20.19 |
| | 2016 | 1.779 | −0.923 | −1.013 | 0.409 | 0.089 | −1.379 | 0.200 | 20.09 |

(continued)

**Table 10.4** (continued)

| Air carriers | Year | Operating revenue/Total assets | Retained earnings/Total assets | Equity/Debt | Liquid asset/Current liability | EBIT/Operating revenues | W | P | % |
|---|---|---|---|---|---|---|---|---|---|
| | | $X_1$ | $X_2$ | $X_3$ | $X_4$ | $X_5$ | | | |
| | 2017 | 2.169 | −0.773 | −0.593 | 0.468 | 0.071 | −2.981 | 0.048 | 4.79 |
| | 2018 | 1.929 | −0.043 | −0.040 | 0.759 | 0.090 | −3.839 | 0.021 | 2.10 |
| | 2019 | 1.901 | −0.407 | −0.359 | 0.765 | −0.029 | −1.079 | 0.248 | 24.80 |

*Source* Calculated from Annual Reports of different Airline companies

**Table 10.5** Probability of bankruptcy for selected air carriers

| Air carriers | Year | % | 0–25% | 25–50% | 50–75% | 75–100% |
|---|---|---|---|---|---|---|
| | | | Low | Average | High | Very high |
| Indigo | 2014 | 3.276 | ✓ | | | |
| | 2015 | 0.382 | ✓ | | | |
| | 2016 | 0.147 | ✓ | | | |
| | 2017 | 0.0715 | ✓ | | | |
| | 2018 | 0.0046 | ✓ | | | |
| | 2019 | 0.0076 | ✓ | | | |
| Jet Airways | 2014 | 70.80 | | | ✓ | |
| | 2015 | 97.20 | | | | ✓ |
| | 2016 | 92.91 | | | | ✓ |
| | 2017 | 94.90 | | | | ✓ |
| | 2018 | 98.10 | | | | ✓ |
| Air India | 2014 | 98.00 | | | | ✓ |
| | 2015 | 72.98 | | | ✓ | |
| | 2016 | 58.01 | | | ✓ | |
| | 2017 | 57.0 | | | ✓ | |
| | 2018 | 71.10 | | | ✓ | |
| | 2019 | 78.90 | | | | ✓ |
| Spice Jet | 2014 | 10.40 | ✓ | | | |
| | 2015 | 20.19 | ✓ | | | |
| | 2016 | 20.09 | ✓ | | | |
| | 2017 | 47.93 | ✓ | | | |
| | 2018 | 2.10 | ✓ | | | |
| | 2019 | 24.80 | ✓ | | | |

### 10.5.3 *Fuzzy Logic Model*

Table 10.6 depicts the fuzzy logic scores calculated for chosen air carriers. From scores, it can be observed that none of the air carriers are in a complete safe zone. Z score for both Jet Airways and Air India is greater than 2.73 for all the years under consideration. This illustrates a very high degree of financial distress. One of the major reasons for this is very high debt coupled with negative net worth.

Spice Jet moved into low-risk zone since 2018 after being in moderate to high-risk zone for the preceding four financial years as shown in Table 10.7. Indigo consistently remained in low-risk zone as per Z values calculated according to calculation equation of this model.

**Table 10.6** Fuzzy logic Z scores for air carriers for 2014–2019

| Air carriers | Year | Shareholders' fund/Total assets | Total liabilities/Total assets | Operating revenue/Total assets | Fixed asset/Total assets | Z score |
|---|---|---|---|---|---|---|
| | | $X_1$ | $X_2$ | $X_3$ | $X_4$ | |
| Indigo | 2014 | 0.061 | 0.448 | 1.427 | 0.576 | 2.197 |
| | 2015 | 0.052 | 0.447 | 1.731 | 0.606 | 2.165 |
| | 2016 | 0.262 | 0.289 | 1.554 | 0.457 | 1.997 |
| | 2017 | 0.284 | 0.181 | 1.401 | 0.286 | 2.016 |
| | 2018 | 0.368 | 0.116 | 1.196 | 0.238 | 1.981 |
| | 2019 | 0.291 | 0.0922 | 1.198 | 0.238 | 2.036 |
| Jet Airways | 2014 | −0.155 | 1.255 | 1.050 | 0.568 | 2.917 |
| | 2015 | −0.229 | 1.279 | 0.619 | 0.490 | 3.000 |
| | 2016 | −0.169 | 1.249 | 0.779 | 0.479 | 2.891 |
| | 2017 | −0.601 | 1.779 | 1.569 | 0.449 | 3.329 |
| | 2018 | −0.615 | 0.572 | 1.669 | 0.247 | 2.845 |
| Air India | 2014 | −0.450 | 0.967 | 0.469 | 0.844 | 3.114 |
| | 2015 | −0.522 | 0.939 | 0.509 | 0.863 | 3.154 |
| | 2016 | −0.480 | 0.901 | 0.551 | 0.692 | 3.133 |
| | 2017 | −0.558 | 0.996 | 0.610 | 0.822 | 3.198 |
| | 2018 | −0.767 | 1.011 | 0.699 | 0.817 | 3.364 |
| | 2019 | −0.947 | 0.358 | 0.820 | 0.821 | 3.187 |
| Spice Jet | 2014 | −0.347 | 0.517 | 2.140 | 0.640 | 2.483 |
| | 2015 | −0.485 | 0.544 | 1.989 | 0.657 | 2.598 |
| | 2016 | −0.365 | 0.360 | 1.779 | 0.572 | 2.487 |
| | 2017 | −0.214 | 0.361 | 2.169 | 0.568 | 2.252 |
| | 2018 | −0.0107 | 0.251 | 1.929 | 0.397 | 2.132 |
| | 2019 | −0.073 | 0.204 | 1.901 | 0.334 | 2.193 |

*Source* Calculated from Annual Reports of different Airline companies

### *10.5.4 Kroeze Model*

Table 10.8 shows the $Y_a$ score calculation as per Kroeze model. This model classifies air carriers only into two categories based on sign of $Y_a$ score. Positive value denotes solvent situation, whereas the negative value implies very high chances of bankruptcy. Based on this model, only Indigo is in solvent stage since 2015 with a positive score. All other three chosen air carriers are showing negative value of $Y_a$ since 2014 till 2019 (for Jet Airways till 2018). Though the performance of Spice Jet has been improving over the period 2015–2018, for Air India and Jet Airways, performance expressed in terms of $Y_a$ score is only deteriorating. The $X_2$ ratio which is calculated

**Table 10.7** Assessment of risk of different air carriers based on fuzzy logic Z scores

| Air carrier | Year | Z ≤ 1.862 | 1.862 ≤ Z ≤ 2.2 | 2.2 ≤ Z ≤ 2.515 | 2.515 ≤ Z ≤ 2.73 | Z ≥ 2.73 | Assessment |
|---|---|---|---|---|---|---|---|
| Indigo | 2014 | | ✓ | | | | Low risk |
| | 2015 | | ✓ | | | | Low risk |
| | 2016 | | ✓ | | | | Low risk |
| | 2017 | | ✓ | | | | Low risk |
| | 2018 | | ✓ | | | | Low risk |
| | 2019 | | ✓ | | | | Low risk |
| Jet Airways | 2014 | | | | | ✓ | Insolvent |
| | 2015 | | | | | ✓ | Insolvent |
| | 2016 | | | | | ✓ | Insolvent |
| | 2017 | | | | | ✓ | Insolvent |
| | 2018 | | | | | ✓ | Insolvent |
| | 2019 | NA | | | | | |
| Air India | 2014 | | | | | ✓ | Insolvent |
| | 2015 | | | | | ✓ | Insolvent |
| | 2016 | | | | | ✓ | Insolvent |
| | 2017 | | | | | ✓ | Insolvent |
| | 2018 | | | | | ✓ | Insolvent |
| | 2019 | | | | | ✓ | Insolvent |
| Spice Jet | 2014 | | | ✓ | | | Moderate risk |
| | 2015 | | | | ✓ | | High risk |
| | 2016 | | | ✓ | | | Moderate risk |

(continued)

**Table 10.7** (continued)

| Air carrier | Year | $Z \leq 1.862$ | $1.862 \leq Z \leq 2.2$ | $2.2 \leq Z \leq 2.515$ | $2.515 \leq Z \leq 2.73$ | $Z \geq 2.73$ | Assessment |
|---|---|---|---|---|---|---|---|
| | 2017 | | | ✓ | | | Moderate risk |
| | 2018 | | ✓ | | | | Low risk |
| | 2019 | | ✓ | | | | Low risk |

**Table 10.8** $Y_a$ scores as per Kroeze model

| Air carrier | Year | Working capital/Total assets | Retained earnings/Total assets | Book value of equity/Total liabilities | $Y_a$ score |
|---|---|---|---|---|---|
| | | $X_1$ | $X_2$ | $X_3$ | |
| Indigo | 2014 | −0.221 | 0.004 | 0.137 | −0.040 |
| | 2015 | −0.134 | 0.218 | 0.117 | 0.159 |
| | 2016 | −0.003 | 0.181 | 0.906 | 0.249 |
| | 2017 | −0.117 | 0.182 | 1.578 | 0.291 |
| | 2018 | −0.109 | 0.193 | 3.158 | 0.479 |
| | 2019 | −0.166 | 0.146 | 3.154 | 0.428 |
| Jet Airways | 2014 | −0.299 | −0.162 | −0.296 | −0.183 |
| | 2015 | −0.212 | −0.254 | −0.430 | −0.317 |
| | 2016 | −0.215 | −0.195 | −0.361 | −0.261 |
| | 2017 | −0.569 | −0.615 | −0.897 | −0.767 |
| | 2018 | −0.533 | −0.624 | −1.368 | −0.818 |
| Air India | 2014 | −6.581 | −0.082 | −0.466 | −2.499 |
| | 2015 | −0.588 | −0.105 | −0.555 | −0.350 |
| | 2016 | −0.433 | −0.160 | −0.533 | −0.259 |
| | 2017 | −0.686 | −0.165 | −0.561 | −0.379 |
| | 2018 | −1.184 | −0.165 | −0.759 | −0.529 |
| | 2019 | −0.177 | −0.165 | −0.759 | −0.978 |
| Spice Jet | 2014 | −0.471 | −0.101 | −0.672 | −0.286 |
| | 2015 | −0.598 | −1.231 | −0.892 | −1.289 |
| | 2016 | −0.584 | −0.923 | −1.013 | −1.039 |
| | 2017 | −0.471 | −0.773 | −0.593 | −0.840 |
| | 2018 | −0.182 | −0.043 | −0.040 | −0.389 |
| | 2019 | −0.204 | −0.407 | 0.359 | −0.410 |

*Source* Calculated from Annual Reports of different Airline companies

as retained earnings/total assets is negative for all the air carriers except Indigo. It is an indicator of financial distress as it highlights negative retained earnings.

As it can be seen from Table 10.9 that except for Indigo, this model indicates very high probability of bankruptcy for all the other three air carriers of which one has already undergoing bankruptcy proceedings.

**Table 10.9** Assessment of air carriers based on Kroeze model

| Air carrier | Year | $Y_a$ score | Positive value | Negative value | Assessment |
|---|---|---|---|---|---|
| Indigo | 2014 | −0.040 | | ✓ | High probability of bankruptcy |
| | 2015 | 0.159 | ✓ | | Non bankruptcy |
| | 2016 | 0.249 | ✓ | | Non bankruptcy |
| | 2017 | 0.291 | ✓ | | Non bankruptcy |
| | 2018 | 0.479 | ✓ | | Non bankruptcy |
| | 2019 | 0.428 | ✓ | | Non bankruptcy |
| Jet Airways | 2014 | −0.183 | | ✓ | High probability of bankruptcy |
| | 2015 | −0.317 | | ✓ | High probability of bankruptcy |
| | 2016 | −0.261 | | ✓ | High probability of bankruptcy |
| | 2017 | −0.767 | | ✓ | High probability of bankruptcy |
| | 2018 | −0.818 | | ✓ | High probability of bankruptcy |
| Air India | 2014 | −2.499 | | ✓ | High probability of bankruptcy |
| | 2015 | −0.350 | | ✓ | High probability of bankruptcy |
| | 2016 | −0.259 | | ✓ | High probability of bankruptcy |
| | 2017 | −0.379 | | ✓ | High probability of bankruptcy |
| | 2018 | −0.529 | | ✓ | High probability of bankruptcy |
| | 2019 | −0.978 | | ✓ | High probability of bankruptcy |
| Spice Jet | 2014 | −0.28557 | | ✓ | High probability of bankruptcy |
| | 2015 | −1.289 | | ✓ | High probability of bankruptcy |
| | 2016 | −1.039 | | ✓ | High probability of bankruptcy |
| | 2017 | −0.840 | | ✓ | High probability of bankruptcy |
| | 2018 | −0.410 | | ✓ | High probability of bankruptcy |
| | 2019 | −0.41 | | ✓ | High probability of bankruptcy |

**Table 10.10** Consolidated scores of selected models for various air carriers

| Air carrier | Year | Z″ score | P-score | Fuzzy score | $Y_a$ score |
|---|---|---|---|---|---|
| Indigo | 2014 | −0.853 | 0.03276 | 2.197 | −0.04 |
| | 2015 | 1.197 | 0.00382 | 2.165 | 0.159 |
| | 2016 | 3.324 | 0.00147 | 1.997 | 0.249 |
| | 2017 | 2.732 | 0.000715 | 2.016 | 0.291 |
| | 2018 | 4.567 | 0.000046 | 1.981 | 0.479 |
| | 2019 | 2.626 | 0.000076 | 2.036 | 0.428 |
| Jet Airways | 2014 | −3.412 | 0.708 | 2.917 | −0.183 |
| | 2015 | −2.716 | 0.979 | 3.000 | −0.317 |
| | 2016 | −1.579 | 0.929 | 2.891 | −0.261 |
| | 2017 | −5.728 | 0.949 | 3.329 | −0.767 |
| | 2018 | −6.953 | 0.981 | 2.845 | −0.818 |
| Air India | 2014 | −44.278 | 0.980 | 3.114 | −2.499 |
| | 2015 | −5.058 | 0.729 | 3.154 | −0.350 |
| | 2016 | −3.384 | 0.580 | 3.133 | −0.259 |
| | 2017 | −5.254 | 0.570 | 3.198 | −0.379 |
| | 2018 | −9.128 | 0.711 | 3.364 | −0.529 |
| | 2019 | −17.86 | 0.789 | 3.187 | −0.978 |
| Spice Jet | 2014 | −6.072 | 0.104 | 2.483 | −0.286 |
| | 2015 | −10.572 | 0.210 | 2.598 | −1.289 |
| | 2016 | −6.631 | 0.200 | 2.487 | −1.039 |
| | 2017 | −4.940 | 0.048 | 2.252 | −0.840 |
| | 2018 | −1.317 | 0.021 | 2.132 | −0.389 |
| | 2019 | −2.305 | 0.248 | 2.193 | −0.410 |

### *10.5.5 Consolidated Results*

The consolidated results of all the four models discussed are depicted in Table 10.10. Apparently, Indigo appears to be the most financially stable among all the four carriers considered in this study. This is also confirmed from the audited financial statement of the company. Indigo showed a consistent improvement in its operating revenue on a year-on-year basis. The operating revenue of INR 13925.30 crore in March 2015 has increased to INR 23020.90 crore in March 2018 and then further to 28496.77 crore in March 2019 as stated in its various annual reports. The company has also reported an increasing net profit after tax continuously from INR 1304.20 crore in FY 2015–16 to INR 2242.4 crore in FY 2018–19. However, in the FY 2018–19, Indigo also reported an operating loss of INR 149 crores.[15]

[15]Annual Report of Indigo FY 2014–15, 2017–18, 2018–19 accessed on 7 February 2020.

Spice Jet showed an improvement in its financial figures in terms of its operating revenues and net profit over a period between 2015 and 2018. This aspect is observed in its scores from various models. The company faced a near-death-like situation in 2014 due to severe financial crunch[16] and was almost on the verge of shutting down its operations. However, Spice Jet showed an improvement in its operating revenue from INR 5201.53 crore for FY 2015–16 to INR 7795.09 crore in FY 2018–19. From reporting a loss of INR 687.05 crore in 2015–16,[17] Spice Jet moved gradually towards a net profit of INR 566.65 crore in FY 2017–18. This was possible due to major efforts towards cost cut and also expansion to newer routes which resulted in increased revenues. However, due to significant down turn observed in aviation sector in FY 2019–20, this company again reported an operating loss of INR 9.09 crores. Spice Jet despite showing improvement is still in danger zone as per different models.

As mentioned earlier, Jet Airways suspended its flying operations since April 2019 due to severe financial crunch. The company is undergoing insolvency proceedings after State Bank of India (SBI), the largest commercial bank of the country, filed a petition for the same in June 2019. All the models have appropriately highlighted the financial plight and probable bankruptcy for this particular air carrier since 2014. Jet Airways got into debt trap after it decided to go in for a debt-based expansion plan which increased its debt significantly from INR 3,000 crores in 2005-06 to INR 16,600 crores in 2009–10. The company owes close to INR 11,261 crores[18] to various domestic and international lenders in addition to money it owes to various operational creditors. Its net worth also became negative since 2012 and continued deteriorating further since then. This negative net worth coupled with a significantly high debt made leverage ratio of Jet Airways unfavourable.

The financial situation of Air India is also very dismal as portrayed by all the chosen models. As this air carrier is funded by Government of India, it keeps getting financial aid from the government on a regular basis. In 2014, Air India received a bailout package of INR 28,000 crore from the government. Despite this huge package for turnaround, this air carrier could only report an operating profit of INR 403.03 crores in succeeding two financial years viz. 2015–16 and 2016–17, respectively.[19] Air India has shown very poor operational efficiency over the years as evident from appropriate X ratios in Altman and Fuzzy Logic models.

To summarise the observations of various models, Indigo is in a relatively low-risk situation. Out of remaining three air carriers, Spice Jet has shown gradual improvement in financial performance, whereas for Jet Airways and Air India, all the models have depicted very bad financial position indicating all likelihood of bankruptcy.

---

[16]https://www.livemint.com/Companies/T2BOBSwziSYSnEDPMJ2xEM/The-SpiceJet-turnaround-story-and-how-it-became-worlds-best.html, accessed on 19 May 2020.

[17]Annual Report of Spice Jet FY 2014–15, 2017–18, 2018–19 accessed on 7 December 2019.

[18]https://www.thehindubusinessline.com/economy/logistics/jets-gross-debt-likely-to-add-up-to-11261-cr/article26905023.ece, accessed on 10 May 2020.

[19]https://www.businesstoday.in/current/economy-politics/a-loss-making-airline-for-almost-a-decade-air-india-has-no-reason-to-exist/story/281813.html, accessed on 5 June 2019.

This is a very significant observation in light of the fact that Jet Airways is grounded since April 2019, whereas Air India is surviving on the support of Government of India. All the four models are depicting more or less the same state of affairs for all the chosen air carriers and clearly portraying their prevailing situation at present.

## 10.6 Implications of the Study

The notion of financial distress in Indian aviation industry has not only developed a considerable amount of research interest among the academicians and research scholars but also among the policymakers and corporates. The current study examines the existence of financial distress among the Indian aviation companies. In other words, this study indicates that the models studied can successfully predict bankruptcy well in advance revealing financial instability. However, financial distress is only an indicator of a possibility of future failure of any company. It does not imply that company will certainly become bankrupt. The situation if identified at the appropriate time can be reversed by taking corrective measures either by the top management of the organisation or by the concerned ministry under the government. Thus, these models through the scores can do a significant job of alerting the management and government timely and provide them with the opportunity to reverse the condition. Considering the impact which failure of any air carriers has on different stakeholders such as employees, customers, government, other allied businesses and on the overall economy, it is only prudent to make this kind of analysis mandatory so that it may serve as an early warning signal. This research technically confirms the applicability, validity and reliability of the chosen models for Indian aviation sector. The findings of this study can serve as a base for further research in this particular sector.

## 10.7 Concluding Observations

The main aim of this study was to assess the financial situation of four major national air carriers operating in India. The results from the various models have indicated the existence of high degree of financial distress in the Indian aviation industry. This is in conformity with some of the previous studies conducted in relation to Indian air carriers (Safiuddin 2017; Kulkarni 2018). Financial situation of Indigo is relatively better as compared to other three air carriers viz. Spice Jet, Air India and Jet Airways.

The study also aimed to explore the applicability of various bankruptcy predicting models like Altman Model, Pilarski Model, Fuzzy Logic Model and Kroeze Model in the Indian context. These models have measured the prevailing financial situation of Indian aviation sector with a great degree of accuracy. All the four chosen models have shown high probability of bankruptcy for Jet Airways right from 2014 to 15 on year-on-year basis. Jet Airways had suspended its operations since April 2019 and presently undergoing insolvency proceedings. Seeing the ability of various models to successfully capture the prevailing financial situation in Indian aviation sector, it can be concluded that these models can be applied to other companies in the same sector to predict the possible bankruptcy.

This study is based entirely on secondary financial data extracted from the annual reports of different companies. It focuses only on the financial aspects of bankruptcy. Although it is true that unstable financials does indicate probable business failure but at the same time it should be noted that bankruptcy in a dynamic sector like aviation is a complex phenomenon depending upon competition to a great extent. The commercial business models used by competitors do act as a game-changer that too in a very short span of time. One of the limitations of this study is that it is based only on four national carriers. This study can be further extended with a larger sample size involving other national and regional carriers. Further research can also focus on identifying critical variables for improving the financial performance of different air carriers on a case-to-case basis. Future studies can also focus on understanding various non-financial indicators of bankruptcy.

## References

Altman, E. (1968). Financial ratios, discriminant analysis and the prediction of corporate bankruptcy. *Journal of Finance, 23*(23), 589–609.

Altman, E. (1983). *Corporate financial distress: A complete guide to predicting, avoiding and dealing with bankruptcy.* New York: Wiley.

Altman, E., & Gritta, R. (1984). Airline bankruptcy propensities: A ZETA analysis. *Journal of the Transportation Research Forum, 25*(1), 150–154.

Altman, E., Haldeman, R., & Narayanan. (1977). ZETA analysis: A new model for bankruptcy classification. *Journal of Banking and Finance, XXVI*(3), 24–56.

Baker, D., Merkert, R., & Kamruzzaman, M. (2015). Regional aviation and economic growth: Cointegration and causality analysis in Australia. *Journal of Transport Geography, 43*, 140–150.

Balcaen, S., & Ooghe, H. (2006). 35 years of studies on business failure: An overview of the classic statistical methodologies and their related problems. *The British Accounting Review, 38*(1), 63–93.

Barki, G., & Halageri, S. (2014). Analysis of financial strength of select firms from Indian textiles industry using Altman's 'Z' score analysis. *Acme Intellects International Journal of Research in Management, Social Sciences & Technology, 5*(5), 1–11.

Beaver, W. (1966). Financial ratios as predictors of failure. *Journal of Accounting Research, IV*, 71–111.

Chen, H. J., Huang, S. Y., & Lin, C. S. (2009). Alternative diagnosis of corporate bankruptcy: A neuro fuzzy approach. *Expert Systems with Applications, 36*(4), 7710–7720.

Chow, G., Gritta, R., & Leung, E. (1991). A new approach to forecasting financial distress in air transportation: The AIRSCORE model. *Journal of the Transportation Research Forum, XXXI*(2), 371–376.

Cultrera, L., & Brédart, X. (2016). Bankruptcy prediction: The case of Belgian SMEs. *Review of Accounting and Finance, 15*(1), 101–119.

Davalos, S., Gritta, R., & Chow, G. (1999). The application of neural network approach to predicting bankruptcy risks facing the major US carriers: 1979–1996. *Journal of Air Transport Management, 5*(2), 81–86.

Fung, M. K. Y., Law, J. S., & Ng, L. W. K. (2006). Economic contribution to Hong Kong of the aviation sector: A value-added approach. *Chinese Economy, 39*(6), 19–38.

Gepp, A., & Kumar, K. (2008). The role of survival analysis in financial distress prediction. *International Research Journal of Finance and Economics, 16,* 14–34.

Goodfriend, J., Gritta, R., Adrangi, B., & Davalos, S. (2004). Assessing the financial condition of the major U.S. passenger airlines over the 1993–2003 period using the P score and Z″ score discriminant models. *Credit and Financial Management Review, 10*(4).

Gritta, R. D., Chow, G., & Lippman, E. (1995). The impact of the capitalization of leases on financial analysis: An issue revisited. *Logistics and Transportation Review, 30*(2), 189–202.

Gritta, R., Davalos, S., & Adrangi, B. (2006). A review of air carrier bankruptcy forecasting methodologies and directions for future research. *Credit and Financial Management Review, XII*(3), 11–30.

Gritta, R. D., Wang, M., Davalos, S., & Chow, G. (2000). Forecasting small air carrier bankruptcies using a neural network approach. *Journal of Financial Management and Analysis, 13*(1), 44–49.

Gudmundsson, S. V. (2002). Airline distress prediction using non-financial indicators. *Journal of Air Transportation, 7*(2), 3–24.

Hanson, R. O. (2003). *A study of Altman's revised four-variable Z & Prime score bankruptcy prediction model as it applies to the service industry.* UMI ProQuest Digital Dissertations. Doctoral Dissertation. Nova Southeastern University, 2003, Ft. Lauderdale, Florida.

Korol, T. (2012). Fuzzy logic in financial management. In P. E. Dadios (Ed.), *Fuzzy logic—Emerging technologies and applications* (pp. 259–286). Poland.

Kroeze, C. (2005). *Predicting airline corporate bankruptcies using a modified Altman Z-score model.* UNLV Retrospective Theses & Dissertations. 2609. Retrieved from https://digitalscholarship.unlv.edu/rtds/2609.

Kulkarni, S. (2018). Analysis of Z score for BSE Listed Airline Companies in India, *Paridnya – The MIBM Research Journal*, 6(1), 24–29.

Kumar, M., & Anand, M. (2013). Assessing financial health of a firm using Altman's original and revised Z-score models: A case of Kingfisher Airlines Ltd (India). *Journal of Applied Management and Investment, 2*(1), 36–48.

Lu, C., Yang, A. S., & Huang, J. F. (2015). Bankruptcy predictions for U.S. air carrier operations: A study of financial data. *Journal of Economics and Finance*, 39(3), 574–589.

Majid, S., Sucherly, & Kaltum, U. (2016). Analysis on the factors causing airlines bankruptcy: Cases in Indonesia. *International Journal of Management Sciences and Business Research, 5*(2), 25–40.

Ohlson, J. A. (1980). Financial ratios and the probabilistic prediction of bankruptcy. *Journal of Accounting Research, 18*(1), 109–131.

Panigrahi, A. (2019). Validity of Altman's "Z" score model in predicting financial distress of pharmaceutical companies. *NMIMS Journal of Economics and Public Policy, 4*(1), 65–73.

Patrick, P. (1932). A comparison of ratios of successful industrial enterprises with those failed firms. *Certified Public Accountant*, October, November & December, 598–605, 656–62 and 727–731.

Pilarski, A., & Dinh, T. (1999). Numerical scoring approach to credit risk analysis. In *Handbook of Airline Finance* (pp. 329–342). New York: McGraw-Hill.

Safiuddin, S. K. (2017). Prediction of insolvency—A study of select companies in Indian aviation industry. *International Research Journal of Management Science & Technology, 8*(10), 304–309.

Silva, V., Respico A., Spiritu Santo, S., & da Silva Portugal, L. (2005). Using the "Hybrid financial statement analysis technique" to rate and monitor airlines financial status. In *Proceedings of the Air Transportation Research Society*, World Conference on Transport Research. Paper presented in Rio de Janeiro.

Timmermans, M. (2014). *US corporate bankruptcy predicting models.* Master's thesis, Tilburg University, Tilburg.

Vasantha, S., Dhanraj, V., & Thiayalnayaki. (2013). Prediction of business bankruptcy for selected Indian airline companies using Altman's model. *International Journal of Research in Business Management, 1*(4), 19–26.

Vasigh, B., Fleming, K., & Humphreys, B. (2014). *Foundations of airline finance: Methodology and practice*. London, UK: Routledge.
Wang, Z., Hofer, C., & Dresner, M. E. (2013). Financial condition, safety investment and accident propensity in the US airline industry: A structural analysis. *Transportation Research Part E: Logistics and Transportation Review, 49*(1), 24–32.
Zmijewski, M. E. (1984). Methodological issues related to the estimation of financial distress prediction models. *Journal of Accounting Research, 22*, 59–82.

# Index

**A**
Agency cost, 112, 116–120, 123–132, 135, 139, 142, 145
Agricultural commodities, 55–60, 63–67
ARDL bound test, 63–67

**B**
Bab factor, 29–31, 34–40, 42
Bankruptcy predicting models, 149, 155, 171
Banks, 1–8, 11, 12, 16, 17, 25, 26, 31, 58, 80, 83, 113, 123–126, 128–145, 170
Behavioral finance, 72, 73, 76
Betting against beta, 29, 30
Business cycle, 15–18, 21–26

**C**
Capital Asset Pricing Model (CAPM), 29, 30, 34, 37, 40, 41
Causal relationship, 19, 24, 55, 57, 59, 60, 65–67
Competitive environment, 149

**D**
Developing economies, 1, 7, 11, 12, 56

**E**
Economic policy uncertainty, 45, 47, 49–52
Emerging economies, 6–8, 46, 55, 56, 79, 111–117, 119, 120
Emerging markets, 1, 2, 4–7, 11, 12, 30, 46, 57, 66, 79, 113, 119
Emotional finance, 73, 74
Emotional intelligence, 74, 75
Equity and bond market, 2, 4

**F**
Fast-Moving Consumer Goods (FMCG), 55–67
Financial cycle, 15–18, 21, 23–26
Financial development, 2, 12, 79, 80
Financial distress, 57, 149–151, 154–156, 159, 163, 167, 171
Financial inclusion, 1, 2, 7, 8, 11, 12, 80

**G**
GARCH models, 46–48
Governance, 111–117, 119, 120, 123, 124, 127, 128
Granger causality test, 15, 16, 19, 24, 26, 55, 57, 58, 60, 63, 65, 66

**H**
Household debt, 81, 84, 89, 97, 101

**I**
India, 3, 5, 8, 9, 11, 15–17, 22, 25, 26, 29–31, 42, 55–58, 66, 67, 79–81, 83, 123–125, 129, 131, 149–153, 155, 160, 170, 171
Indian aviation sector, 149–151, 155, 171, 172
Institutional and non-institutional credit, 80, 83

 
A. K. Mishra et al. (eds.), *The Financial Landscape of Emerging Economies*,
Accounting, Finance, Sustainability, Governance & Fraud: Theory and Application,
https://doi.org/10.1007/978-3-030-60008-2

**J**
Johansen cointegration, 58, 59, 64, 66

**L**
Leverage constraint, 31, 38

**M**
Multi-level mixed-effects regression model, 81

**N**
Neuroscience, 73, 76

**P**
Principal-principal conflict, 111, 113–116, 118

**S**
Spectral Granger causality, 15, 16, 19, 24, 26
Stock market volatility, 45, 46, 50–52

**T**
Toda and Yamamoto approach, 55, 65
Turning point, 15, 16, 18, 21–24, 26

The manufacturer's authorised representative in the EU is Springer Nature Customer Service Centre GmbH, Europaplatz 3, 69115 Heidelberg, Germany. If you have any concerns regarding our products, please contact ProductSafety@springernature.com

Printed and bound by CPI Group (UK) Ltd, Croydon, CR0 4YY
30/09/2026
02225697-0003